The Social Philosophy of Gillian Rose

VERITAS

Series Introduction

"... the truth will set you free" (John 8:32)

In much contemporary discourse, Pilate's question has been taken to mark the absolute boundary of human thought. Beyond this boundary, it is often suggested, is an intellectual hinterland into which we must not venture. This terrain is an agnosticism of thought: because truth cannot be possessed, it must not be spoken. Thus, it is argued that the defenders of "truth" in our day are often traffickers in ideology, merchants of counterfeits, or anti-liberal. They are, because it is somewhat taken for granted that Nietzsche's word is final: truth is the domain of tyranny.

Is this indeed the case, or might another vision of truth offer itself? The ancient Greeks named the love of wisdom as *philia*, or friendship. The one who would become wise, they argued, would be a "friend of truth." For both philosophy and theology might be conceived as schools in the friendship of truth, as a kind of relation. For like friendship, truth is as much discovered as it is made. If truth is then so elusive, if its domain is *terra incognita*, perhaps this is because it arrives to us—unannounced—as gift, as a person, and not some thing.

The aim of the Veritas book series is to publish incisive and original current scholarly work that inhabits "the between" and "the beyond" of theology and philosophy. These volumes will all share a common aspiration to transcend the institutional divorce in which these two disciplines often find themselves, and to engage questions of pressing concern to both philosophers and theologians in such a way as to reinvigorate both disciplines with a kind of interdisciplinary desire, often so absent in contemporary academe. In a word, these volumes represent collective efforts in the befriending of truth, doing so beyond the simulacra of pretend tolerance, the violent, yet insipid reasoning of liberalism that asks with Pilate, "What is truth?"—expecting a consensus of non-commitment; one that encourages the commodification of the mind, now sedated by the civil service of career, ministered by the frightened patrons of position.

The series will therefore consist of two "wings": (1) original monographs; and (2) essay collections on a range of topics in theology and philosophy. The latter will principally be the products of the annual conferences of the Centre of Theology and Philosophy (www.theologyphilosophycentre.co.uk).

Conor Cunningham and Eric Austin Lee, *Series editors*

The Social Philosophy of Gillian Rose

ANDREW BROWER LATZ

CASCADE *Books* • Eugene, Oregon

THE SOCIAL PHILOSOPHY OF GILLIAN ROSE

Veritas 27

Copyright © 2018 Andrew Brower Latz. All rights reserved. Except for brief quotations in critical publications or reviews, no part of this book may be reproduced in any manner without prior written permission from the publisher. Write: Permissions, Wipf and Stock Publishers, 199 W. 8th Ave., Suite 3, Eugene, OR 97401.

Cascade Books
An Imprint of Wipf and Stock Publishers
199 W. 8th Ave., Suite 3
Eugene, OR 97401

www.wipfandstock.com

PAPERBACK ISBN: 978-1-5326-1837-6
HARDCOVER ISBN: 978-1-4982-4390-2
EBOOK ISBN: 978-1-4982-4389-6

Cataloguing-in-Publication data:

Names: Brower Latz, Andrew

Title: The social philosophy of Gillian Rose / Andrew Brower Latz.

Description: Eugene, OR: Cascade Books, 2018 | Series: Veritas 27 | Includes bibliographical references and index.

Identifiers: ISBN 978-1-5326-1837-6 (paperback) | ISBN 978-1-4982-4390-2 (hardcover) | ISBN 978-1-4982-4389-6 (ebook)

Subjects: LCSH: Rose, Gillian | Philosophy, British | Political science, philosophy | Hegel, Georg Wilhelm Friedrich, 1770–1831 | Frankfurt school of sociology | Christianity and politics

Classification: B1649.R74 B768 2018 (print) | B1649.R74 (ebook)

DECEMBER 27, 2017

Contents

Acknowledgments

THIS BOOK BEGAN LIFE as a PhD thesis at Durham University. I am grateful to Christopher Insole and Marcus Pound for supervising it, Brian O'Connor and Thom Brooks for examining it, and the UK Arts and Humanities Research Council for funding it.

For conversations about Rose and/or comments on draft sections of the thesis I am indebted to Keith Ansell-Pearson, Deirdre Bower Latz, Robert Fine, Josh Furnal, David Held, Owen Hulatt, Stephen Houlgate, Kimberly Hutchings, Simon Jarvis, Anthony Jensen, Vincent Lloyd, Sebastian Luft, Thomas Lynch, Wayne Martin, Hermínio Martins, John Milbank, Maggie O'Neill, Peter Osborne, William Rasch, Anna Rowlands, Andrew Shanks, Nigel Tubbs, and Rowan Williams.

My gratitude is happily due to my parents and parents-in-law for their immeasurable support over the years. My greatest thanks go to my wife, Deirdre, to whom I dedicate this work.

Abbreviations

Works by Gillian Rose

TMS	*The Melancholy Science: An Introduction to the Thought of Theodor W. Adorno* (1978)
HCS	*Hegel Contra Sociology* (1981)
DN	*Dialectic of Nihilism: Post-Structuralism and Law* (1984)
BM	*The Broken Middle: Out of Our Ancient Society* (1992)
JAM	*Judaism and Modernity: Philosophical Essays* (1993)
LW	*Love's Work: A Reckoning With Life* (1995)
MBL	*Mourning Becomes the Law: Philosophy and Representation* (1996)
P	*Paradiso* (1999)

Works by Hegel

PhR	*Philosophy of Right*
PhSp	*Phenomenology of Spirit*
EL	*Encyclopaedia of the Philosophical Science*, part 1, *Logic*
SL	*Science of Logic*

Introduction

If you could create a phenomenology of consciousness, some part of it would be the systematic falsification of the foundations of our culture.

—Marilynne Robinson

1 Introduction

THIS BOOK PROVIDES AN original interpretation and reconstruction of Gillian Rose's work as a distinctive social philosophy within the Frankfurt School tradition. Rose's social philosophy has multiple achievements. It holds together the methodological, logical, descriptive, metaphysical, and normative moments of social theory. It provides a critical theory of modern society. It includes a distinctive version of ideology critique based on the history of jurisprudence, and offers interesting modulations of mutual recognition as the internal moral norm of modern society.

Rose's philosophy integrates three key moments of the Frankfurt tradition: a view of the social totality as both an epistemological necessity and normative ideal; a philosophy that is its own metaphilosophy because it integrates its own logical and social preconditions within itself; and a critical analysis of modern society that is simultaneously a critique of social theory. Rose's work is original in the way it organizes these three moments around absolute ethical life as the social totality, its Hegelian basis, and its metaphysical focus on law and jurisprudence. I construe Rose's Hegelian philosophy as an account of reason that is both social and logical without reducing philosophy to the sociology of knowledge, thereby steering between dogmatism and relativism. Central to this position are the historically developing nature of rationality and knowing, and an account of the nature of explanation as depending on a necessarily, and necessarily imperfectly, posited totality. Said positing is always provisional and can be revised through the combination of several different kinds of social theorizing. No totality is ever fully attained, in practice or theory, but is brought to view through the Hegelian-speculative exposition of history, of dirempted experience, and of the tensions immanent to social theories.[1] I thus call such totalities "implied" or "provisional." For example, any adequate understanding of the contemporary world must include a grasp of the global capitalist economy but no such grasp can be complete. Rose posited and explored one main social totality within her own social philosophy—absolute ethical life—as the implied unity of law and ethics, and of finite and infinite. In her trilogy (*Hegel Contra Sociology*, *Dialectic of Nihilism*, *The Broken Middle*) absolute ethical life enables a critique simultaneously and immanently of society and social philosophy in three ways. First, of both the social form of bourgeois property law and social contract theories reflective of it. Second, of social theorizing that insufficiently appreciates its jurisprudential determinations and/or attempts to eliminate metaphysics. Third, the broken middle shows the state-civil society and the law-ethics diremptions as two fundamental features of modern society and as frequently unacknowledged influences on social theorizing.

Rose's social philosophy speaks to a number of debates. In the field of social theory and sociology it provides a critical theory of modern society revolving around the law-ethics and state-society diremptions, which are also foci for empirical investigations. It provides a logical grounding for social theory, explains the presence of contradiction and appearance (*Schein*) in sociology, accounts for the historical nature of sociological knowing, foregrounds the need for an interplay between different sociological methods and between philosophy and sociology, and is exemplary in handling the relation between metatheory and theory. It shows that social philosophy cannot escape metaphysics or ethics, and that ethics must take on board at the ground floor the all-pervasive inevitability of mediation. It adds important textures to the ethics of mutual recognition, and suggests several aspects of practical wisdom for citizens

1. "Speculative" denotes, approximately, Hegel's logic and its way of handling contradictions (see ch. 1, §4.3). "Diremption" is a Hegelian term for a split between two things; Rose means a split that cannot be mended between two things that are nevertheless related and, as it were, yearn for unity (see especially ch. 4, §2.2 and §2.3).

of modern societies. It provides a significant contribution to the development of Hegelian-Adornian Frankfurt theories, including how such theories could be open to religion. It includes a unique version of ideology critique based on jurisprudence. It calls for a broad vision of philosophy of law, in which relations between legal, ethical, and metaphysical questions are foregrounded and addressed. Finally, its distinction between "Holocaust ethnography" and "Holocaust piety" addresses discussions in continental social philosophy about power and subjectivity after the Holocaust.

I use the term "social philosophy" to describe Rose's work because Rose preferred the term "philosopher" as a self-description since it covered the breadth of her interests—ethical, legal, political, metaphysical, epistemological and social: "Only philosophy as I conceive it can accommodate my intellectual endeavors across their range."[2] She also used the self-appellation "social theorist."[3] Rose placed herself within the Frankfurt School tradition in a lecture given in 1986: "There are now generations of Frankfurt School students who occupy posts as sociologists and philosophers throughout the world. I really consider myself to be one of them."[4] She was, more specifically, part of the Hegel-Adorno strand of the second-generation of the Frankfurt School. In line with this tradition she opposed the separation of philosophy and sociology. "My current and recent research and publishing has a common core: to investigate the separation of sociological thinking (methodological and substantive) from philosophical thinking which leads to the posing of sociological questions without a sociological culture."[5] For the purposes of my argument, therefore, I use "social philosophy" and "social theory" (and their derivatives) synonymously.

2. In a letter to Paul-Mendes Flohr, dated 5 August 1992, replying to his question about where Rose saw herself fitting in the university, she wrote, "I think my departmental allegiance must be philosophy—this is the bane of my life: only philosophy as I conceive it can accommodate my intellectual endeavours across their range." Gillian Rose Archive, Modern Records Centre, University of Warwick, MSS.377 box 19. Hereafter, references to archive material will be given by box number only.

3. In a letter from John Milbank to Gillian Rose, 12 June 1992, he notes that at her request he has amended his description of her (in his review of *BM*) to "philosopher and social theorist," box 11.

4. "Introduction to Critical Theory," cassette 7658, a lecture in the *Sociological Theory and Methodology* series at Sussex University, 1986.

5. Letter to Warwick University's registrar (26 October 1989, box 52).

My interpretation has five main advantages over the alternatives.[6] First and above all it presents Rose's work as a coherent social theory and shows how she deployed it in various ways, thereby making Rose's work more available for use as a social theory. It shows Rose sophisticatedly relates the main moments of critical social theory, has a critical theory of modern society, and it reveals for the first time her distinctive versions of mutual recognition and ideology critique. Second, it explains how and why Rose regarded *Hegel Contra Sociology*, *Dialectic of Nihilism* and *The Broken Middle* as a trilogy. Each is a way of pursuing the critique-of-society-and-sociology in relation to the social totality on the basis of a Hegelian philosophy and metaphilosophy. Third, by showing how Rose appropriated Hegel, Adorno, the Frankfurt School, the jurisprudential tradition, Marx, and Weber, it reveals her work as an original synthesis of all her main sources rather than concentrating only on some. Fourth, it is the most comprehensive and detailed interpretation available, encompassing not only her written works but also archive material, and recollections of former friends, colleagues and students. I have made the most extensive use to date of the Gillian Rose archives at Warwick and her taped lectures at Sussex. In the course of my research, I have retrieved the text of a paper she gave at a conference in Sweden in the early eighties that was heretofore unknown.[7] I also register the influence of her teachers Dieter Henrich and Leszek Kołakowski. Continuities between Rose's work and these philosophers are revealing and noted where they occur. This comprehensiveness matters because the scope and ambition of Rose's work is crucial to it: her social philosophy is only properly understood in a synoptic vision; concentrating on only parts of it, rather than the whole, distorts those parts. Fifth, due to its comprehensive nature, my interpretation is able to answer the debate within the secondary literature about the role of religion in her work and her work's relation to religion. I show that religion was not a major source for her thinking but was rather material on which she exercised her mature social philosophy; at the same time Rose articulates a Frankfurt Hegelianism open to religion and theology.

6. Shanks, *Against Innocence*; Lloyd, *Law and Transcendence*; Schick, *Gillian Rose*; the articles by Tony Gorman, Peter Osborne and Rowan Williams listed in the bibliography; the special issue of *Telos* 173 (winter 2015); and the work of Nigel Tubbs, especially *Contradiction of Enlightenment*.

7. Rose, "Parts and Wholes."

2 Rose's Life and Work

Gillian Rose was born Gillian Rosemary Stone in London on 20 September 1947 to a secular Jewish family originally from Poland. She studied philosophy, politics and economics at Oxford, then continental social philosophy, sociology and the Frankfurt School at New York's Columbia University and the *Freie Universität* of Berlin. She also attended the New School for Social Research while in America. Her introduction to German philosophy began at Oxford, in a seminar set up by Hermínio Martins; continued in America and Germany; and resumed in Oxford when she returned to complete a PhD on Adorno under the supervision of Leszek Kołakowski and Steven Lukes. Rose studied Hegel with Dieter Heinrich in Germany.[8] She was reader in sociology at Sussex University from the mid-seventies to 1989 and professor of social and political thought at Warwick University from 1989 to 1995, a chair created especially for her. All ten of her PhD students moved with her from Sussex to Warwick. Rose was "one of a number of Jewish 'intellectuals' chosen to advise the Polish Commission on the Future of Auschwitz."[9] Rose published eight books, two articles and four book reviews. She made interventions into many fields, including German idealism, the Frankfurt School, Marxism, postmodernism and poststructuralism, sociology, Christian theology, Jewish theology and philosophy, Holocaust studies, architecture and jurisprudence, and offered original readings of many figures, including Hegel, Kierkegaard, Nietzsche, Heidegger, Arendt, Luxemburg, Varnhagen, Girard, Mann, and Kafka. She read German, French, Latin, Hebrew and Danish. She died in Coventry on 9 December 1995, aged forty-eight, after a two-year struggle with ovarian cancer. She was baptized into the Anglican Church moments before her death by the then-bishop of Coventry, Simon Barrington-Ward. This was surprising and troubling to some, creating a debate about how or whether Rose's conversion related to her work. "Conversion," however, may be the wrong term, since she wrote in her final weeks in hospital, "I shall not lose my Judaism, but gain that more deeply, too . . . I am both Jewish and Christian."[10]

8. *LW*; see the various obituaries listed in the bibliography. I thank Hermínio Martins and Wayne Hudson for additional biographical information (private communication, 20 December 2012 and 20 January 2013 respectively).

9. *LW*, 12.

10. Rose, "Final Notebooks," 7.

Rose applied her social theory to Judaism and Christianity as she became both increasingly interested in religion and, indeed, religious. Some of her close friends were important religious figures or theologians (Julius Carlebach, John Milbank, Rowan Williams, Simon Barrington-Ward), and her work has been used theologically by figures such as Milbank, Williams, Andrew Shanks, Vincent Lloyd, Anna Rowlands, Marcus Pound, and Randi Rashkover. This has created a debate within the secondary literature about the role and status of religion in her thought. Does religion (especially Anglicanism) emerge as a *telos* for her whole corpus (Andrew Shanks)? Or is its role overplayed when she instead developed a "secular faith" (Vincent Lloyd)? Did her interest in religion make her work less coherent and less powerful (Tony Gorman)? Or does her work provide useful insight and resources for theology (Milbank, Pound, Rashkover, Rowlands, Williams)? Rose was not a theorist of religion per se and did not develop a separate theory of religion. Only in her posthumously published texts do explicit religious remarks appear. I will show she used the social philosophy she had already developed to assess certain aspects of religious philosophy and political theology. Thus theology was not a major source for Rose in forming her social philosophy but material on which she exercised it. This, along with the various uses by theologians of her work, clearly supports the view that her social philosophy provides useful insights for theology, without being itself directly theological (except in the record of her personal religious experiences in her posthumous writings). Hence her work's relation to theology cannot be understood apart from a proper understanding of her social philosophy. Yet Rose does show the possibility of a Frankfurt version of self-limiting rationality that is open to religious views. Rose does not develop this connection at length, however.

3 Outline of the Argument

I argue that Rose integrated the methodological, descriptive, metaphysical and normative moments of social theory, as well as three core Frankfurt School requirements for social philosophy—a view of the social totality,[11] that philosophy be its own metaphilosophy,[12] and that a critique

11. See, e.g., Frankfurt Institute for Social Research, *Aspects of Sociology*, 5; Wheatland, "Debate about Methods in the Social Sciences."

12. Or: "Any science in their view must also be its own metascience" (Gebhardt,

of society be at the same time a critique of sociology[13]—around absolute ethical life. I argue further that she provides a critical theory of modern society and advances distinctive versions of ideology critique and mutual recognition. Rose's theory is also open to religion based on the Frankfurt doctrine of self-limiting reason.

Absolute ethical life is for Rose a central component of Hegel's Absolute, an impossible unity of law and ethics we are nevertheless compelled to posit by a speculative exposition of experience of society. In her trilogy she brought out three main aspects of this. First, Hegel's view of absolute ethical life as a critique of the bourgeois property form and its hold over the social contract philosophy of Kant and Fichte. Second, social philosophy's unavoidable entanglement in metaphysics and jurisprudence. Third, the diremptions between law and ethics and between state and civil society as fundamental to modern society and influencing social theories. I explore these in chapters 1, 3, and 4, respectively. Chapter 1 explains the Hegelian foundation of Rose's social philosophy, showing its integration of philosophy and metaphilosophy to supply methodological and logical guidance in sociology. Chapter 2 shows how, from the beginning, Rose's conception of the social totality was of a self-consciously imperfect grasp of a fissured whole, thus avoiding many of the problems associated with "totalizing." Her Frankfurt view of self-limiting rationality supported this conception and her reception of religion. I examine her versions of ideology critique and mutual recognition in chapters 3 and 4, respectively. Chapter 4 elucidates the state-civil society and law-ethics diremptions as Rose's theory of modern society.

Chapter 1 exposits Rose's Hegelian framework for social philosophy as found in *Hegel Contra Sociology*. I begin by relating Rose's work to contemporary and earlier Hegelian scholarship in order to locate her controversial and somewhat eccentric interpretation of Hegel. I then explain the argument of *Hegel Contra Sociology* and her appreciative critique of classical and Frankfurt School sociology. Since any totality (both as social reality and our epistemological grasp thereof) is necessarily imperfect, Rose accepts the complementarity of different sociological approaches but aims to account for the good practice of social theory better than

"Critique of Methodology," in *Essential Frankfurt School Reader*, 372). Cf. Adorno, introduction (1–67), and Habermas, "Positivistically Bisected Rationalism" (198–225), in Adorno et al., *Positivist Dispute*; Habermas, *On the Logic of the Social Sciences*.

13. E.g., Frankfurt Institute, *Aspects*, 119: "A theory of society must be at the same time a critique of sociology."

the self-understanding of many other social theorists. This prepares the ground for Rose's own Hegelian social philosophy. Through her (somewhat particular) interpretation of Hegel's phenomenology, triune logic and speculative identities, Rose justifies and integrates the three central moments of her account (the social totality, a philosophy that is its own metaphilosophy, a simultaneous critique of society and social theory). The key issue is the difference in the circular natures of transcendental and speculative explanation and positing. Transcendental explanation is penultimate by starting from a given precondition; speculative explanation (better, comprehension) is ultimate by historically informed reference to the social totality. The totality Rose develops is absolute ethical life, which introduces mutual recognition as her main normative ideal and provides a critique of the role of private property and bourgeois property law in society. She uses this to explain Hegel's critique of the political philosophy of Kant and Fichte as possessed of substantive errors prompted by metatheoretical misunderstanding, especially the way individualism in social contract thinking relates to the bourgeois property form. To demonstrate the sociological gains of Rose's theory, I relate it to contemporary work in social theory, including emergence, the status of contradictions within sociology, and the sociology of philosophy. I also adduce the work of Wayne Martin as an example of the way her approach could be used constructively.

Chapter 2 refines the picture of Rose's social philosophy via those elements of the Frankfurt School tradition most important to her work but which she does not defend at length because they were well-established Frankfurt ideas. These were a Weberian analysis of modernity, a combination of sociology and philosophy, a realist-idealist epistemology rather than positivism or relativism, and immanent critique aiming at emancipation and reflexive self-knowledge. I describe Rose's social philosophy more precisely as part of the Hegelian-Adorno line of this tradition, partly by drawing on the work of her intellectual colleague J. M. Bernstein. Her speculative philosophy led to an aporetic ontology; a vision of philosophy as a modernist cultural practice opening the way to modern forms of *phronesis* and *praxis*; and a self-limiting rationality. The latter produced an unusual form of Frankfurt theory that was open to religion. I further define her notion of the social totality to show it avoids totalizing. I explain the difference between her speculative philosophy and Adorno's negative dialectics. Some of the difference turns on Rose's reactivation of the role of recognition and appropriation from Hegel, one consequence of which is revealed in Rose's work on theoretical responses to Auschwitz.

Chapter 3 shows how Rose pursued the reciprocal critique of sociology and society in *Dialectic of Nihilism* through "the antinomy of law." This names the permanent but changing tension between law and ethics, foregrounded by absolute ethical life and manifested socially in tensions between customs and constitution. Rose does not attempt to solve or dissolve the antinomy, by synthesizing its poles or making one primary. She analyzes its appearance in social philosophies as an ideology critique of said philosophies based on historical legal epochs influencing their work. Rose critiques Kant, neo-Kantians, and poststructuralists in this way, showing the effects of social forms ("objective spirit") on consciousness, relating the soul and the city, as she put it. By examining Rose's critique of Kant I show how her novel ideology critique is intended to work and how in Kant's case it fails, but suggest her critiques of poststructuralism are nearer the mark. This failure is nevertheless instructive insofar as it reveals some of Rose's constructive aims, namely, support for a social and political philosophy inspired by Hegel's *Philosophy of Right*, the use of law to gain a view of the social totality, and an expansive view of jurisprudence as examining the links between the metaphysical, ethical and legal. I explore the latter in dialogue with the work of Sean Coyle, as a positive example of "jurisprudential wisdom."

Chapter 4 shows how, in *The Broken Middle* and later works, Rose developed in her mature position both the relation between philosophy and metaphilosophy and the reciprocal critique of sociology and society through the two fundamental diremptions of modern society: between state and civil society (using Marx and Arendt), and between law and ethics (using Weber). She examines how social philosophies of various stripes do not adequately reflect on these diremptions and so are determined by them in ways that undermine their intentions. In this way both postmodern political theologies and Levinasian forms of ethics are mirror images of one another, in flight from the rationalization of law and society. At this stage in the argument, with a view of Rose's social theory as a whole, it becomes apparent Rose applied her social theory to political theology rather than wrote directly theological material. I expand on the constructive side of Rose's theory as an analysis of modern society by drawing on the work of Sara Farris and Zygmunt Bauman to defend the enduring importance of the state-civil society diremption. I show the way in which Rose began to develop the law-ethics diremption in relation to ethics, politics and mutual recognition. I briefly explore the modulation Rose gave the latter.

The conclusion summarizes Rose's mature social philosophy of the broken middle.

1

Rose's Hegelianism

You do have to have a system.

—Harry Hill

1 Introduction

This chapter has two main tasks. First, it sets out the Hegelian basis of Rose's social philosophy to show how it holds together the methodological, logical, descriptive, metaphysical and normative aspects of social theory. Second, it exposits absolute ethical life as an implied and imperfectly posited social totality. Rose's Hegelian philosophy requires a totality as integral to any satisfactory account or explanation of society; this is the formal source of absolute ethical life. Its substantial source is that absolute ethical life both emerges from and critiques the diremptions of society's bourgeois property form and the antinomies of social contract theory. It is, for Rose, key to the Absolute in Hegel: "Hegel's philosophy has *no* social import if the absolute . . . cannot be thought."[1] This chapter advances three parts of my interpretation: the basis for the coherence of Rose's social theory, one of the ways it can be used to critique society and social theory, and how both are part of the unity of her work as a whole and her trilogy in particular.

1. *HCS*, 45.

A principal question of the first task is whether Rose was right to claim Hegelian speculative philosophy offers not only a better approach to social theory than both the classical sociological and Frankfurt School traditions but "a wholly different mode of social analysis."[2] In *Hegel Contra Sociology* Rose critiqued both traditions for their transcendental or neo-Kantian structure and proposed a Hegelian speculative philosophy as an alternative way of doing social philosophy. Transcendental theories (including empirical sociology) are necessary but penultimate;[3] their explanations must be taken up into a wider pattern of thought. This is a bold claim and a potential misunderstanding should be confronted immediately. Rose does not argue that transcendentally structured social theory has no worth or that its explanations fail. She argues instead that the logical foundation and the practice of social philosophy are best articulated by Hegelian speculative logic and that a more conscious appreciation of this would improve the practice of sociology to some extent. She said of *Hegel Contra Sociology*: "The first and longest chapter of my book is devoted to discussing the 'neo-Kantian paradigm,' in order to derive the conditions of *intelligibility* of sociological reason, not its 'uncomprehendability.' . . . My whole book is a defence and restatement of the view that Hegelian heights are . . . the most 'sensational' in offering a perspective on the recurrent issues of social theory."[4]

Rose's speculative logic, then, offers itself as a better articulation of what social theory does at its best than the self-understandings of neo-Kantian social theories, and accounts for sociological error derived from their self-misunderstanding. In other words, her theory sublates them; it preserves some elements and negates others.[5] In this, she continued the

2. *HCS*, 1.

3. Cf. McCarthy notes (in the introduction to Habermas, *Logic of the Social Sciences*, ix) that the classical sociologists such as Marx and Weber "were unable to grasp the methodological specificity" of their own work so attempted mistakenly to imitate the natural sciences.

4. Rose, letter to *London Review of Books*, 24.

5. *TMS*, 78, 95–96, 102–8, 51: Adorno "shows how various modes of cognition, Marxist and non-Marxist, are inadequate and distorting when taken in isolation; and how by confronting them with each other precisely on the basis of an awareness of their individual limitations, they may nevertheless yield insight into social processes"; 96: "No one method could produce conclusive results concerning any object of investigation, but the results of several methods, qualitative as well as quantitative, would need to be collated." Cf. *BM*, 182–83; *TMS*, 84.

Frankfurt School tradition.[6] This goal and her admiration for the classical sociological tradition are articulated in a lecture at Sussex University in 1986 entitled "Does Marx Have a Method?"

> The general statement of our rules always presupposes the results which are to be explained. They are an essential and deadly exercise. Sociological rationalism is this paradox. A scientism which knows that it is historically specific; that it is always both separate from and part of its object. And this seems to me equally true of all the great classic sociologists: Mannheim, Simmel, Tönnies, as well as Marx, Weber, Durkheim, Lukács, and phenomenology. Sociology must be disciplined or methodological in order to be rational, but equally it must recognize its inherent tendency to lose its object if it becomes excessively instrumental. Hence it must constantly radicalise its methods. The particular claim of Marxism to be methodological and sociological is that it exposes the illusion that experience is immediate, in a way that is more comprehensive than its rivals, more inclusive. It sees the paradoxes of other theories as contradictions, which themselves have a social origin. Thus in an important sense, the varieties of sociologies are complementary not competing. Sociology does not impose abstract schemas, it provides an exposition of the abstract experience we are already living as immediate experience.[7]

Rose's belief that different areas of social theory cannot be hermetically separated led her to favor the systematic ambitions of the founders of classical sociology above the fragmented status of much (then) current sociology. Rose's argument concerns whether and how reason, truth, ethics and politics may be legitimately grounded, or whether some form of dogmatism (rationalism) or skepticism (nihilism) are inevitable: "This book, therefore, remains the core of the project to demonstrate a nonfoundational and radical Hegel, which overcomes the opposition between nihilism and rationalism."[8] Rose also argues against positivism in sociology, arguing for an essential moment of hermeneutic understanding (*Verstehen*) for understanding human society. Indeed, insofar as social theory has progressed since 1981, thereby avoiding some of Rose's criticisms, it has tended to confirm her core thesis that the issue is the choice between neo-Kantian and Hegelian social theory. Insofar as

6. E.g., Horkheimer, "Traditional and Critical Theory," 231.

7. Rose, "Does Marx Have a Method?"

8. *HCS*, preface (1995 ed.).

theories like those of Giddens and Bourdieu succeed it is because they approximate to the Hegelian speculative rationality Rose sets out.[9] Likewise many continuing sociological debates are set within German idealist terms, knowingly or not,[10] often in ways that repeat the original debates, though sometimes with less sophistication.[11]

In order to answer the question about the success or failure of Rose's alternative social philosophy I first situate Rose's Hegelianism within the contemporary field of Hegelian studies, in relation to non-metaphysical approaches to Hegel (§2). These interpretations rose to prominence in English-language scholarship after 1989, almost a decade after Rose's own Hegel book but they are nevertheless the most useful way of expositing her thinking. Then I explain the nature of the argument in *Hegel Contra Sociology*, and expound its criticisms of social theory by reference to the work of Richard Biernacki and Nigel Pleasants, who have independently made similar critiques to Rose against, respectively, social science (§3.2.1) and critical theory (§3.2.2). Having thus corroborated Rose's complaints against social theory, I explain Rose's version of Hegelian speculative philosophy (§4). Programmatically put, Rose's speculative social theory involves a phenomenological exploration of ethics, society and politics (§4.1); a triune rather than dichotomous way of thinking (§4.2); and speculative propositions (§4.3). I then show Rose's Hegelian philosophy in action as it critiques society and social theory (§5.1) and posits an implied social whole, absolute ethical life (§5.2). In the course of the chapter I elucidate Rose's work by comparing it to other social theories and suggesting some examples of work that could be regarded as meeting Rose's requirements for social philosophy. I will also show the utility of Rose's social philosophy by going beyond her own use of it by relating it to questions in contemporary sociology she did not directly address: emergence, the status of contradictions within sociology, and

9. Pierre Bourdieu's concept of *habitus* ("structured and structuring structure") works like a Hegelian concept (*Begriff*): "When one speaks of the aristocratic asceticism of teachers or the pretension of the petite bourgeoisie, one is not only describing these groups by one, or even the most important, of their properties, but also endeavouring to name the principle which generates all their properties and all their judgments of their, or other people's, properties." *Distinction*, 166.

10. E.g., Bloor, "Anti-Latour," 81–112, and Latour, "For David Bloor," 113–29. Latour and Bloor talk as if the German Idealists were subjective idealists. Further, Rose's version of phenomenology can incorporate Latour's idea of the influence of non-human beings on human ideas and agency.

11. The same claim is argued against postmodern philosophy in *DN* and Pippin, *Modernism as a Philosophical Problem*.

the sociology of philosophy. I answer two criticisms of Rose's early and late work (§6), that her phenomenology is unable to address specific determinations and that absolute ethical life is too vague to do any substantive work.

Within the larger argument of the book, this chapter lays out the main theoretical architecture for Rose's social theory. Although she would revise her thought in various ways, she never fundamentally departed from the Hegelianism she expounded in 1981. Her later thought therefore cannot be properly understood apart from the Frankfurt-School-influenced-Hegelianism set out here. Rose's second book reaffirmed her commitment to the Frankfurt School but in a critical manner. She distanced herself from Adorno and Lukács though remaining strongly influenced by them even in her interpretation of Hegel. In the preface to a new printing of *Hegel Contra Sociology* in 1995 she expressed its role as the foundation of her work in *Dialectic of Nihilism*, *The Broken Middle* and *Judaism and Modernity*. In those books she repeats the speculative critique first aimed at sociology against, respectively, poststructuralism; political theology, anthropology, modernism, architecture, political philosophy, etc.; and various forms of Jewish theology and philosophy, or uses thereof. In the process, her position was elaborated and refined, the results of which will occupy chapters 3 and 4. This order follows the chronological and conceptual development of Rose's social theory. To understand Rose, one needs first to grasp her background in and commitment to her Frankfurt Hegelianism, then her mature position and its appropriation and critique of its competitors.

2 Situating Rose's Hegelianism

Hegel Contra Sociology was one of the first books of the English-language Hegelian renaissance of the last few decades.[12] Rose, in 1981, took more seriously than most of her contemporaries the systematic nature of Hegel's thought and the centrality of the Absolute to it, but simultaneously altered the details of his overall philosophy.[13] Rose's Hegel should not be conflated with Hegel himself. Her work asks to be judged not as a strict exegesis of Hegel but as a contribution to social theory.[14] As she would

12. Harris, "Hegel Renaissance," 77–105 (esp. 90–91).

13. I follow Rose's use of "Absolute" as a shorthand for absolute ethical life.

14. Bernasconi, review of *HCS*, 43: "I understand her book as an attempt to repeat

later write, her version of speculative philosophy was partly a criticism of Hegel.[15] Further, her interpretation of Hegel is at times controversial and even eccentric. My argument is not that Rose offers the best reading of Hegel but that the elements she took from Hegel's philosophy are assembled in a useful and coherent manner.

Rose interprets Hegel's later thought as consistent with his early writings, though most commentators agree there is a shift in Hegel's thought, dating his mature work from the 1807 *Phenomenology*. Rose does not deny Hegel changes his mind or that his thought matures; her argument is only that his earlier works display more obviously the links between the form of thinking employed by Kant and Fichte and the content of their political, ethical and legal philosophies, and that this connection between the form and substance of thinking remains in play in all of Hegel's later work.[16] Since she believes Kant and Fichte's form of thinking are shared by sociology, Hegel's critique of his predecessors can also be made to work against the sociological tradition. Her approach to Hegel is less concerned with discovering exactly what Hegel meant than with Rose's intention to "retrieve Hegelian speculative experience for social theory."[17] As Rose pointed out, Hegel's phrase "absolute knowing" (like Nietzsche's "absolute method") is an oxymoron, and should have alerted readers to Hegel's (and Nietzsche's) "facetious" presentation.[18] The same is true of Rose's conception of "absolute ethical life."

Rose's Hegelianism approximates to the inaccurately named "non-metaphysical" interpretation. Robert Pippin, the *locus classicus* of the non-metaphysical interpretation, refers to Rose's work as similar to his approach.[19] This is true in three broad senses: Rose understands Hegel in a "non-metaphysical" way, that is, she interprets *Geist* as something like the mindedness of culture, not as divine or originating from beyond the

---

Hegel's philosophy as social theory in order to destroy it as onto-theo-logy."

15. *HCS* is not entirely clear about this but in a letter dated 12 June 1991, Rose wrote that her version of "*speculative* exposition . . . (arising from my *criticism* of Hegel see *Hegel Contra Sociology* last two chapters esp. 199) can accommodate everything post-modernity is convinced it omits, and still *produce a critical account of modernity*" (Box 11, original emphasis).

16. A view substantiated by Speight, "'Metaphysics' of Morals," 379–402; and Avineri, *Hegel's Theory of the Modern State*.

17. *HCS*, 1.

18. *MBL*, 56.

19. *Philosophical Problem*, 194n29; 195n42; *passim*; *Hegel's Idealism*, 262n9; 276n34.

world;[20] she views Hegel's social and political philosophy as a historical self-understanding of modern society and thought; and she regards his system as in some way incomplete, open, revisable, inherently negative.

Rose says the dialectical progression of ideas and forms of life proceeds by surprise, contingency and error, which means she favors the weaker sense of rational necessity in dialectics.[21] (The strong sense is that B improves on A in being the necessary and only possible next position to take. The weak sense is that B can be shown retrospectively to be an improvement on A, though other options are available. In the strong sense, everything later *must* follow from everything earlier and so is contained therein.)[22] For Hegel "the thought of the totality of what is . . . [is] the Absolute [that] must be thought of . . . as *process* and transition rather than *thing* or entity."[23] Rose viewed the Absolute as a "broken middle," and Hegel's system as one that "acknowledges both its circularity and the breaks in the circle."[24] Hegel believed he had found the basically complete form of the philosophical idea—i.e., of logical and ontological categories—although further development was possible.[25] Rose described this later as "aporetic philosophy" aware of its gaps and problems.[26]

Although Rose can be described as a "non-metaphysical" Hegelian she insisted on the importance of metaphysics, but this discrepancy is

20. Such mindedness occurs in various forms: in objective spirit in institutions; in subjective spirit in individuals; in Absolute spirit in the self-knowing of the concept through individuals and cultures at a certain reflexive stage. Pippin, *Hegel's Idealism*, 147: Spirit is Hegel's "term of art for social existence, for collectively achieved practices." For the antecedents of this, see Hartmann, "Hegel," 101–24.

21. *MBL*, 72.

22. Pippin, *Philosophical Problem*, 76, says Hegel's is the stronger version but probably fails, but only the weak version is required to defend Pippin's (and, I add, Rose's) version of Hegelianism.

23. Duquette, "Kant, Hegel and the Possibility of a Speculative Logic," 1–16 (7–8).

24. *HCS*, 199. Many commentators now argue Hegel himself had a view of the Absolute and/or Being as intrinsically incomplete. E.g., Carlson, *Commentary to Hegel's* Science of Logic.

25. *PhR* §216 and Addition. Exactly how these two claims could be reconciled continues to be debated. See Kolb, "What Is Open," 29–50; Pippin, *Philosophical Problem*. It is enough for Rose's position to say that with Hegel's philosophy thought reaches a certain formal self-awareness that has a certain completeness but remains to be refined and applied. It has this completeness because it becomes fully aware for the first time of the sociopolitical conditioning of thought (thought's conditions of possibility in a much wider sense than Kant allowed) and the role of thought in constituting objects.

26. *MBL*, 7–15.

quite easily defrayed. For Rose "metaphysics" means a general account of how we take the world to be, which is elaborated from our various commitments when we try to put them into practice amid the contention and difficulty they inevitably occasion, and when we try to relate them coherently to one another.[27] These commitments and their articulation are known to be historical products, though some of them seem non-reversible, like the importance of freedom, that "no belief (action, norm, etc.) can be valid apart from our authorizing of it, self-legislating it"; that "significant human values, practices, and institutions" emerge "historically as the intended or unintended consequence of particular human activities"; and that we are part of the natural world.[28] "Modernity *has once and for all* set the world in perpetual motion and change."[29] Just this, however, is how the non-metaphysicals interpret Hegel. The disparity is entirely verbal, resulting from the general ambiguity of the term "metaphysics." Both metaphysical and non-metaphysical Hegelians accept there is metaphysics in Hegel, they disagree over how much and how separable it is from other parts of his thinking. The non-metaphysical Hegelians wanted to show that Hegel had not regressed to pre-critical metaphysics but had intensified and radicalized Kant's critical philosophy by questioning givenness *tout court* and challenging the assumptions latent in Kant's Copernican turn. Hegel accepted Kant's Copernican turn in at least two senses: that our conceptual categories were the condition of possibility of objects and objective reality, and that thought was essentially apperceptive (that any judgment is in principle accompanied by the awareness that I am making that judgment). *Geist* is not a divine reality or a natural given but a way of thinking about how the meaningfulness of the world is dependent upon historically and socially changing conditions and human intellectual categories. At the same time, there is no permanently hidden reality as in Kant's noumenal realm.

Lumsden avers the "question for Hegel that constitutes *the* modern problem of philosophy is *not* an epistemological question concerned with how consciousness could know anything about external realities but the question of how a finite being can find a meaningful place in a world set in constant motion,"[30] which means Hegel is "concerned with capturing

27. Williams, "Between."

28. Bernstein, *Adorno*, 236.

29. Lumsden, "Rise of the Non-Metaphysical Hegel," 51–65, 59.

30. Ibid., 58.

a kind of modern self-understanding, which would enable the modern subject to identify with the self-transforming nature of norms."[31] Rose saw this as continuous with the ancient Greek concern with the soul and the city, but her more immediate influence was the Frankfurt School's inheritance of Hegel in their investigations into ideology and reification as the contemporary forms of the determination of consciousness by society and objective spirit. In fact, Lumsden's characterization is partly misleading, since Hegel was equally concerned with both epistemological and social questions. Hegel began with an interest in religious and political reform, seeking to be a man of letters like Lessing, who would bring the philosophical and political changes afoot in universities into popular consciousness and acceptance, and felt that the details of Kant's epistemological revolution could be left to scholars. But he came to realize that the two sides were inextricably bound together, and that changes in one had to be worked through in the other.[32] The post-Kantian German idealists were all very interested in how our intellectual categories could correctly connect with the external world. These terms are vague but important because German idealists are still, even now, sometimes construed as subjective idealists, as if their claim was that our thoughts create or invent reality.

It is the German idealist combination of logic, epistemology and social theory that is at work in Rose's own thinking from 1981 onward. She, like Pippin, thinks intellectual and political modernity (including postmodernity) is best understood by going back to Kant and Hegel. Both favor Hegel but see him as following and extending Kant. Both think the *Phenomenology* and *Logic* should be understood together, and that Hegel's core project can work without defending every claim he makes in those texts. Both saw postmodernism as misunderstanding the German idealist tradition and failing to realize their dependency on some of its central notions (freedom, the subject, metaphysics). Neither thinks Hegel offers a philosophical or theological theodicy; neither accepts that modernity is completely to be rejected. Both think institutions are a key element in the practical and theoretical criticism and defense of modernity. Both regard thought as intrinsically incomplete.[33]

31. Ibid.

32. Pinkard, *Hegel: A Biography*, 33–37, 59–64, 80.

33. William Rasch compares *HCS* and Pippin thus: "Pippin agrees with Rose on the desirability of being able to think the simultaneity of dichotomies (of being able to think, for instance, the simultaneity of the self-determining and yet determined nature

3 The Nature and Scope of the Argument in *Hegel Contra Sociology*

3.1 *Hegel Contra Sociology* in-itself

The enduring antinomy of sociology—variously thought as agent/structure, freedom/determination, system/actor—is: do people make society or does society make people? Does Rose's version of Hegelian speculation provide a better way to think through this antinomy and its implications? She wrote: "The speculative proposition that substance is subject refers to a reality in which subject does not know itself as substance but is, nevertheless, a determination of substance."[34] The historical dimensions of speculation "reveal the *aporia* of subjectivity: the subjective standpoint is criticized by means of the exposition of its formation; but the absolute is thought as subject."[35] That is, individual subjects are shaped by the substance of society, yet society itself can only be properly understood as a kind of subject, that is, as a totality that is more than the sum of its parts (we will refine this thought over the next two chapters). As Pippin noted,

> The foundational issue [in *Hegel Contra Sociology* is] . . . the way in which a subject can be said to determine itself (to *be* a subject), . . . what . . . could be called the "Fichtean dimension," and yet how a subject can be said also to be a real, concrete, and so, in some sense, determined subject (. . . Fichte's aporia). To think both aspects together, indeed even to be able to recognize that they must be thought together, requires, as Rose points out with great thoroughness and insight, the move to Hegel's "speculative" position.[36]

Central to any proper social explanation is to see that people make society and society makes people. Hegel's speculative way of handling that duality emerged from his critique of Kant and Fichte and can be used, Rose thinks, as a critique of the way the duality is handled in much sociology, which she considers neo-Kantian in its founding logic. The

---

of subjectivity). . . . Indeed, an ineradicable Kantian impossibility remains in Pippin's Hegel, for what Rose sees as an inevitable consequence of attempting to think the absolute from within the space of bourgeois society, Pippin seems to see as constitutive of thought itself" (*Niklas Luhmann's Modernity*, 7). Rose in fact thinks all societies, not only bourgeois society, create and are constituted by aporia.

34. *HCS*, 112.

35. Ibid., 113.

36. *Hegel's Idealism*, 272n49.

heart of Rose's claim that Hegel offers a different kind of social theory from the mainstream tradition is therefore in the meaning of the speculative handling of this pair of terms.[37] In order to get to this, I summarize Rose's argument, then discuss her critique of non-speculative sociology (§3.2) and then treat of her speculative philosophy (§4).

Hegel Contra Sociology set out a reading of Hegel with several aims. It argued that Hegel's fundamental goal as a philosopher remained constant from the late eighteenth century on: to critique contemporary philosophy and society in order to reveal a different ethical life. It read Hegel systematically, which involved three interrelated tasks: to unite Hegel's *oeuvre* around his speculative logic and view the early and late works as a piece; to combat thereby the various Hegel myths that were prominent in English philosophy at the time; and to use this Hegelian philosophy as a basis for social philosophy. Hegel criticized the logical and philosophical basis of the practical philosophies of Kant and Fichte, in his natural law essay, in the *Differenzschrift*, and throughout his later writings; Rose performs the same sort of critique on neo-Kantian sociology, postmodern thought, political theology, etc. Rose thought the philosophical issues she addressed fed into substantive theorizing, and she believed she had shown how Hegel's thought of the Absolute affected thinking in various areas of social thought (religion, art, work, etc.). Rose believed some of the fundamental justifications for and forms of society were the same in the late eighteenth century as now, including: a distinction between state and civil society, a capitalist economy, private property law, a culture of "reflection" (that is, of making fixed divisions between opposites). Insofar as these and other similarities remain in place, Hegel's thought is directly relevant to contemporary social theorizing. Rose took Hegel's attempt to unify theoretical and practical reason to be superior to the later attempts of Weber and Durkheim and the earlier attempts of Kant and Fichte to do the same. Kant and Fichte were understood by Hegel and Rose as representing the summation and consummation of their time and culture: the culture of reflection or understanding (*Verstand*).[38]

37. *PhR*, preface, 3: "But in this book I presuppose that philosophy's mode of progression from one topic to another and its mode of scientific proof—this whole speculative way of knowing—is essentially distinct from any other way of knowing." Contrast the view that to explain a social phenomenon is to reduce it to natural scientific explanations.

38. Hegel's early works give "reflection" a negative denotation, whereas later he saw reflection as a necessary moment of the concept.

Rose's outline of the *form* or structure of Hegel's philosophy is accordingly offered in contrast to Kant, because the latter's critical philosophy sets the terms of debate for German idealism and later sociology. (She nevertheless opposes the *content* of Hegel's thought more often to Fichte's than Kant's.[39] Such distinctions are at best heuristic, since in speculative philosophy "content is essentially bound up with *form*,"[40] but the impression remains that in Rose's mind Kant and Hegel were closer on ethics and politics than Hegel and Fichte.) Hegel replaced Kant's transcendental method of argument with a phenomenology; his moral philosophy with the idea of (absolute) ethical life; and his disjunction between theoretical and practical philosophy with their unity as expressed in the *Science of Logic*.[41] Here we should distinguish two ways in which Kant's arguments have transcendental form or structure. In discussing the transcendental structure of neo-Kantian sociology, Rose has in mind arguments of the form: "we know we have *p*, what else must be the case for us to have *p*?" For example, Kant began from the fact that morality is binding, and argued that God must exist and we must presuppose ourselves to be (noumenally) free for morality to work as it does. A second feature of transcendental arguments is both less common and more controversial. A transcendental argument may gesture toward a transcendental object, which is an object that cannot be known (*wissen*) but may be thought (*denken*).[42] In Kant's case, we cannot know God or freedom but *must* (not simply *may*) think them. The controversies around whether the noumenal realm and its transcendental objects can be coherently thought caused many post-Kantian theorists to abandon both doctrines and so leave Kant's transcendental idealism behind. Metacritical theories, as we shall see, are transcendental in the first sense but not the second: they take a feature of society as given or conditioned (say, morality) and seek to explain it by recourse to something that conditions it (say, the economy), but that precondition is immanent not transcendental. (Hence, the term "quasi-transcendental.")

Rose exposits Hegel's whole thought as speculative, as an alternative to the dualism of his idealist predecessors and later sociology, and as intrinsically bound up with the Absolute; hence her oft-repeated line

39. E.g., *HCS*, 215–17.

40. E.g., *PhR*, preface, 4; cf. *EL* §160, §162, and the preface.

41. *HCS*, 48–50.

42. Kant, *Critique of Pure Reason*, B166 and note.

that Hegel's philosophy has no social import if the Absolute cannot be thought.[43] Such philosophy interprets experience speculatively and expresses it in speculative propositions. The main speculative proposition of Hegel's thought, according to Rose, is: "In general religion and the foundation of the state is [*sic*] one and the same thing; they are identical in and for themselves."[44] That is, the main speculative experience for Hegel was the harmony *and* disharmony (or unity and difference, as Rose often puts it) between political legitimacy and ideology; between political structures and institutions on the one hand and the inner dispositions, the customs, ethos and ethics of a people and culture, on the other.[45]

In the first chapter of the book she clears the ground to enable the speculative reception of Hegel as opposed to neo-Kantian forms of sociology that dominate the tradition and the imposition of which on Hegel have created so many misunderstandings. She then explains, via his early writings, speculative propositions and Hegel's central concern with absolute ethical life, which is substantial freedom, the unity of finite and infinite and of theoretical and practical reason (ch. 2).[46] Next she offers a reading of the rest of his corpus to elaborate what is involved in absolute ethical life so conceived: his lectures on religion and history (ch. 3), on art (ch. 4), the *Phenomenology* (ch. 5), the *Logic* (ch. 6). Chapter 7 returns to the questions of understanding society and how philosophy has a role in social change, suggesting a speculative Hegel provides a better grasp of the theory-praxis relationship than Marxism, though Rose interprets Hegel as close to Marx, and combining idealism and materialism. The result of her exposition enables the possibility of a "critical Marxism," which would combine Marx's analysis of capital with a philosophy of subjectivity and culture in capitalism, which Rose believed deficient in Marxism.

43. *HCS*, 45, 98, 218, 223, cf. 101, 221.

44. Ibid., 51, citing *Philosophie der Religion*, 16, 236, tr. I 297 (Rose's own translation and square brackets).

45. Ibid., 224. Cf. *PhR* §267. This reappears in *DN* as "the antinomy of law" and in *BM* as the diremption between law and ethics.

46. *EL* §214: "The idea can be grasped as *reason* (this is the genuine philosophical meaning of *reason*), further as *subject-object*, as the *unity of the ideal and the real, of the finite and the infinite, of the soul and the body*, as the *possibility that has its actuality in itself*, as that the *nature* of which *can only be conceived as existing*, and so forth, because in it [the idea] all relationships of the understanding are contained, but in their *infinite* return and identity in themselves."

3.2 Is Hegel contra sociology? Rose's critique of classical and critical social theory

3.2.1 Classical social theory

Rose's title is misleading if understood as simplistically opposing Hegelian philosophy to sociology. On Rose's reading Hegel is a social theorist and Rose valued the classical sociological tradition. She spoke highly of it in her lectures, used it in her books, and praised Weber, Marx and Durkheim as better at integrating sociological and philosophical concerns than many later thinkers. The reviewers of *Hegel Contra Sociology* in the early eighties could not know that, however, and Rose unfortunately appeared to some to be arguing that the neo-Kantian structure of sociology voided its conclusions.[47] Yet Rose states explicitly on the first page: "The neo-Kantian paradigm is the source of both the strengths and weaknesses of Durkheim's and Weber's sociology."[48] Neo-Kantian sociology does provide information about and insight into society but is incomplete. Its transcendental circularity posits a condition of possibility (e.g., the economy) and a conditioned (e.g., moral philosophy), but does not sufficiently allow the conditioned to redound onto the condition: "A transcendental account necessarily presupposes the actuality or existence of its object and seeks to discover the conditions of its possibility."[49] Again: "Empirical reality or experience of it cannot be specified apart from concepts. Experience of social reality is mediated by concepts, thus there is no independently definable reality to pit against concepts in order to 'test' them . . . to stipulate *a priori*, that is apart from experience, what is to count as empirical evidence for a concept, is merely to register what the methodology is equipped to register. . . . A circle is unavoidable."[50] As Adorno had it, "an object gets investigated by a research tool which,

47. Knapp sums up the worry (201): "Even if she has correctly formulated the first principle of modern social theory, this still forgets the difference between a first principle and a developed science, between an acorn and an oak."

48. *HCS*, 1. Cf. 31, where she argues that Lukács was neo-Kantian but nevertheless his work had "great sociological force."

49. Ibid., 1. Notice that the non-redounding of precondition onto conditioned is a feature of neo-Kantian sociology but not something she attributes to Kant, since Kant did allow such redounding (*JAM*, 112).

50. *TMS*, 101.

through its own formulation, decides what the object is: a simple circle."[51] Hence Rose:

> With instruments in general we can demonstrate their use without setting about using them. . . . But designing, building and examining sociological tools can only be done by the same rationality that is sociology's object. Rationality means rules, and sociology is the study of the rules and conventions of social life. So we are in a vicious circle. We are assuming the validity of the operation whose validity is to be questioned. This [neo-Kantian] approach is claiming that it is neutral and makes no assumptions but it has overlooked a major assumption: that logic, here socio-logic, is distinct from the rest of reality and that it can be used to grasp that reality, or at least part of it. The very metaphor of tool in sociology is suspect. The power of sociology, especially Marxist, is that scientific rationality and subjective consciousness are themselves part of the whole to be apprehended. Instrumental method, however, seeks to know before it starts knowing. This is absurd—this is what Hegel said about Kant.[52]

There are five substantive implications of the transcendental form of social theory that are of importance for Rose's case. Each is to some extent related to a lack of historicality, insofar as they involve reifying either a feature of society or a concept for interpreting or explaining society. Rose's social philosophy, by contrast, is intentionally historical in its phenomenological approach. Each is also related to the circularity of social theorizing, which is worked out differently in transcendental and speculative social philosophies.

First, in a transcendental account, that which explains other terms does not explain itself, such that one term tends to become unknowable. For example, Fichte and Kant considered variously the ego, categorical imperative and transcendental unity of apperception as unknowable. They saw this as a limit of knowledge itself, rather than a resting point of a historical formation of reason within modern society. This in turn bleeds into their political philosophies and so has substantive, not simply formal, implications. Similarly John Milbank, on the basis of *Hegel Contra Sociology*, argued in *Theology and Social Theory*[53] that the charac-

51. *Soziologie*, cited in the introduction to "Critique of Methodology," by Gebhardt, in Frankfurt Institute for Social Research, *Essential Frankfurt School Reader*, 376.

52. Rose, "Does Marx Have a Method?"

53. Milbank, *Theology and Social Theory*, 101–44.

teristic gesture of sociology of religion was to "explain" (away) religion by reducing it to society, which obfuscated the nature of both religion and society, and took the concept of society for granted, when in fact society itself requires explanation.[54] Rose discerned a similar difficulty in late nineteenth-century neo-Kantian jurisprudence.[55] Thus Eike Gebhardt: "Without a theory of what mediates between social and cognitive factors, i.e., of the 'transcendental' constitution of consciousness and reality, their relation had to remain accidental—or exemplify a cultural truism which begs the very question it pretends to answer."[56] Rose's speculative philosophy uses phenomenological history to discover various "third" terms mediating between society and individuals.[57]

Second, any precondition is itself conditioned and so in need of a further precondition, thus creating an infinite regress.[58] Speculative circularity, as we shall see below, substitutes the bad infinite regress for a good infinite regress.

Third, Rose repeats Adorno's criticism of prioritizing either philosophy—such that truth becomes untouched by history—or sociology—such that truth is lost because philosophy is replaced by sociology of knowledge. Writes Adorno:

> What are alleged to be the most highly abstract and universal factors governing knowledge, the factors that must be present for knowledge to be conceived of in the first place, presuppose the element of factuality, of actual existence, that they are supposed to explain. Thus reflection on the fact that subject and object or transcendental factors and human reality are mutually interdependent is at the same time a necessary pointer to the fact that I must not make absolutes of these transcendental factors, I must not hypostatize them. This means that I may not separate them from their genesis, their origins in factual reality, any more than I can detach factual reality or judgments about the world of things from their subjective mediation and hence

54. Rose and Milbank made these criticisms in the early eighties, since then things have moved on (e.g., Beckford, *Social Theory and Religion*, 2–3) although the fundamental approach is arguably still widespread (see Brown, *Death of Christian Britain*).

55. *DN*, 25–49.

56. Introduction to Frankfurt Institute, *Essential Frankfurt School Reader*, 356.

57. Adorno criticized the tendency to absolutize one term and remove it from mediation since mediations give it its meaning (*Metacritique of Epistemology* excerpted in *Adorno Reader*, 112–36).

58. *DN*, 70.

> from their historical roots . . . just as it is impossible to see the categories other than in relation to their origin and to history, it is equally impossible simply to *derive* concepts like space, time and the categories from history and to reduce them to social phenomena.[59]

Rose's Hegelian speculative philosophy, by contrast, examines its own positing more thoroughly than neo-Kantian social theory and, as we will see below, is circular in a way that avoids making one side of the condition/precondition prior to the other. Indeed, *Hegel Contra Sociology* is a kind of sociology of sociology.[60] Rose, following Hegel, makes the social determination of thought intrinsic to the very logic of thinking itself, without reducing thought to the sociology of knowledge. By contrast, the neo-Kantian "transformation of Kantian transcendental epistemology into a series of *methodologies* concerned with ascertaining the basis of validity implied that epistemological problems could be transformed into problems of the sociology of knowledge."[61] As a result, the force of practical reasons is much reduced and Rose thus doubts the quasi-transcendental form of social theory can fully account for ethics, especially if it is used as the basis of philosophy as a whole and as the way to hold together practical and theoretical reason. The neo-Kantians conceded they could not explain the unity of fact and value; these had to be taken on faith.[62] "Behind [Weber's] demand for value free science lies an epistemological conception derived from the neo-Kantians, namely, that value judgments are not the result of cognitive acts. In fact Weber later saw the justification of practical judgments as meaningless."[63] Weber and Durkheim accept the fact-value distinction in a way that assumes mind and world are separate, and so fail properly to understand their mutual mediation. Weber, following Rickert, saw the world itself as irrational, and the values and categories used to understand it imposed on it by human minds.[64] Rose's Hegelian social philosophy does not take the fact-value distinction so rigidly, and sets it within a different mind-world relationship in which

59. Adorno, *Kant's* Critique of Pure Reason, 167–68.

60. I owe this phrase to Nigel Tubbs, in private correspondence, 22 October 2013. On the sociology of sociology, see Ritzer, *Explorations in Social Theory*.

61. Israel, "Epistemology and Sociology of Knowledge," 116.

62. Cf. Beiser, "Normativity in Neo-Kantianism," 9–27; and Adorno, "Actuality of Philosophy," 121.

63. Frisby, introduction to *Positivist Dispute*, ix–xliv (xxiv; cf. xxxix).

64. Habermas, *Logic of Social Sciences*, 4–5, 13–16.

the aim is to see all the multiple mediations through which subject and object, individual and society, create one another.[65]

Fourth, neo-Kantian sociology is problematic when the "notion of the limitations of knowledge simply turns into positivism of a generally scientific or, more specifically, psychological or sociological kind."[66] An interesting corollary of Rose's critique of sociology is that one of the sources of the repeated recurrences of positivism[67] within sociology may be the lack of appreciation by sociologists about the transcendental form of their thinking.[68] Neo-Kantians retained the transcendental form of enquiry developed by Kant but rejected his transcendental idealism. As a result, the objectivity of knowledge—the way in which thought relates to the world—became a problem. As Max Horkheimer put it, in neo-Kantianism

> particular traits in the theoretical activity of the specialist are here elevated to the rank of universal categories, of instances of the world-mind, the eternal "Logos." More accurately, decisive elements in social life are reduced to the theoretical activity of the savant. Thus "the power of knowledge" is called "the power of creative origination." "Production" means the "creative sovereignty of thought." For any datum it must be possible to deduce all its determinations from theoretical systems and ultimately from mathematics.[69]

In other words, the touchstone for a system of thought is thought itself, in a way that tended to insulate thought from receptivity to thought's other.[70] (Rose viewed poststructuralism's attitude to truth as reproducing

65. *HCS*, 194: "Absolute knowledge is a path which must be continually traversed, re-collecting the forms of consciousness and the forms of science. This idea of a whole which cannot be grasped in one moment or in one statement for it must be experienced is the idea of the system."

66. Pippin, *Hegel's Idealism*, 58 (referencing *HCS*).

67. On which, see Steinmetz, *Politics of Method in the Human Sciences*.

68. Cf. Habermas, *Logic of Social Sciences*, 109.

69. Horkheimer, "Traditional and Critical Theory," 198. Horkheimer is here discussing the Marburg school of neo-Kantians, whereas Weber was more influenced by the Heidelberg or Southwestern neo-Kantians, but Rose felt the same problem was discernable in both (which she traced back to the influence of Lotze). She thought Marburg neo-Kantianism, however, developed "a logic of thought which is independent of the process of cognition," which "heralds the end of transcendental logic" (*HCS*, 10) and was thus not Kantian enough.

70. *Hegel's Idealism*, 185.

this neo-Kantian problem.) Validity, values and cognition of the world are separated from one another. Validity becomes an *a priori* matter, separable from conditions of experience; values are based only on conviction. Weber's value neutrality, for example, while legitimate if methodologically constrained, "makes independent scientific access to empirical reality a logical impossibility and ultimately reduces science to just one more value."[71] (Rose believed poststructuralism's use of Nietzsche replicated this neo-Kantian problem.) Now of course sociologists know they should test their theory against the evidence and alter it accordingly if it does not match.[72] In that sense, their theory is not at all trapped within thought; but two problems may arise. The first problem occurs when the circularity of the *explicans* and *explicandum* is left untroubled. Since the theory is supposed to explain the data, the data is taken to support the theory rather than disturb it. A virtuous circle may turn vicious. The second problem is to regard the externality between mind and world as fundamental, rather than a useful method for specific activities. Experience and representation are then no longer part of cognition and method becomes external to its object. As William Rasch summarizes:

> Rose reads modern sociology as a bad infinite based on the neo-Kantian abstract opposition of validity and value. . . . If the "structural metacritique of validity (Durkheim)" leads to the absolutizing of the "totally conditioned agent," then the "action-oriented metacritique of values (Weber)" results in the absolutizing of the "unconditioned actor." . . . On the one hand we have the primacy of theoretical reason, the "structured" realm of necessity that is nature; on the other, the primacy of practical reason, the free, supersensible, self-positing "Ich" that simultaneously posits its conditioned other. The former leads to an "empty" structural sociology, the latter to a "blind" action theory.[73]

This is all the more worthy of critique for Rose because the classical sociologists rightly retained Hegel's ambition to unite practical and theoretical reason, but were not as successful as Hegel in prosecuting the aim. Once again, it is a question of refinement rather than outright rejection.

71. Crane, "Habermas and Hegel," 638.

72. Rose spoke approvingly of Weber: "Weber's sociology is circular, but it is a virtuous not a vicious circle, a journey, a *hodos*, which ends where it began, after of course a lot has happened on the way" (Rose, "Does Marx Have a Method?").

73. *Luhmann's Modernity*, 4.

Fifth, neo-Kantian sociology has a tendency to treat the appearance of society as its reality.[74] This is not simply a matter of dissatisfaction with first-order statements made by individuals about their experience.[75] Rose shares the Frankfurt view of social forms as not-fully-actualized-forms or forms-in-process. For Hegel, the social forms not fully realized ("actualized") are those based on the concept and the concept has both rational and ethical normativity[76] (for example, a state *should* be like *x* and do *y*). Further, Rose uses Hegel's logical category of *Schein* ("show," "seeming" or "appearance") as a fundamental feature of social philosophizing. *Schein* is the appearance of something, and thus presents a limited truth of that something, but conceals a fuller truth—the essence behind the appearance—to see which a more comprehensive view is necessary. The appearance is not left behind but retained in the more comprehensive view. As a category of social philosophy, then, *Schein* means that a phenomenon is not fully understood unless its connections to and mediations in the social totality are known (making it "more concrete" in Hegel's terms). *Schein* is also used to ground the idea of necessary illusions (or fetishism), in which a society structurally produces certain appearances, which are both true in a limited sense and yet mask its real structures. For example, capitalist societies systematically foster the view of individuals as atomized and self-constituted rather than intersubjectively formed, and this both expresses a significant feature of experience (hence the illusion can take hold) and yet hides the multiple dependencies between people. They are necessary to the society because they play an important role in the reproduction of the society. Revealing necessary illusions (or fetishisms) is one of the two main forms of ideology critique taken from Marx by the Frankfurt School.[77] A failure to do social philosophy thoroughly leavened by the category of *Schein* and forms-in-process can result in work that is insufficiently critical of society and rescinds from normative

74. *TMS*, 23.

75. Although the first-order/second-order distinction is common in sociology, it can be difficult to make in practice: Greiffenhagen and Sharrock, "Where Do the Limits of Experience Lie?," 70–93.

76. Beiser, *Hegel*, 211–13.

77. Arato, introduction to "Esthetic Theory and Cultural Criticism," in *Essential Frankfurt School Reader*, 201. The second main form (mistaking theory for reality) is discussed at the beginning of chapter 3.

judgment:[78] "social conformism is smuggled in as a criterion of meaning for the social sciences."[79]

Is Rose's critique justified? Peter Knapp voices two important problems: "Rose deals not with contemporary sociology but with Durkheim, Weber and the Frankfurt school, and she does not deal with their substantive theories but with one aspect of their methodological self-understanding . . . [she] tends to portray Hegel's own social theory as a simple stamping of philosophical positions by property relations, a picture which is vulgar-Marxist and ultimately anti-Marxist."[80] The preceding paragraphs make clear that theoretical (or methodological) and substantive issues cannot be separated, hence Rose's focus on the theoretical level is not only legitimate but has implications for substantive theories themselves (we will see below further examples of interaction between these two levels). Rose thinks Hegel can help social theory improve by being more aware of the form of thought it uses and how thought and reality relate.[81]

On Knapp's second point, there are moments where Rose strays into vulgar-Marxist pronouncements,[82] or lays herself open to misunderstanding, as when she writes that the neo-Kantians shared the problem of "the transformation of Kant's critical method into a logic of validity (*Geltungslogik*), a general method, [which] *excluded any enquiry into empirical reality*."[83] How can this be, when the whole purpose of sociology is to enquire into the empirical reality of society? Rose's protest is more subtle than a simplistic reading of this sentence indicates. The problem with a "method" in the human (or *geistig*) realm is its external relation to what it analyzes. Hence her doctoral supervisor Kołakowski: "What we properly call a method should be a sequence of operations which, when applied to the same subject, will give the same or approximately

78. Cf. Thornhill, "Political Legitimacy," 135–69 (164n1, and the references there): "Sociology might be seen as *in toto* founded in a primary hostility to normative political analysis."

79. Adorno, introduction to *Positivist Dispute*, 17.

80. Knapp, review of *HCS*, 201–3.

81. See §5.1 below.

82. Especially *HCS*, 79–84, where Rose repeatedly uses the word "only" in sentences such as: "As long as bourgeois property relations and hence formal recognition prevail religion can only be a form of misrepresentation" (83). In fact, her treatment of religion in *HCS* is methodological in the way she criticizes. The problem is the move from condemning one particular version of religion to condemning religion per se.

83. *HCS*, 10, my emphasis. Cf. *PhSp* §50.

the same results. In the humanities, the identification and collation of sources apart, this is far from being the case."[84] The so-called methods in the humanities are really only general guidelines such as "the way people think is usually influenced by their social relations, the values accepted within their community"; thus "no explanatory method exists in the study of cultural history."[85] "A method is simply a question . . . and surely no method will yield information which it does not ask for (through its very formulation). . . . Methods/questions are thus as dependent on the cultural paradigm as are 'satisfactory' explanations."[86] Further, over the course of the neo-Kantian period, methodology became detached from and began artificially to dominate substantive study.[87] This is the sense in which Rose worried about theory (see below her comments on Marxism being problematic precisely *qua* theory). Yet Rose was not arguing against empirical enquiry, explanation or theory per se. She was opposed only to the unreflexive use of theory, to its reification into a rigid schema, which is then imposed on experience. The dialectical combination of different methods or forms of sociology could prevent such ossification. Once again, the transcendental form of method is both a strength and weakness: "Methodologies are either relative (adequate) to predefined object domains, and thus share their transcendental organization, or they must claim to be universal, in which case the question of their adequacy is undecidable and irrelevant. In either case, their validity cannot be determined regardless of their relation to their subject matter."[88] The strengths may be used and weaknesses avoided if the method is used in the right way, for which a good meta-philosophy or meta-theory is required. Then one can say with Adorno, "Method is really the substantive, complete understanding."[89]

84. Kołakowski, *Modernity on Endless Trial*, 244. Cf. *HCS*, 2: "The very idea of a scientific sociology, whether non-Marxist or Marxist, is only possible as a form of neo-Kantianism." Rose regards Marxism as suffering from the same problems as neo-Kantian sociology because of its claim to scientific status.

85. Kołakowski, *Modernity on Endless Trial*, 245.

86. Gebhardt, introduction to *Essential Frankfurt School Reader*, 379.

87. Frisby, introduction to *Positivist Dispute*, xxviii and n57.

88. Gebhardt, introduction to *Essential Frankfurt School Reader*, 379.

89. Cited in Wheatland, "Debate about Methods," 128. Cf. Rose's remark about *Negative Dialectics* as "an experimental attempt to state a method apart from its practice when the special nature of that method is that it is inseparable from its practice" (review of *Negative Dialectics*, 599).

One of Rose's examples is how to think of the finite and infinite. Weber and Durkheim separate concepts for thinking about the finite world of society from larger metaphysical questions. Thus, Durkheim treats values as given social facts; Weber treats values as coherent and justifiable only from within the form of life embodying them, but the choice between values as arbitrary. From a Hegelian point of view, their logic assumes too much and imposes itself on the world rather than knowing it immanently. This is apparent from Hegel's critique of Fichte and Locke in *Faith and Knowledge*. "Finite" in this text refers to the seemingly neutral, descriptive, empirical aspects of humanity, and the infinite refers to the endlessly controverted realm of beauty, morality, truth—those aspects of humanity by which it transcends itself. More technically, finite refers to the Kantian stipulation of knowledge's need for sensuous content (spatiotemporal intuition) if it is to be knowledge, in contrast to the illusions and antinomies that are generated when thought attempts to work without such reference.[90]

The problem with treating the finite and infinite as opposites is that knowledge is limited to the sensuous realm; empirical happiness is treated as humanity's only goal; cognition (or Reason as Hegel calls it in this essay) then "consists solely in calculating the worth of each and every thing with respect to the singularity, and in positing [i.e., subsuming] every Idea under finitude."[91] "Locke and the eudæmonists transformed philosophy into empirical psychology"; they ask merely "what the universe is for a subjectivity that feels and is conscious by way of calculations typical of the intellect, or in other words, for a Reason solely immersed in finitude, a Reason that renounces intuition and cognition of the eternal."[92] For Hegel, the parts must be understood within the whole; thus human possibilities and capacities, what may be expected from the world and people, should not be decided on the basis of a narrowly-viewed anthropology and rationalized reason[93] but in connection with the widest metaphysical and ontological questions. This is, as it were, Hegel's critique of

90. Duquette, "Speculative Logic"; Beiser, *Hegel*, 166.

91. Hegel, *Faith and Knowledge*, 60–61. The square parentheses are original to the Cerf and Harris translation. Hegel is being rather unfair to Kant here.

92. Ibid., 63. The similarity with Adorno and Horkheimer's *Dialectic of Enlightenment* should be apparent. The dialectic between Enlightenment and religious faith appears in *PhSp* B.I–II.

93. This term is anachronistic but captures Hegel's objection to philosophy that apes after maths in *PhSp* §38.

positivism, with which he connects form and substance in social and political philosophy. Hence: "What we tend to think of as immediate (sense) perceptions are in Hegel's view the product of complicated mediations. Furthermore, ideas that commonsense [*sic*] regards as concrete, because particular, are normally abstract for him, because they are unmediated; the truly concrete is not a particular, isolated phenomenon, but an aspect or 'moment' of a totality. Thus in his usage 'concrete' pertains more properly to 'totality,' while 'abstract' is related to the partial and one-sided, the individual and unmediated."[94] To understand things immanently is to allow all their mediations to present themselves.

The occasional, vulgar-Marxist slip notwithstanding then, Rose's considered opinion is that the exact nature of the relation between social forms and philosophy is the "most important and difficult" part of Hegel's thought[95] and "everything depends on how they are determined."[96] This refinement becomes even clearer in Rose's later work. Knapp's objection can thus be put to rest. Furthermore, Rose's rejection of external methods and her detection of their recurrence in sociology, can be supported by Richard Biernacki's work on textual coding in social science.[97] Biernacki shows the ways in which qualitative and quantitative methods are combined in three important (because widely influential) sociological studies of literature to produce viciously circular arguments that simply confirm and justify prior assumptions and in some cases interpret the meanings of texts exactly opposite to their plain meaning. This can be read as a detailed confirmation of Rose's warning about the adoption of general methodology (*Geltungslogik*) that ends up distancing a sociologist from the real world and empirical data—exactly the opposite of what sociology intends.[98] The use of a method can induce complacency or overconfidence and lead to bad results. Biernacki cites Clifford Geertz: "Keeping reasoning wary, thus useful, thus true" is the best kind of approach.[99] "The only intellectual building material is self-vigilance, not the reified

94. Livingstone, "Notes to English Edition," in Lukács, *History and Class Consciousness*, 344.

95. *HCS*, 60.

96. Ibid., 119.

97. Biernacki, *Reinventing Evidence in Social Inquiry*.

98. Anthony Giddens provides other examples of this problem in his introduction to *New Rules of Sociological Method*, 10–11.

99. Biernacki, *Reinventing*, 8.

ingredients 'theory' or 'method.'"[100] For Rose, "the aim is simply to be fully alert, to know the score."[101] (It is important to remember this is neither an argument against quantitative methods nor transcendental arguments per se.) Biernacki's thesis is bold: that "humanist" approaches to literature and history are truer to the ideals of science than the scientific seeming mixture of quantitative and qualitative methods:[102] "The nonsystematizing humanists still appreciate the obstacles to induction, the gift of an acute trial, the insurance of shared documentation, and the transformative power of anomalies . . . such interpretation better fulfills the consecrated standards to which social 'scientists' ostensibly subscribe."[103]

Rose's Hegelianism, lacking the guarantee of method, is more open about its risk: it knows it must start its judgments in the middle, in an already contested space, in a mixture of error and truth. It knows that sociology does not generate universal laws but only rules of thumb. Moreover, it knows there is no unfiltered or raw data, but moves from what appears as such into a more comprehensive view, from the seemingly immediate to awareness of mediation, from natural consciousness to speculative thought, from real illusion to awareness of determination. The importance of *Schein* thus reappears; in Stephen Houlgate's words: "Illusion is in fact real . . . seeming does occur—and . . . reflexivity (negativity) is actually at work in our world."[104] In short, Rose saw the value for social theory of "Hegel's critique of the methodological mind,"[105] which is lost if his system and method are divorced. Rose noted how Adorno had previously attacked "methodologism *per se*. This refers to any neo-Kantian kind of pure logic, which grants validity to an autonomous method and its objectifications, which is 'positive' in the general sense of suppressing the social and historical preconditions of its own possibility. Methodologism or 'positivism' in this metacritical sense may be found in any approach: phenomenology, Marxism, as well as in the positivist methodology of the standard verificationist kind."[106]

100. Ibid.

101. *DN*, 7.

102. Biernacki, *Reinventing*, 151.

103. Ibid., 3–4.

104. Houlgate, introduction to *Encylopaedia Logic*, in *Hegel Reader*, 131.

105. *HCS*, 36.

106. *HCS*, 35. Cf. *EL* §227.

It is by attention to particulars, beginning with immanent analysis and including ever-deepening or widening awareness of determination, that Rose's Hegelianism avoids the crude determinism of vaguely referring to an unanalyzed term (such as society or capitalism) to explain phenomena. Put otherwise, as noted above, there are various levels of mediation before jumping to society, or culture, etc., as cause—this is why Hegelian dialectics proceeds immanently and works outward.[107] If this difficulty is lost, then any phenomenon or piece of "data" can be fit into the overall scheme, losing proper contact with "empirical reality":[108] just this is the vicious circularity and divorce between universal and particular against which Rose complains.[109] Rather than making one pole of the antinomy fundamental and the other epiphenomenal to it, or collapsing the distinction, the best thinking keeps both in play through different forms of mediation. Rose's position was thus similar to Adorno's as she described it in *The Melancholy Science*:

> Since our access to empirical reality and our conceptual apparatus are inseparable and equally restricted, the idea of testing theoretical propositions by means of independently-defined indicators is incoherent. However, Adorno does not therefore abandon empirical research as irremediably circular, but utilizes a range of empirical means to explore the divergences between the ways in which social reality is understood and the ways in which this illusory intelligibility is determined. This exposition of empirical procedures is designed to eschew not only the "scientistic" understanding of them, but also any adaptation of them which takes account merely of an interpretive circle between theory and its designated indicators.[110]

Milbank well sums up Rose's distrust of neo-Kantian sociology:

> It treats society as an "external," empirical reality, whose ahistorical form is governed by eternal laws. . . . Only since Comte has an object called "society," amenable to scientific treatment, been isolated. As Gillian Rose . . . has shown, the means of this isolation is to elevate some aspect of given social reality—either a structural pattern, or a subjective understanding of meaningful action—into a *categorical* role in the Kantian sense . . .

107. Cf. Kolb, *Critique of Pure Modernity*, 47.

108. *HCS*, 10; Biernacki, *Reinventing*, 28, 127.

109. Cf. Biernacki, *Reinventing*, 16–17.

110. *TMS*, 145.

> If, for example, a social structure is interpreted as a category, as a "quasi-*a priori*," then this means that it can be appealed to as a sufficient way of categorizing and "explaining" the social facts that fall within its scope. In this way one is excused from the "difficult labor" of searching for genuinely historical interpretations.[111]

As we will see, Rose's historical version of phenomenology avoids such ahistoricism, and of course inherits a great deal from Adorno's critique of identity thinking. Biernacki's response to the problems with social science is to return to the "wary" or alert use of Weber's ideal types, providing ways of organizing and understanding research while remaining conscious of the risks of reification. Rose's social theory, we shall see, has a great deal in common with Weber here.[112] Yet Rose is clearer than Weber on our ability to know the truth about reality and moral norms. Others, such as Giddens, Bourdieu and Habermas, have echoed her complaints against classical sociology, in various attempts to harmonize subjective and objective dimensions of society, or individual experience and structures of experience.[113] For example, Giddens argues that agent and structure are the two fundamental, connected but distinct elements in any sociological analysis, and are always implicated in meaning, norms and power. Knowledge is always mediated, particularly through language, but not in hermetically sealed universes of meaning (the problem of some Wittgensteinian or Heideggerian interpretive sociologies like Peter Winch's).[114] Giddens also affirms the need to examine different levels between macro- and micro-structures. This is very like Rose's view that society and subject are in a speculative identity; that various levels of mediation between the two are required; her focus on truth, morality and law; and her realist critique of epistemologies of hermetically sealed communities. They share very similar critiques of the traditions of sociology stemming from Durkheim and Weber. Giddens argues against functionalist sociologies that focus solely on structure (Durkheim, Parsons) for reducing or eliminating subjectivity, but he

111. "An Essay Against Secular Order," 201. Whereas with Hegelianism "There is . . . no social 'given' at the categorical boundary of our understanding" (203).

112. See her Sussex lectures "Does Marx Have a Method?" and "Dispute over Marx and Weber" and *TMS*, 90–91, in which she compares ideal types to Adorno's constellations.

113. Grieffenhagen and Sharrock, "Limits of Experience."

114. Giddens, *New Rules*, 50–57.

also thinks Weberian *Versetehen*-style sociologies (understanding action through empathetically understanding the intentions of the actor) pay insufficient heed to structures. This is very similar to Rose's critique of the separation of validity and values.

Once again it is important to recall that Rose valued the classical sociological tradition. Her social theory aims to explicate better the logical basis of the good practice of Weber, Giddens, Bourdieu, etc., than they achieved in their own methodological statements, and to sublate neo-Kantian social theory. With this reminder of the measured nature of Rose's critique—in contrast to her polemical tone—we can turn to her critique of the Frankfurt School.

3.2.2 Frankfurt School social theory

As Peter Osborne noted, Rose's "reading of Hegel functions as a reformulation of the foundations of Critical Theory."[115] To see how, consider Tony Gorman's statement:

> On Rose's interpretation of Hegel, phenomenological criticism is, as it were, immanent critique of metacritique. To explain: metacritique aims to reveal the socio-historical conditions of possibility of given theoretical and social disciplines and practices (for example, philosophy, science, morality, art, etc.), on the assumption that the latter lack either the interest or self-reflective capacity to acknowledge these wider preconditions of their own activity. . . . Unfortunately, metacritique founders upon the problem of circularity. There is, it appears, simply no non-question-begging way to validate the unobservable transcendental fact or value that is postulated to explain the observable social reality—whether it be "economic determinism" (Marx), "social facts" (Durkheim) or "meaning" (Weber)—independently of the theory in which the stipulated postulate is inscribed. . . . By contrast, phenomenological criticism attempts to comprehend the repetition of the antinomy of sociological reason without repeating it, or, more exactly, by repeating it differently.[116]

Metacritiques repeat neo-Kantian circularity in sociological form, positing some sociohistorical entity as the (quasi-)transcendental feature making possible and explaining experienced realities. Again, Rose views

115. Osborne, "Hegelian Phenomenology," 8.

116. Gorman, "Gillian Rose," 28.

this structure as both a strength and weakness. "A philosophy of reflection is at the heart of . . . all sociological metacritiques of the neo-Kantian kind. What is regrettable is not the presence but the denial of this element of [their] thought."[117] Metacritiques structurally leave the question of the epistemological validity and ontological reality of the transcendental (or conditioning) factor necessarily undecidable (or else posited as unquestionable and to be taken on faith).[118] They also give the transcendental condition of possibility an ambiguous form: it is both transcendental and empirical (Habermas explicitly recognizes this in calling his argument "quasi-transcendental").[119] Metacritiques have difficulty accounting for "the status of the relation between precondition and condition."[120] They hover between offering society-specific preconditions and universal, atemporal preconditions.[121] When the latter wins out, the "point of mediation between precondition and conditioned becomes the pivot of a *theory*,"[122] with the problems of external method just noted. The danger is to conflate or level off the transcendental and empirical in a way that reproduces a kind of positivism. Consider, for example, a Marxist view of law: "Law gives effect to, mirrors or is otherwise expressive of the forms of economic relations."[123] If this is taken as a guide for investigations into law, it is very useful. If it is read as the prescription of a scientific law, as if every piece of legislation was chiefly economic in ultimate derivation, it becomes implausible.

Garbis Kortian explains the structure of Habermas's work as a way of expounding Frankfurt School thinking more generally. He independently confirms Rose's analysis of the quasi-transcendental structure of their argumentation, though he embraces it: "The more precise coordinates which define the Frankfurt School thesis are, on the one hand,

117. *HCS*, 42.

118. Rose takes this from Hegel's critique of Fichte in *Faith and Knowledge* but Nigel Pleasants makes the same charge without reference to idealism in *Wittgenstein and the Idea of a Critical Social Theory*. The question is whether some metacritiques meet the Hegelian criteria Rose stipulates.

119. *HCS*, 36–43. On Habermas's theory as another version of *Geltungslogik*, based on Rose's analysis in *HCS*, see Israel, "Epistemology and Sociology of Knowledge."

120. Ibid., 41.

121. Cf. *DN*, 125.

122. *HCS*, 44. Rose thought Habermas's theory had become methodological in this sense.

123. Hunt, "Marxism, Law, Legal Theory and Jurisprudence," 102.

the two fundamental concepts of the *Phenomenology of Spirit*, speculative experience and the speculative proposition, and, on the other, the fact that the dissolution of German Idealism threw these concepts into question."[124] Rose begins her Hegel book: "This essay is an attempt to retrieve Hegelian speculative experience for social theory" and she goes on to explain speculative propositions as fundamental to the whole enterprise. She takes exactly the opposite view to the Frankfurt School's rejection of speculative experience and speculative propositions.[125] Again, in Kortian's view, contemporary philosophy must understand the implications of the dissolution of Hegel's idea of absolute knowledge, and must "denounce one of the constitutive moments of Hegelian speculative experience: the moment of recognition and appropriation (*Anerkennung und Aneignung*) of the phenomenalized totality of the absolute concept in its otherness."[126] This is precisely contrary to Rose's view in which the Marxist distinction between "radical method" and "conservative system" has obscured "the centrality of those ideas which Hegel developed in order to unify the theoretical and practical philosophy of Kant and Fichte. . . . These ideas, recognition and appropriation (*anerkennen* and *aneignen*), are fundamental to Hegel's notion of a system, and their importance cannot be appreciated apart from Hegel's critique of the methodologism and moralism of Kant and Fichte."[127] Hegel's system and method cannot be separated because Hegel "demonstrated the connection between the limitations of the idea of method in Kant and Fichte and the limitations of the kind of social and political theory which they produced."[128] Hence: "the 'absolute' is not an optional extra, as it were. . . . Hegel's philosophy has *no* social import if the absolute is banished or suppressed, if the absolute cannot be thought."[129]

124. Kortian, *Metacritique*, 26. Rose regarded his book as "excellent" (*HCS*, 244n181). She thought Habermas was "half-way on the road between Kant and Hegel" (Rose, Letter to *London Review of Books*).

125. Cf. *PhSp* §47–48, §56–57. *EL* §82 and Addition. Since I am expositing Rose's Hegelianism, the extent to which the Additions reflect Hegel's own thought remains moot for my discussion.

126. Kortian, *Metacritique*, 41. Cf. Jürgen Habermas's discussion of totality in *Theory of Communicative Action*, 1:339–99.

127. *HCS*, 45.

128. Ibid.

129. Ibid.

To return to Osborne's comment, Rose was reformulating the foundations of critical theory away from neo-Kantian transcendental circularity toward Hegel's speculatively circular logic in combination with his phenomenology (i.e., the logic of the concept).[130] Pippin encapsulates the heart of Rose's position: "The Hegelian experiment . . . involves entertaining and thinking through the view that, in accounting for the fundamental elements of a conceptual or evaluative scheme, there is and can be no decisive or certifying appeal to any basic 'facts of the matter,' foundational experiences, logical forms, constitutive 'interests,' 'prejudices,' or guiding 'intuitions' to begin or end any such account."[131] There are no formal rules or ultimate criteria for the (meta)rules for creating categories for judgments; rather we have the categories we have as a response to the failure of previous categories. These two claims combined mean "the justification of our most authoritative claims to knowledge is 'dialectical,' not logical or formal."[132] When Rose speaks of the "validity" of a sociology's transcendental precondition (as she frequently does throughout the book) she is referring to Kant's question (in the first *Critique*) of whether the categories can be used in conjunction with experience to create knowledge (i.e., whether the categories are objective). Kant argues in the affirmative in his section titled "Transcendental Deduction." Hegel replaced Kant's transcendental deduction with a phenomenological deduction: rather than combining *a priori* categories with intuitions (sociologically: precondition with condition), Hegel argues the categories develop increasing objectivity over time through attempts to apply them, the break downs of those attempts and formulations of more successful categories. Neo-Kantian sociology treats its transcendentally circular knowledge as valid; speculative sociology treats its knowledge as historically sufficient. Hegel's speculative logic builds that status into its very conception of knowledge, whereas the transcendental form of neo-Kantian sociology cannot do full justice to the historical nature of reason and knowledge (even if a sociologist explicitly thinks of reason and knowledge as historical, the transcendental form of thinking works against that insight).

130. Ibid., 197–217.

131. Pippin, *Idealism as Modernism*, 163.

132. Ibid., 166.

Nigel Pleasants has independently criticized Habermas, Giddens and Roy Bhaskar for their transcendentally structured theories.[133] Like Rose, Pleasants considers these theories to be Kantian in form, with an "emphasis on universal and transcendent rules, structures and mechanisms, and its method of transcendental theoretical analysis."[134] He, too, thinks much of "both first- and second-generation 'critical theory' is rooted in Kantian ontological pictures of subjectivity and agency."[135] The "'craving for generality' which motivates the construction of these pictures is . . . a 'reaction formation' to the widespread acceptance . . . of the doctrine of fallibilism . . . critical social theorists react to this by seeking to combine epistemic fallibilism with 'ontological' *infallibilism*—thereby claiming that we can achieve certainty at the most abstract, transcendental level because things *must* be the way that their theories depict."[136] Pleasants summarizes his critique of transcendental arguments in social theory thus:

> This type of reasoning involves the postulation of various mechanisms, powers, structures, etc. at a level which is logically unexperienceable because it supposedly constitutes the very conditions of possibility of experience. These transcendental entities are then taken to be, in a sense, more "real" than the reality which can be and is known; the former is understood to generate the latter. In critical social theory this form of reasoning issues in a conjunction of theoretical assertions which purport to explain how people do what they do, how social order is sustained, and how social change is possible. Critical social theory is respectably fallibilist about *particular* kinds of knowledge-claim, but assumes infallible authority over *generalised* transcendental knowledge-claims. Wittgenstein tried to show that the transcendental form of reasoning is delusory and unsatisfactory because it ultimately does not provide the kind of understanding that we (as philosophers) hanker after.[137]

This echoes Rose's critique that preconditions in sociology, the terms that are supposed to explain the conditions, tend to become reified.

133. As has King, *Structure of Social Theory*.

134. Pleasants, *Wittgenstein*, 171.

135. Ibid.

136. Ibid., 178; "craving for generality" is Wittgenstein's phrase.

137. Ibid., 181–82.

Second, both Rose and Pleasants question the strength of the connection between correct description and social change. Giddens, Bhaskar and Habermas employ a "double hermeneutic," focused simultaneously on understanding both society and individuals' capacity to understand themselves differently via understanding social theory (and the interaction between these two levels). These thinkers know the complications involved here but nevertheless focus more on description than on how their work connects with non-specialists. Pleasants discerns a latent positivism in the relentless concern with accurate description and failure to appreciate how the technical nature of the presentation of the theories inhibits its reception by people in the society it wishes to change: "Theories of people's behavior *can* feed back into that behavior, thereby becoming a factor in sustaining or changing it. But this should be seen as an empirical connection, not a transcendental, ontological presupposition."[138] Rose inherited this concern from Adorno via the question of style, and criticized Giddens and Habermas on this basis:

> This jettisoning of speculative thinking by recent "critical theory" of modernity has also meant the abandonment of that methodological reflexivity, which is equally substantive, and which learns by coming to know its own formation in the culture it explores. Habermas and Giddens write in the severe style, having disqualified not only Marx and Hegel, but also Weber, Horkheimer and Adorno, who are read without any attention to their difficult and facetious presentation. This lack of attention to form and style leads to the functionalism of the subject: to the critical theorist who becomes a sociologist, his own authoritative voice a neutral, unimplicated discourse of its object.[139]

Rose and Pleasants differ on how best to respond to their shared dissatisfactions with such social theory. Pleasants stresses that he, like Wittgenstein, does not have a "substantive alternative" view of "the way things really are" with which to replace the philosophical pictures that he "deconstructs."[140] He thinks the problems matter more than the theories, and philosophy as therapy should replace philosophy as theory.[141] From Rose's point of view this is a little too easy. It is not that there are no preconditions or explanations to be had; it is that explanations should

138. Ibid., 177.

139. *BM*, 245.

140. Pleasants, *Wittgenstein*, 181.

141. Ibid., 182, 14–15.

be more complex than is usually admitted, by reference to a totality (see below). Put otherwise, Pleasants has no concept of *Schein*. Further, how could social and political "problems" be tackled without some sense of how things really are and how things should be? And then how could those views be justified? Descriptions in Hegel's view take their meaning from wider contexts in which they are embedded in a way that circumvents the description/explanation distinction Pleasants wishes to draw:[142] "Speculative logic contains the former logic and metaphysics, preserves the same forms of thought, the same laws and objects, but at the same time in doing so it develops them further and transforms them with the help of additional categories."[143] Pleasants suggests that Milgram's obedience experiments and Bauman's *Modernity and the Holocaust* are two examples of work that can be described more accurately as critical social theory than the work of these others precisely because they have affected how many people think about themselves and their society. But this proves Rose's point. Milgram and Bauman both produced such important work only by making use of a great deal of theory (quantitative, qualitative, sociological, philosophical).[144] Further, Bauman ends his book by recommending Levinasian ethics; that is, by endorsing a theory to guide action. Rose thinks Levinasian ethics suffers from an inability to grapple fully with the mediations of ethics and politics,[145] and this may be true of Pleasants's Wittgensteinian approach.

4 The Substance of Rose's Hegelianism

Thus it appears Rose's criticisms of sociology and critical theory express genuine worries within the disciplines, and that the main thrust of her understanding of Hegel coheres with Pippin's approach in making the

142. This sounds a little misleading as Pleasants does allow some role to explanation and theory: 19–26.

143. Hegel, *EL* §9. Hegel notes in *EL* §214, that the idea itself passes over from speculative reason into abstract understanding and back, and just so is it the idea.

144. Pleasants says "transcendental knowledge of transcendental entities is just irrelevant to *critical* self- and social reflection" (*Wittgenstein*, 182), whereas Rose, as we have seen, says that transcendental social theory has both strengths and weaknesses rooted in its transcendental form. Notice the parallel in form between Pleasants's attitude to theory and Rose's critique of "Holocaust piety": use of theory and scholarship ends with rejection of theory and scholarship (*MBL*, 41–48).

145. For an elaboration of Rose's critique, see Alvares, *Humanism After Colonialism*.

phenomenological rather than transcendental deduction of the categories of thought one of the central Hegelian issues. If these aspects of her project are well motivated, we are in a better position to understand Rose's intention to present "a repristination of the Hegelian project in something like its full ambition."[146] At the start of this chapter I mentioned the three main pillars of Rose's speculative thought: a phenomenological justification of ethics, society and politics; a triune rather than dichotomous way of thinking; and reference to absolute ethical life. As Rose put it:

> Hegel put a trinity of ideas in place of Kant's idea of transcendental method: the idea of phenomenology, the idea of absolute ethical life (*absolute Sittlichkeit*), and the idea of a logic. The idea of phenomenology can be seen as an alternative to Kant's theoretical *quaestio quid juris*, while the idea of absolute ethical life can be seen as an alternative to Kant's justification of moral judgments. This, however, would be to concede the Kantian dichotomy between theoretical and practical reason. The idea of all Hegel's thought is to unify theoretical and practical reason. In his *Logic*, as in all his works, the unification is achieved by a phenomenology and the idea of absolute ethical life.[147]

For Rose, Hegel's thought was a response to perceived failures with Kant's transcendental idealism while remaining committed to transcendental philosophy itself. How Kant's failure is construed will naturally shape the response. If the failure is one of logic—transcendental idealism cannot fully account for its precondition—then one answer, favored by Houlgate and Winfield, is a presuppositionless, *a priori* speculative logic that derives logical categories from complete indeterminacy rather than taking certain things for granted. If the failure is linked to the failure of theory per se, as with Pleasants, then a therapeutic response is called for. Rose does not quite take either of these routes. In the final sentence of the above quotation Rose refers the *Logic* to phenomenology and absolute ethical life, not vice versa. That is, she takes the view, like Pippin, that the justification for the *Science of Logic* depends on the *Phenomenology of Spirit*. The *Phenomenology* provides a developmental justification of current categories of thought and their constitution of experience; while the *Logic* is an immanent development of the categories necessary for

146. Williams, "Between," 9.

147. *HCS*, 48. The *quaestio quid juris* is the question of whether Kant's categories have objective validity.

thinking (now motivated by the phenomenology).[148] Neither is committed to the view that Hegel's every move in the *Logic* or his every application of the logic to social philosophy is correct, but both regard his work as nevertheless extremely fruitful for understanding the concepts by which we understand being (or reality).[149] Speculation not only accounts for the determination of the conditioned by the precondition but also accounts for the very act of accounting (positing).[150] It is thus a self-validating logic and ground of thinking and knowing, providing categories for thinking being, in a more expansive and thorough way to Kant, without having attained completion or perfection. As Klaus Hartmann shows, there is no non-circular way into transcendental philosophy, but Hegel's response to this is to apply the transcendental philosophy to everything. What appears at first as a non-transcendental introduction to thought turns out later to have been transcendental and justified as such. There is no fixed and given ground from which all else is derived, but the "whole domain [of knowledge] is self-grounding, self-validating. From 'outside' it looks like a petitio principii, but only from outside. From inside we can demonstrate its systemic virtues."[151] Rose calls this "beginning in the middle." Pippin expresses it thus:

> The question of what comes to count as, in general, an authoritative explanation of objects and events, the decisive classificatory procedure, or evaluative criterion, can never itself be resolved by appeal to an ultimate explanatory principle, or general regulative ideal, or basic argumentative strategy. There are, finally, no rules to tell us which rules we ought to follow in regulating our discursive practices, no intuitions certifying the axioms out of which such rules should be constructed, and no transcendental argument for the necessary conditions of any experience. What we always require is a narrative account of why we have come to regard some set of rules or a practice as authoritative. In Hegel's "phenomenological" version, such an account must always appeal to a pre-discursive context or historical experience (sometimes simply called "life") as the origin of such authoritative procedures and rules (even while Hegel also maintains that such a context or experience is itself the "product" of a kind of prior

148. Pippin, *Hegel's Idealism*, 38.

149. Pippin, "Hegel and Category Theory," 839–48.

150. Hartmann, "On Taking the Transcendental Turn," 223–49, which Rose cites in *DN*, 111n3.

151. Hartmann, "Transcendental Turn," 238.

> reflective principles, now become implicit, taken for granted, in everyday social life). Our account of our basic sense-making practices is thus tied to an account of the *aporiai* "experienced in the life of Spirit," and so such a justification is everywhere . . . "dialectical," and not "logical."[152]

For Rose, then, Hegelian speculative logic therefore provides a theory of categories (the concepts by which we understand being) on the basis of phenomenology. These concepts are both a logic and metaphysics.[153] Her reliance on the phenomenological motivation and justification for Hegel's categorial logic is evident in that at every point she indicates her alternative to neo-Kantian social theory or poststructuralism it is by reference to (political) history.[154] Consider: Hegelian speculative philosophy "comprehends the dualisms and deconstructions of the first response as the dynamic movement of a political history which can be expounded speculatively out of the broken middle."[155]

Or: in

> the erstwhile critical reduction of "religion" . . . the object "religion" is given as a positivity. . . . Criticism, *Kritik*, was quasi-transcendental in its inquiry into the preconditions or possibility of its object, but it was restricted to independently specifiable conditions, and did not address the formation of its object; and it was, of course, negative and destructive. It did not produce a *speculative* exposition of the historical separation of the institutions of Caesar from the institutions of God, which

152. *Philosophical Problem*, 68. At 194n29, Pippin confirms the similarity between his and Rose's readings of Hegel: "This approach to Hegel obviously places a very great emphasis on Hegel's theory of sociality, an issue as relevant to his doctrine of 'Absolute Knowledge' as to his more familiar discussions of morality, the state, etc. . . . one of the few commentators on Hegel to have discussed his account of knowledge as, in effect, a social institution, and so to have interpreted his intimidating theory of 'the Absolute' in terms of social reconciliation (and to have connected his position with many of the *aporiai* of the modern social science tradition), is Gillian Rose in her original and persuasive book (1981). See especially her claims about the relation between the Kantian themes of intuition/concept and the young Hegel's doctrine of 'recognition.' There is a parallel between her claim about the way the social science tradition replays so many of the original issues in Hegel's critique of Kant (structural sociology is 'empty,' liberal, individualist political theory is 'blind,' . . .) and the claim I am making about the history of the modernity problem."

153. See ch. 2 §4 and ch. 4 §3.1.

154. Cf. *DN*, 124, 208–12.

155. *MBL*, 71; cf. *HCS*, 214.

> would require neither a sociology nor a philosophy of religion, but an investigation into the changing relation between meaning and configuration, revelation and realization.[156]

Or: to "mediate Christianity with speculative thought . . . would call for the expounding of the truth and untruth of Christianity world-historically."[157] And: "Not that comprehension completes or closes, but that it returns diremption to where it cannot be overcome in exclusive thought or in partial action—as long as political history persists."[158] Rose pits the "political history which would come to know" itself against the various "deconceptualizations and displacements" of political history in the theories she examines in *The Broken Middle*.[159] One reason for the brokenness of the middle is (as Pippin stated above) the central role of the experience of *aporiai* in social reality.

A phenomenological reading of political history thus grounds Rose's social theory, and marks its difference from neo-Kantian social theories. Her motto could have been "no social theory without history,"[160] or better, "social theory ultimately depends on phenomenology," on phenomenological accounts of ethics and meaning—not given moral-social facts (Durkheim), not arbitrarily-individually chosen meanings (Weber), but sociohistorically narrated accounts of changed views of reason with an assessment of which configuration's concepts are more rational and better resolve the difficulties in earlier accounts. When social theory takes the longer historical view, its object (such as "society" or "religion") is no longer given but seen to result from earlier forms and changes. On a Hegelian view, the only finally adequate form of justification and explanation is historical-phenomenological. "In Hegel's thought, 'spirit' means the structure of recognition or misrecognition in a society. 'Objective spirit' is inseparable from absolute spirit, the meaning of history

156. *JAM*, 37–38.

157. *BM*, 39.

158. Ibid., xiv.

159. Ibid., xii.

160. Cf. *JAM*, 51. Cf. Pippin, *Philosophical Problem*, 70: "No reliance in a philosophical account on any principle or faculty or axiom or procedure, without a 'phenomenology' of why we have come to regard such a procedure as indispensable, and a 'logical' reconstruction of the categorial commitments of such an enterprise." Also *Idealism as Modernism*, 168: "No sociology of knowledge, no genealogy of the play of power, and so on, at least . . . not without a 'logical' reconstruction and deduction of the Notions presupposed in such strategies. Anything else would be a regression to positivism."

as a whole."[161] Although this sounds grandiose, it follows from the view of rationality Hegel developed. What, then, is the precise nature of this speculative, historical, phenomenological theory?

4.1 Phenomenology

Rose's speculative social theory proceeds somewhat like Hegel's *Phenomenology*: at once the immanent critique of current social forms and the historical-philosophical reconstruction of past forms: beginning in the middle. Rose regards many of Hegel's works, especially his early writing, as phenomenological, because "the illusions and experiences of moral and political consciousness are presented in an order designed to show how consciousness may progress through them to comprehension of the determination of ethical life."[162] For example, Hegel often begins with what appears most natural or immediate to natural consciousness (e.g., the family) in order to show how in fact such social forms "presuppose an overall economic and political organization which may not be immediately intelligible."[163] In the *Phenomenology*, "natural consciousness" is the consciousness that either does not recognize it is determined, or misrecognizes how it is determined. "Philosophical consciousness" examines the range of forms of misrecognition and the way natural consciousness learns from them, then draws certain conclusions. It concludes *inter alia*, that: a phenomenological and historical mode of categorial justification comes to replace an *a priori* mode; misrecognition is intrinsic to any recognition, so the process of trying to learn must continue; any social theory and ethics has to account for the mixture of passivity and activity in subjectivity (hence *Sittlichkeit* is placed alongside *Moralität*); dichotomies must not be rigidly employed. The result is "absolute knowing," which is comprehensive thinking not omniscience. In contrast to natural consciousness, the "absolute is the comprehensive thinking which transcends the dichotomies between concept and intuition, theoretical and practical reason."[164] This learning from immanent critique, which entails the possibility of theories and improvement in theories, parallels Hegel's move from the *Phenomenology* to the *Logic* and is the reason Osborne's

161. *HCS*, 44.
162. Ibid., 53.
163. Ibid., 54.
164. Ibid., 218.

and Gorman's charges that Rose cannot account for either social theory or social determination do not work.[165]

Dario Parinetti's summary of the key components of Hegel's phenomenology as a conceptual rather than causal history will clarify Rose's position:

> 1. Hegel's theory of concepts is a conceptual history and, as such, like naturalistic conceptions of logic, is descriptive rather than prescriptive.
>
> 2. The descriptive character of Hegel's logic does not imply that the theory is non-normative. A conceptual history will be shown to be a description of relations between concepts, rather than of facts about concepts.
>
> 3. Hegel's position does not entail a rejection of naturalistic accounts of concept acquisition. It only entails a rejection of the naturalistic stand-point as an adequate one for grounding a philosophical understanding of concepts.[166]

In contrast with phenomenology, normal historiography or "pragmatic history looks for the sense or meaning of a series of facts. . . . Pragmatic history, in Hegel's view, is mostly concerned with providing causal explanations for historical events. . . . To represent historical events as following from causes such as the contingent intentions of agents or the climate of a nation—as pragmatic historians did—is to miss the point of what we want to understand in history."[167] In the realm of spirit (*Geist*), reasons and not simply causes are at work (a Kantian point). As Houlgate explains, "only those sequences of events which have been brought about by the development of human self-consciousness and by the pursuit of consciously articulated goals can really count as *historical*. . . . Change is historical when those involved in it understand it as fitting into a narrative scheme of things, when they are conscious of its having historical significance."[168] Gorman argues that Rose's theory of modernity and her approach to the Holocaust may be defended only on a "weak teleological philosophy of history" that maintains a central place for mutual

165. Osborne, "Hegelian Phenomenology"; Gorman, "Critical Marxism"; Tubbs, "Rose and Education," 125–43, also defends Rose against Osborne and Gorman.

166. "History, Concepts and Normativity in Hegel," in *Hegel's Theory of the Subject*, 60–61. Cf. *PhR* §3.

167. Parinetti, "History," 66. Cf. Macdonald, "What Is Conceptual History?," in *Hegel: New Directions*, 207–26.

168. *Introduction*, 19.

recognition.[169] A weak teleology of history does not trace the multiple contingent causes of events but involves retrospectively "reconstructing the dialectical intertwinement of justificatory conceptual systems and the forms of life they legitimize, by tracing the pattern of their emergence, development, breakdown and reconfiguration in history."[170] Historical events "do not have an immanent telos" but "become historical only when they enter into narratives" and "world-historical" when they are judged to shift us from one phenomenological phase to another that better accounts for ourselves than previous ones.[171]

Rose related *Sittlichkeit*, history and ethical theory in a particular way. Her language of the "form" of ethics is a question of its historical appearance and preconditions, which "shows how speculative thinking is social/political/historical."[172] Rose sometimes uses speculative thought and experience as synonyms for phenomenology, since Rose's version of speculative philosophy is intrinsically historical.[173] For Hegel the *Logic* and the philosophies of nature and spirit are rationally commensurable, but the *Logic* presents the *a priori* development of the categories that are necessary for any thought or experience, whereas the historical realization of the movement of the absolute idea occurs within the realm of contingency and error.[174] Likewise, when Rose says speculative thought is intrinsically historical, she means both the historical expression of the categories of the absolute idea in society and politics and the categories themselves.[175] The difference between the rational necessity and

169. Gorman, "Whither," 48, which he takes from the work of Pinkard and Pippin (Pinkard, *Hegel's* Phenomenology, 331–43; and *Hegel's Idealism*). He thinks Rose's later work does not have this philosophy of history, whereas I am about to argue it does. He argues her later work is genealogical rather than phenomenological, but I think he ignores the way Rose assimilates genealogy to phenomenology. For the same reason I disagree with his view that Rose's later work is perspectival.

170. Ibid., 66.

171. Ibid.

172. Letter from Rose to J. M. Bernstein, 27 March, 1987, box 36. On "form" see below, ch. 3 §2.2.

173. *HCS*, 52.

174. E.g., introduction to *PhR*.

175. There is, though, also a historical precondition for Hegel's presuppositionless derivation of the categories, on which, see Houlgate, *Opening*, and Kolb, *Critique*. Houlgate, *Introduction to Hegel*, 24: "The categories of modern consciousness are *historical* products, but they are not therefore intrinsically *limited* categories because they are the categories through which we have become fully aware of our historicity and freedom."

completeness of the logical categories and their necessarily imperfect sociohistorical realization explains Rose's comments about the surprise involved in reason and reason's moveable boundaries.[176] The rational reconstructions of shapes of spirit and the categories therein, which is phenomenology, cannot be deduced *a priori* (Hegel is not deducing nature or history from *a priori* categories).[177]

The historical nature of speculative thought in Rose's social theory includes the recognition that the ethical, political, religious and aesthetic terms in social theory have a history.[178] In Rose's interpretation, speculation is similar to Nietzschean or Foucaultian genealogy but without the risk of genetic fallacies.[179] "Without any necessary assumptions of linearity or progression, this alternative description of mutual positings and their breakdown also reopens the way to conceive learning, growth and knowledge as fallible and precarious, but risk-able. This risk refers to the temporarily constitutive positings of each other which form and reform both selves."[180] Hence her claim that the two terms of a speculative sentence are filled in over periods of history, such that Hegel "suspends the history of philosophy within the philosophy of history, and the philosophy of history within the history of philosophy."[181] (A speculative sentence is of the form "A is B," while meaning that A is identical to and different from B. See the next section.) Social theory and explanation are therefore primarily historical-philosophical rather than scientific demonstration of highly probable correlations. The latter are only moments within a larger whole.

History is also the basis of Rose's distinction between the Aristotelian and Hegelian forms of aporia. Aristotle's aporia concentrated on the difficulty (metaphysical and epistemological) of connecting universal and particular,[182] whereas "the re-construction of the history of [ethical]

176. E.g., *JAM*, 1–10. Hardimon, *Hegel's Social Philosophy*, 78: "Imperfection is a necessary condition of the social world's being as it ought to be."

177. Pippin, *Hegel's Idealism*, 139.

178. *HCS*, 180. *PhSp* §41.

179. Cf. Bierbricher, "Critical Theories of the State," 388–405; Adorno's idea of objectivity as "sedimented history," *Negative Dialectics*, 163; O'Connor, "Adorno and the Problem of Givenness," 85–99.

180. *MBL*, 13.

181. *DN*, 3.

182. See Booth, *Aristotelian Aporetic Ontology*, cited in *BM*, 165–69. Booth shows Aristotle was not rigid in applying the laws of the excluded middle and

form, the recognition of experience, must be intrinsic to any abstract statement of how there is aporia in Hegel."[183] As J. M. Bernstein put it in a paper expressing their joint views, the absolute is "the fate of subject and substance, the experience that has developed from Sittlichkeit to Legal Status to Morality. . . . Institutional history and metaphysical history are the same and different."[184] Here again, what subjects are, how they live and think, are deeply bound to social institutions (substance). The changes Bernstein enumerates are changes of shapes of spirit throughout European history as phenomenologically reconstructed by Hegel, to which Rose remained committed. It is important to note, then, that the content of the terms of a speculative proposition in social theory do not simply yield themselves through pure *a priori* thinking (marking a difference from logical speculation). Their content is revealed through their historical use, which is the entry point for (the necessity of) contingency, surprise, inversions.[185]

Rose's historical version of speculation entails a philosophy of history—nicely described as "weak teleology"—the nub of which she puts thus:

> This is how the philosophy of history should be conceived, not as a teleology of reconciliation, not as replacing the exhausted attempt to create a Christian civilization, but as perpetual repetition, as the perpetual completing of the historic Good Friday by the speculative Good Friday. There is no end of religion and no end of history, but a perpetual "speculative justification" to complete the faith which "justifies nothing."
>
> Hegel is not sanguine that the rational completing of the meaning of religion will make possible a rational ethical life in the way a realization of the principle of the Christian religion would have done. But he is sure that misrepresentation and irrational political life will continue in history, and that philosophy will have to be more armed against its irrationality not less. But this philosophic rationality may not bring freedom.[186]

non-contradiction precisely because he recognized the aporetic nature of metaphysics.

183. Rose, letter to J. M. Bernstein, 27 March, 1987.

184. "Speculation and Aporia," 2 April 1987, box 36, 5.

185. See Pippin, "Logic of Experience."

186. *HCS*, 127.

Once an idea is realized in the world the idea's own conceptual necessity has a certain force.[187] To take one of Hegel's examples, once the idea of the infinite worth of the individual is brought into history by Christianity, it can be seen that slavery is rationally untenable, although this takes quite some time.[188] The idea itself plays a role in the eventual end of slavery's sanction by the state. There is merely surface tension between saying a concept can only be understood through its history of use and that a concept has a kind of independent force once it is unleashed in the world. Both are aspects of (the movement of) the concept. To understand a concept through its use and development is to understand the concept itself, its inner necessity. Coming to see that slavery is wrong is coming to understand better what the infinite worth of individuals means. Hence Rose's is a social theory that provides rational justification for institutions, not simply descriptions. This is how Rose and Hegel avoid the genetic fallacy, prevent philosophy collapsing into sociology of knowledge, and manage the tension between historicism and realism in epistemology:

> *We* do not form the concepts at all and . . . the concept in general is not to be considered something that has a genesis at all. . . . It is wrong to assume, first that there are objects which form the content of our representations and then our subjective activity comes along behind them, forming the concepts of objects by means of the earlier mentioned operation of abstracting and gathering together what is common to the objects. On the contrary, the concept is what is truly first and the things are what they are, thanks to the activity of the concept dwelling in them and revealing itself in them. In our religious consciousness this surfaces in such a way that we say, "God created the world out of nothing" or, to put it otherwise, "the world and finite things have gone forth out of the fullness of divine thoughts and divine decrees." In this manner it is recognized that the thought and, more precisely, the concept is the infinite form or the free, creative activity, which is not in need of some stuff on hand outside itself, in order to realize itself.[189]

Hegelian philosophy is historically rational: developmental justification occurs by reference to past forms of life and their reason-giving,

187. *EL* §147.

188. Ibid. §163.

189. Ibid. §163 Addition 2. Cf. §213 Addition.

but it does not thereby lose the concept of objectivity and thus may enquire after the rationality of contemporary life forms.[190] The combination is designed to avoid dogmatism (or foundationalism) and skepticism. Hegel's position refuses the restriction of epistemological options to the dogmatic view that the truth is out there to be had directly or the skeptical alternative of reason as pragmatic, relative or sophistic.[191] Rose thus makes phenomenological reconstruction essential to any rational justification in social theory (one sees here the Hegelian roots of the Frankfurt motto that epistemology is social theory). The shape of spirit and its justification emerge from a history of experiences of contradiction, determinate negation, reformulation and readjustment. This enables a way of understanding how we are determined subjects:

> This perspective is comprehensive, *Begreifendes*, conceptual in the sense of complete, not in the sense of the abstract concept. It conceives or grasps the absolute as it is determined in all the shapes of consciousness. It is not a static or prejudged knowledge but comprehends the shapes of consciousness as they appear in their contradictions. . . . The absolute or substance appears as consciousness and its oppositions or differentiations. To know that consciousness divides itself into abstract concept and oppositions is not the same as consciousness' knowing of that opposition. It is a knowing which knows consciousness and its oppositions and is therefore comprehensive.[192]

A more comprehensive social theory will have a grasp of both consciousness and its oppositions as both part of the same shape of spirit. Hence Rose's claim that the "identity of religion and the state is the fundamental speculative proposition of Hegel's thought, or, and this is to say the same thing, the *speculative experience of the lack of identity* between religion and the state is the basic object of Hegel's exposition."[193] The religion-state speculative identity is intended to direct attention to the whole history of the harmony and disharmony between "subjective disposition

190. O'Connor, *Adorno's Negative*, 60: "By virtue of the significance of the object in the social totality its meanings necessarily transcend the individual subject. As the individual subject confronts the object, the latter contains an irreducible independence that, in the orders of experience and explanation, grants it, so Adorno's argument concludes, the status of priority."

191. Pippin, *Philosophical Problem*, 44, 192–93n7. Rose accused poststructuralism of reducing epistemology to these two options (e.g., *MBL*, 10–13).

192. *HCS*, 192.

193. Ibid., 53.

(*die Gesinnung*)" and "absolute ethical life,"[194] custom and constitution. Other modulations of this appeared as the "antinomy of law" (in *Dialectic of Nihilism*) and as the diremption between law and ethics (in *The Broken Middle*); each a way of thinking about the relation between formal law and informal ethical life, as mediated by the "third" of theory or the individual (respectively). We will return to speculative sentences below; for now, the main point is Rose's social theory asks and has the means to answer what makes social forms and institutions rational and whether they are more or less rational than other forms. Its historical-rational form is both more thoroughly historical than transcendental sociology and more explicit about making normative-because-rational assessments. That is why it better expresses the experience of coming to learn, on a group and historical level (not just individually).

The question can always be raised, however, as to whether the phenomenological account is sufficiently historical or whether it has filtered out the messy reality of the past in order to make conceptual sense. Rose would answer the latter is always partially the case. Any totality and any position are always only provisional and, as David Elder-Vass notes, explanations are always abstractions in which we make judgments about which are the most important causal factors, and we may err significantly.[195] Yet phenomenology as Rose construes it foregrounds this feature of theory and judgment, which is the best way to address it, since error is ineliminable.

If the phenomenological learning process is the motivation and justification for the standpoint of the *Logic* then Hegel provides the most profound logical grounding for sociology because logic is social. Hegel's *Phenomenology* was the first work to relate internally epistemology, sociology of knowledge and the sociology of philosophy. In one sense, socio-logic just is logic; though to accept this is to deny any complete epistemological grounding in formal logic.[196] Rose's social philosophy, then, may prevent certain intellectual missteps just because it appreciates the logical as well as the social underpinning of sociological thought. This is apparent if one compares to Rose Randall Collins's *Sociology of Philosophies: A Global Theory of Intellectual Change*. Collins seeks to op-

194. Ibid.

195. Elder-Vass, *Causal Power of Social Structures*, 177–78. In this way Rose's relation of objective spirit to the "meaning of history as a whole" (p. 60 above) is much less alarming than it may first appear.

196. See, e.g., Harris, *Formal, Transcendental, and Dialectical Thinking.*

erate with a minimal of theoretical and normative baggage, observing the operation of philosophers in their various contexts, across history and culture, in order to draw immanent lessons from the process. Some of his conclusions coincide with Rose's; for instance, "we are always in media res, in the middle of things" such that the "successive layers of context for the minds of philosophers display no sharp borders. There is no criterion for arbitrarily stopping."[197] Increasingly comprehensive explanations are a central component of Rose's speculative philosophy, as is "beginning in the middle." *The Broken Middle* is in part an essay on the way in which social philosophies are determined by fundamental features of modern societies. But Collins's empiricism will only take him so far, and problems occur as he attempts to extend his work into philosophy. In the epilogue, Collins seeks to draw out epistemological lessons from his huge survey. He concludes that conceptual universals come from the external world rather than the mind's spontaneity; he reverts, in other words, to pre-Kantian empiricism. In this case, the "error" is not serious for Collins's sociological findings, but is not much use philosophically. Collins is attempting to justify the use of universal concepts against what he regards as postmodern skepticism about universals. He thus aimed at the same philosophical result as Rose, but with less sophistication. Collins's second mistake is more sociologically deleterious, however. Collins underplays the force of ideas themselves within philosophy, by leaving out the question of the truth of ideas. That is, at times he inadvertently reduces philosophy to sociology of knowledge. As Austin Harrington observed, his account then becomes circular and question begging: he seeks to explain the social success of ideas through their social success.[198] We have already seen Rose's critique of this. One of advantages of Rose's social philosophy is an appreciation of Hegel's logic and phenomenology in order to help avoid these sorts of glitches. A further advantage of Hegel's logic is its ability to account for its own logical and social preconditions, and thus to be its own metatheory, which relates to what Rose termed its triune rather than dualistic or dichotomous nature.

197. Collin, *Sociology of Philosophies*, 860–61.

198. Harrington, "From Hegel to the Sociology of Knowledge," 131: "Truth—in a classical Durkheimian gesture—turns out to be the continuous, mutually reinforced tissue of social communication." Harrington himself contrasts Rose and Collins.

4.2 Triune rationality

A common response to the central antinomy of sociology—whether society makes people or people make society—is, "both." This employs the category Hegel terms "reciprocity." It prevents the chicken-and-egg situation between the two terms. "Reciprocity is, to be sure, the proximate truth about the relationship of cause and effect and it stands, so to speak, on the threshold of the concept."[199] The problem is it leaves each side "as something immediately given" rather than "coming to know them as moments of a third, higher [dimension], which is precisely the concept."[200] He continues:

> If we consider, for example, the customs of the Spartan people as the effect of its constitution and then, vice versa, this as the effect of its customs, this consideration may for all that be correct; but this construal, for this reason, does not provide any ultimate satisfaction, since by this means neither the constitution nor the customs of this people are in fact comprehended. That happens only by virtue of the fact that those two sides, and equally all the remaining particular sides revealed by the life and history of the Spartan people, are known to be grounded [*begründet*] in this concept.

What is this third moment called the "concept" (*der Begriff*) and how does it provide better comprehension of sociology's central antinomy? Two ways of thinking about the concept are helpful to bear in mind before approaching Hegel's *Logic* directly, after which I will outline Rose's appropriation thereof. One way to think about Hegel's idea of the concept is as an emergent whole.[201] An emergent social structure is an entity within a society, which endures for a time as relatively stable or self-identical, which has causal powers. Such entities are emergent insofar as they exist only by virtue of the arrangement of their parts. By contrast, an aggregate of parts is indifferent to its arrangement (the mass

199. *EL* §156 Addition.

200. Ibid. §156 Addition. Square brackets from the translators.

201. See Elder-Vass, *Causal Power*, and his discussion of the literature. Cf. Adorno, introduction (1–67), in *Positivist Dispute*, 12: "Totality is not an affirmative but rather a critical category . . . totality is what is most real. Since it is the sum of individuals' social relations which screen themselves off from individuals, it is also illusion—ideology. A liberated mankind would by no means be a totality." This critical edge perhaps marks off Rose's philosophy from some other uses of emergence theory. Cf. Adorno, "Sociology and Empirical Research," in the same volume, 68–86 (esp. 81).

of a whole, for instance, is just the sum of the mass of the parts). Emergent properties are explained *by* parts-in-relations. That does not explain *away* the whole (or higher level, if you prefer) because the whole just is the parts-in-relation. A whole may be therefore more than the sum of its parts and its emergent properties have real causal powers. For Hegel, this is the difference between a mechanical whole and its parts, and an organic whole.[202] The importance Rose attached to the institutions of the middle—that is, of civil society—could be seen to stem in part from their role in social causation (though this is to go beyond Rose's own statements). Her view coheres with Adorno's that the social totality is "a reality. He does not posit it as an interpretative heuristic, as something whose status concerns us only in so far as it assists our understanding. Rather . . . it is the case that society acts as a totality and it is only when we begin to read social phenomena as its moments that their deeper significance can be appreciated."[203] Rose would insist that causally efficacious social entities within society historically arise and pass away.

Indeed, Roy Bhaskar, the creator of the emergence paradigm within contemporary sociology, later turned to dialectics as a conceptual form of emergence providing "an analogue of real material emergence"[204] and as a corollary saw material emergence as "a genuine ontological analogue of Hegelian preservative determinate negation."[205] Bhaskar wished to distinguish his own version of emergence from Hegel's, because he thought the "Hegelian totality is constellationally closed, completed."[206] Rose had already moved away from this version of Hegel by 1981, undoubtedly under the influence of Adorno, and it is now of course a mainstream position within Hegelian scholarship. William Outhwaite called Bhaskar's critical realism, "a model which attempts to bring together metatheoretical and substantive theoretical considerations, and which can do justice to the multiplicity of social relations under conditions of advanced modernity."[207] I am arguing this characterizes Rose's work too.

If one way to think about the Hegelian concept is as an emergent whole, another is to ask after the nature of an adequate explanation. Kant

202. Neuhouser, *Foundations of Hegel's Social Theory*, 124–25.

203. O'Connor, *Adorno*, 27. On the differences between Rose and Adorno's views of the totality, see the next chapter.

204. Roy Bhaskar, *Dialectic*, 21.

205. Ibid., 45.

206. Ibid., 22.

207. Outhwaite, *Future of Society*, 75.

had pointed out the necessity for presupposing teleology in order to understand some systems (such as nature or history or a blade of grass),[208] and Hegel agreed. There is no need to read this as a crude version of teleology, and one of the achievements of *Hegel Contra Sociology* was to offer one of the earliest Anglophone interpretations of Hegel to avoid this error. Causal explanations explain one thing in terms of another, but thereby create an infinite regress. Richard Winfield comments that since cause and effect are indifferent to their content, even mutual cause/effect relations, such as reciprocity, lead to infinite regresses.[209] By contrast, to understand something conceptually is to see its parts and the relations among them as internally connected. Rather than the relations between contents being indifferent to the contents, the relations are an unfolding of the content; the unfolding is a self-unfolding; the causality is final as well as efficient. To understand the whole is to understand how everything connects. That is a virtuously circular understanding, because any part of the system leads eventually to every other. Precisely because we are led around the system we avoid the infinite regress of cause and effect. This is the difference between Hegelian and neo-Kantian circularity. For Hegel "it was precisely the distinguishing feature and ultimate aim of every philosophical science to comprehend a 'whole' in accordance with its immanent self-organizing character, that is, as an organism, *and* simultaneously through this comprehension to unfold itself as a methodically structured and organized system."[210] Complete knowledge of this kind is clearly impossible, which is why Rose emphasizes the provisional nature of such knowledge, what I have here called "implied totalities." It is a system without totalization.[211]

Hegel's *Science of Logic* is divided into three parts: the Logics of Being, Essence and the Concept. Concept translates *Begriff*, a holding together, comprehension. The section on the concept examines various ways of thinking about self-differentiated unity: the universal, concept,

208. E.g., in his essay "What Is Orientation in Thinking?": "*The right of the need* of reason supervenes as a subjective ground for presupposing and accepting something which reason cannot presume to know on objective grounds" (in *Political Writings*, 240–41).

209. Winfield, *Hegel's* Science of Logic, 183–85.

210. Wolff, "Hegel's Organicist Theory of the State."

211. Cf. Adorno, *Negative Dialectics*, 20: "The absolute knowledge that is already, involuntarily, claimed in each succinct individual judgment."

judgment, syllogism and absolute idea.[212] The concept is defined by the interrelation of universal, particular and individual (Rose uses "singular" rather than individual).[213] Rose calls this thinking triune, rather than trichotomous, precisely because the three terms form a unity. "The three moments of the concept are the universal, the particular, and the individual. These terms approximately parallel the traditional genus, species, and individual."[214] "Socrates" is an individual, "man" is a particular. Hegel's universals exist in individuals as a concrete universal. The normal use of "concept" to designate ideas such as "tree" or "person" is in Hegel's view an abstract understanding of concept because it does not employ fully developed concepts with all their determinations—the combination of universal, particular and individual.[215] Hegel's particular is "a definite content or quality defined over against other such qualities, but now that content is seen as a particularization of some universal unity."[216] His individual is a single subsistence, a "type of organic internally-articulated and self-sufficient individual in which the dichotomy between 'particularity' and 'universality' was somehow resolved."[217] The differentiated unity of universal, particular and individual is the unity of the concept.

The unity of the concept is Hegel's equivalent to Kant's unity of apperception.[218] The unity is negative: Kant's transcendental unity of apperception and Hegel's concept are not identical with any of their moments but do require those moments to exist because they are (at least potentially) the self-reflexive awareness of those contents. In Kant's apperception the knower both judges and (potentially) knows she is making a judgment in this way. In Hegel's logic, a judgment is both a positing of a relation between the three moments of the concept and the awareness of this positing. In idealism the judger simultaneously judges and takes herself to be making a judgment using certain categories. And this raises the question not only of the truth or validity of the specific judgment

212. This sentence paraphrases Kolb, *Critique*, 57, on whom this interpretation of triunity heavily depends.

213. *Das Allgemeine, das Besondere, das Einzelne.*

214. Kolb, *Critique*, 60–61. For a complementary account, see Pinkard, *Hegel's Dialectic*, 72–84.

215. *EL* §164; *TMS*, 60–61.

216. Kolb, *Critique*, 61.

217. Redding, "Systematic Reading," 6.

218. Hegel, *Science of Logic*, 12.18 (p. 515 in Giovanni). This is central to Pippin's interpretation in *Hegel's Idealism*, which I follow in this paragraph.

but also of the criteria for the categories by which judgments are made. Whereas Kant had twelve categories based on classical logical forms of judgment, in Hegel's logic the categories are derived rather than taken as given.[219] The shift from the logic of essence to concept is therefore not the discovery of an extra thing in the world but a different way of viewing the moments: as taken-to-be-moments-of-a-whole rather than as immediately given moments. But this means one must at the philosophical level think simultaneously about the world and categories for how to think about the world. Hegel saw that the rationality of the latter is historically and socially formed and justified. Hence for Rose epistemology is social theory and Hegel is one of the first great modern social theorists, who, like Rose after him, had an expansive conception of social theory. In this way, by combining phenomenology and logic, Hegel's philosophy is its own metaphilosophy.

Hegel viewed the *Logic* as the immanent exploration of the structures and content of the categories that constitute both reason and the world.[220] The *Logic* develops "the concepts of particular areas of the experienced world by deriving pure, *a priori* conceptual determination immanently from the logical structure of reason, and by then looking to experience to find the particular empirical phenomena which manifest those determinations and which provide us with the contingent details that extend and fill out our understanding of those determinations"—a combination of both empirical investigation and *a priori* dialectical generation of categories.[221] This logical derivation of categories is immanently, dialectically developmental. The categories of thought dialectically sublate themselves in a process of increasing complexity and refinement, until, at the end, they are seen as various "definitions of the absolute."[222] Hegel himself, then, combines empirical investigation with speculative

219. On the difference between a foundation and a starting place for thought, see *EL* §1; on the meaning of presuppositionlessness in Hegel's logic, see Houlgate, *Opening of Hegel's* Logic, 103–14.

220. This, like any characterization of *SL*, is contentious but guided by my aim of making sense of Rose's social theory. Hegel's only explicit writing about speculative propositions is in the preface to the *Phenomenology*, §59–66, and *Spirit of Christianity*, 256–58 (in *On Christianity: Early Theological Writings*). See *HCS*, 51–55. My interpretation relies on Stephen Houlgate in *Hegel, Nietzsche and the Criticism of Metaphysics*; *Opening*; *Introduction*, 26–66; Burbidge, *Logic of Hegel's Logic*; Giovanni, *Essays on Hegel's Logic*; Surber, "Hegel's Speculative Sentence."

221. Houlgate, *Criticism*, 126.

222. Ibid., 135, citing *EL* §85.

logic, and keeps the latter open to revision by the former (though to what extent speculative logic is or could be finished or completed is an ongoing debate). Hegel acknowledges that speculative logic is often not necessary in everyday reasoning, geometry or the natural sciences, but it is "the only method for determining the inherent character of thought."[223] Conceptual thinking does not replace explanation in terms of reciprocity but contextualizes (sublates) it in the whole-as-self-relating-and-developing (the concept). It switches the bad infinite (regress) of reciprocity for the good infinite (regress) of conceptual/speculative thinking. But just this is the "formulation of fundamental concepts and principles which govern all conceptual explanation."[224] So Hegel's philosophy does not necessarily give different empirical explanations of social phenomena from those provided by transcendental sociology but it can account for itself better: it is the "most general conceptual framework for all the sciences."[225] As a philosophy that includes its own derivation and ground, it is its own metaphilosophy.

In Hegel's view, the threefold division of the *Logic* is reflected in modern society's threefold division between individual/family, civil society and state, which is why modern society better reflects the concept. In premodern societies, the universal (the whole society) is immediate: there is too much unity, insufficient provision for the differences of individuals and social roles (see his discussion of Antigone in *Phenomenology*). In modern society, these differences have been accommodated: now the universal is quite formal, largely procedural, thinner on content, and more content comes from the individuals themselves. This difference is built into the institutions and social structures of modern society. This room for difference is a great achievement of modernity but is one-sided. The state should be a way of addressing this one-sidedness by its role as the larger context within which civil society and individuals attain full rationality.[226] The individuals (and their families) and civil society are more immediate than the state but presuppose and depend on the state to work in the way they should, namely, as means to and modes of freedom. In the state the individuals and their particular desires and roles have reference to the universal, the common good. This larger unity must already exist

223. Ibid., 138.

224. Duquette, "Speculative Logic," 12–13n9.

225. Ibid., 13.

226. See Neuhouser, *Foundations.*

for civil society to be there in the first place. "To think about civil society we need to be able to distinguish a formal process of interaction from the particular content and particular interactions of its members."[227] This is "not a fragmenting of unity so much a new kind of unity."[228] The diremptions of modern society are part of its unity; it is a broken middle.[229]

In Hegel's syllogisms each moment can mediate between the others: universal-particular-individual, universal-individual-particular, particular-individual-universal.[230] As Hegel remarks,[231] the particularity of individuals (their physical and spiritual needs) mediates them, via civil society, to the universal state. But equally the individual is the middle term between state and civil society insofar as her will and activity realizes (we could say, reproduces) the law and economy while simultaneously satisfying her needs by use of civil institutions. And finally the state mediates between individual and civil society by making both possible. "Since the mediation joins each of the determinations with the other extreme, each joins itself precisely in this way together with itself; it produces itself and this production is its self-preservation.—It is only through the nature of this joining together, through this triad of syllogisms with the same *terminus*, that a whole is truly understood in its organization."[232] For Rose these are schematic rather than exhaustive statements, intended to direct sociological investigation, yet they do so in a slightly altered way from neo-Kantian sociology. Some of the main meanings of Rose's term the "third" are now visible: teleology, differentiated unity and emergence as contexts for relating two terms (a condition and precondition). The third can thus be the speculative social totality, or it can be specifically a third thing alongside two others, or the intersubjective positings between two (or more) people.[233]

The essential structure of modern societies for Hegel is the triangular relation between individual, civil society (which includes the economy)

227. Kolb, *Critique*, 58.

228. Ibid., 68.

229. The "entirety of society" is, for Adorno, a "unity containing contradictions": "Lyric Poetry and Society," in *Adorno Reader*, 211–29 (214).

230. *EL* §198. For an excellent discussion of this feature of conceptual thinking as it relates to historical societies, see Henrich, "Logical Form and Real Totality."

231. *EL* §198 Remark.

232. Ibid. §198 Remark.

233. *MBL*, 12, 36.

and state.[234] Individuals (from families) are related to two different kinds of structures, each in a fundamentally different way and with different forms of mediation: civil society is the realm in which individuals may rightly pursue their individual needs and goals, the state is the sphere wherein they relate themselves to the universal needs and goals. Hegelians know this as the result of, and to gain its justification from, a history. It is a more complex structure than the individual-society dichotomy. It is not a trichotomy because it does not split the terms from one another but is triune because it understands the terms through one another.[235] Hence we exist in "a *triune structure* in which we suffer and act as singular, individual and universal; or, as *particular*, as represented in institutions of the *middle*, and as *the state*—where we are singular, individual and universal in *each position*."[236] As the Frankfurt Institute put it, "Insight into the dynamic structure of society requires the untiring effort to attain the unity of the general and the particular."[237] It is the internality of the individual, singular and universal to one another that marks conceptual thinking, which in reference to the state, means individuals and state constitute one another, are internally not externally related.

> The syllogistic form of mediation for the political constitution resulted . . . from the fact that it can be understood not as a kind of free-floating power hovering over and above the individual members of civil society, but only as something that expressly requires these individual members as its bearers and functionaries. It is always singular individuals who have the task of mediating the particular interests of an estate or class with the universal interest of the state. These individuals are identical with the bearers of the political powers, and thus with the government functionaries and officials and the individual members of the legislative body (or bodies).[238]

Sparta's customs and constitution can in this light be seen as the unfolding of a self-moving whole, not simply the back-and-forth between two predefined terms; in the whole understood conceptually the parts are

234. Cf. Neuhouser, *Foundations*, 122.

235. Rose's emphasis on triunity does not carry a theological meaning in this context.

236. *JAM*, 48; cf. *BM*, xii.

237. *Aspects of Sociology*, 26.

238. Wolff, "Hegel's Organicist Theory," 308–9.

essential to the whole, not accidental properties.[239] The picture is not of an enduring substrate with subtractable predicates; rather a conceptual whole is "organic": each part is necessary to the whole and is itself only in the whole; in this sense, each part is or expresses the whole.[240] The concept also names what it is that makes the thing the thing that it is. The concept is similar to Aristotelian form: it is what makes, say, an eye an eye; what it is we understand by "eye" that is not the same as listing all its properties. If the eye is removed from the body (the whole) it dies, and is no longer properly an eye, but a piece of flesh. Contrast this to a cog as part of a machine: separate from its whole, it remains what it is. The difference between reciprocal and conceptual thinking is the difference between understanding the relation between things in terms of "efficient causes all the way down" versus their relation in terms of "what they are."[241] Hegel suggests we need to posit (retrospectively, phenomenologically) something like "the concept (or spirit) of Sparta" as what develops and expresses itself in the reciprocal interaction between customs and constitution: "It is a specific spirit which makes itself into an actual world which now exists objectively in its religion, its ritual, its customs, constitution and political laws, and in the whole range of its institutions, events and deeds. That is its creation—that *is* this people."[242] The purposiveness or teleology—that is, the self-organizing nature—of the state, is internal to the state itself because it is a product of human will (it is not a regulative idea, externally imposed, as Kant's teleology of nature in Hegel's view).[243] This is the whole that reciprocal thinking does not yet see.[244] "In this respect, the absolute idea is comparable to the old man who says the same religious sentences as the child does, but for the old man they have

239. Rose's position is substantiated by Williams, *Hegel's Ethics*, esp. 293–333.

240. Society is "a sort of linking structure between human beings in which everything and everyone depend on everyone and everything; the whole is only sustained by the unity of the functions fulfilled by all its members" (Frankfurt Institute, *Aspects of Sociology*, 16).

241. Schick, "Freedom and Necessity," 84–99 (96), on which this section heavily depends.

242. Houlgate, *Introduction*, 21, discussing the third volume of *EL*.

243. Wolff, "Hegel's Organicist Theory," 306.

244. If one objects that reciprocity be rephrased as "society is such that it causes people and people are such that they cause society" one has just thereby transitioned from reciprocity to the concept. As Adorno noted, introduction to *Positivist Dispute*, 20: "According to pre-dialectical logic, the constitutum cannot be the constituens and the conditioned cannot be the condition for its own condition."

the meaning of his entire life."[245] Again, conceptual circularity is different from transcendental circularity. "To escape the clutches of the Logic of Essence, the determiner has to become both determiner and determined, and the determined has to be both determiner and determined. Only then will the defining distinction between determiner and determined determinacy be removed. Once this occurs, the determination of determined determinacy will give way to self-determination, to which Hegel will link the concept and the universal."[246] One may say it is ungrounded in the sense that each part is both ground and grounded; it is a "chain . . . of syllogisms returning into themselves . . . a form of thinking that can be described best as a 'synoptic conceptualisation.'"[247] This is the difference between Rose's conceptual critique and the quasi-transcendental metacritique. Both accept that transcendentally functioning preconditions for empirical features of society are themselves empirical but the fluidity of conceptual thinking is less prone to reifying the precondition into something non-immanent. Weber, for example, arguably remains at the level of logic of essence insofar as his dichotomies (structure versus will, procedure versus content) prioritize one term over the others.[248] This applies to his methodological individualism although his ideal types could be used in a conceptual manner. Whether all the metacritiques Rose accuses of this mistake actually commit it is debatable, but the import is clear.

Thus far, this account of the concept as an emergent or organic whole, with both ontological and epistemological components, has emphasized the unity of the totality and concept, arguably like Hegel himself. (In fact, Rose thought, "Hegel himself provides an account of why his view is not secure.")[249] For Rose, however, the concept is always internally fractured, dirempted, both ontologically and epistemologically. What in *Hegel Contra Sociology* she calls the circle and the breaks in the circle,[250] she later thought of as the broken middle. Thus any social totality always contains tensions and diremptions, never perfectly realizes itself. Modern society's diremptions are a key focus for Rose, not only as essential to the nature of modernity (though, she would also argue, to human society

245. *EL* §300 Addition.

246. Winfield, *Hegel's* Science of Logic, 190.

247. Wolff, "Hegel's Organicist Theory," 317.

248. Kolb, *Critique*, 14–23.

249. Rose, letter to *London Review of Books*.

250. *HCS*, 199.

tout court, albeit in different forms) but also to critiquing social philosophy where it imagines its theories can mend these socially produced and existing diremptions. (In chapter 4 we will see the implications of this for ethics and mutual recognition. In chapter 2 I will further refine Rose's view of the social totality in comparison to Adorno.) This is why the category of *Schein* from the Logic of Essence remains central to Rose's social philosophy: modern society includes moments of conceptuality and essentiality, such that categories from both are needed to understand it. Thus whereas the concept makes a thing what it is, insofar as it defines what something really is (and for idealism human consciousness has a constitutive role in the process), any concept of the *Geist* of a people will always be a provisional, retrospective reconstruction, a far more complex judgment than the biological metaphors may suggest. Only after the development has occurred, for instance, can the social theorist begin to grasp the concept of Sparta. There is a large measure of contingency in the coming to be of any form of *Geist*. Hegel regarded Sparta's concept (as with all the Greek world) as substantial unity (*Sittlichkeit*), and the concept for modern society as freedom. But for Rose the freedom is one that can never fully work, there will always be unbalance between individual, state and civil society: the broken middle. "These institutions of the middle *represent* and configure the relation between particular and state: they stage the *agon* between the three in one, one in three of singular, individual, universal; they represent the middle, broken between morality and legality, autonomy and heteronomy, cognition and norm, activity and passivity."[251] Rose's stress on the disunity within the whole avoids the over-simplification that organic language for the modern state could entail. Rose's stress on the breaks between universal, particular and singular express the fact that the state and its members not only express one another internally but also differ from one another. The state is both internal and external to its members, hence the importance of the speculative rather than simple identities (or disjunctions) between politics and ideology, state and religion.

It is clear from this example just how different phenomenological conceptual history is from normal, causal history. If the concept or spirit of Sparta as substantial unity or *Sittlichkeit* were supposed to explain (or deduce) its entire history in detail, Hegel's theory would clearly be incredible. Instead, Hegel is focused on the rationality of the shape of spirit,

251. *JAM*, 48.

the fundamental way of thinking that underlies and is produced by ethics, politics and epistemology. Speculative or phenomenological social theory is thus only one line of enquiry, and it cannot replace other kinds of history or sociology (Rose, we have seen, has no illusions about this). Yet that does not make its rational basis irrelevant to other kinds of social theorizing. Indeed, three years after Rose's book both Anthony Giddens's *Constitution of Society* and Pierre Bourdieu's *Distinction* were published in English. Each of these theories—structuration and *habitus*—was an attempt to get past the prioritizing of one side of sociology's antinomy and the objectivism-subjectivism dichotomy then dominating sociology and its classical tradition. In that sense they are close to Rose's own position.[252] As Simon Binney pointed out in a letter to her, with Hegel's philosophy she had "deconstructed" the usual dichotomies of "individual/society, freedom/necessity, idealism/materialism," and was therefore very close to Bourdieu, Giddens and Bhaskar.[253] Thus it appears that as social theory advanced it did so in the Hegelian direction Rose set out. Her reply to Binney was not a model of perspicacity: "The quest must be for the third position which I have continued to seek to formulate, not by turning to those works of my contemporaries which you mention but more to the different traditions of historical jurisdictions which emerge, recognized and unrecognized, in the works of those you mention."[254] When the phenomenological approach to political history and law is seen as central to Rose's social theory, however, her remark makes more sense.[255]

4.3 Speculative propositions

Rose relates the triune rationality of speculative philosophy to speculative propositions or sentences. Speculative sentences in the *Logic* combine

252. Compare the preface and introduction of Giddens, *Constitution of Society*, and Bourdieu's "Structures, *Habitus*, Practices," in *Logic of Practice*, 52–65.

253. Letter dated 1 November 1983, box 49.

254. Letter dated 22 November 1983, box 49.

255. Both Giddens and Bourdieu see the need for history in various ways. Bourdieu, says, "The *habitus*—embodied history, internalized as a second nature and so forgotten as history—is the active presence of the whole past of which it is the product. . . . The *habitus,* is a spontaneity without consciousness or will, opposed as much to the mechanical necessity of things without history in mechanistic theories as it is to the reflexive freedom of subjects 'without inertia' in rationalistic theories" ("Structures, *Habitus*," 56).

subject and predicate terms both of which are "logical categories or universal concepts."[256] That is, speculative sentences are about categories of thought, such as "being is the indeterminate immediate."[257] The speculative sentence states identity *and* difference between the two terms.[258] The subject and predicate are conceptually different but not distinct.

There is also a related but distinct "pre-systematic"[259] dimension of speculative thought: dialectical attention to the *form* of ordinary subject-predicate sentences already reveals the complexity of speculative philosophy (without the need for any particular theory of language). Here the subject-predicate sentences do not combine only two universals but may combine a universal and particular, such as "God is love." These sentences begin with the subject as a "meaningless sound, a mere name" and only the combination of subject and predicate provides any meaning.[260] Why, then, bother with the subject at all? In part because ordinary consciousness implicitly knows there is a difference between the subject and predicate, even though the predicate is supposed to express the essence of the subject: "It is not simply the universal which we want directly given, but *the universal as manifested in a concrete manner*."[261] Once again there is difference but not complete distinction. Thus speculative sentences express the movement of triune rationality through the tension between their form "A is B" and their content "A is B *and* not B."

In each case, systematic or pre-systematic, the identity between subject and predicate is more complex than initially realized; and only the "dialectical movement of the proposition . . . is . . . a speculative account."[262] In each case, the idea of the subject as a substance supporting accidents falls away in the face of this movement of the subject and predicate:

> Since the concept is the object's own self, that is, the self which exhibits itself as the *object's coming-to-be*, it is not a motionless subject passively supporting the accidents; rather, it is the

256. Houlgate, *Criticism*, 146.

257. Ibid., 145.

258. Cf. *EL* §166ff.

259. Surber, "Hegel's Speculative Sentence," 213. For the relation between systematic and pre-systematic, see 224ff.

260. *PhSp* §23. Pinkard's translations unless otherwise stated.

261. Surber, "Speculative," 214. This is one sense in which Rose's social theory and Weber's ideal types are similar.

262. *PhSp* §65.

> self-moving concept which takes its determinations back into itself. Within this movement, the motionless subject itself breaks down; it enters into the distinctions and the content and constitutes the determinateness, which is to say, the distinguished content as well as the content's movement, instead of continuing simply to confront that movement.[263]

For example, "the tulip is red" is usually taken to indicate a self-sufficient subject (the tulip) to which is ascribed an accidental predicate (redness), though the tulip could imaginably be yellow, and so redness cannot be taken to be essential to the nature of what it is to be a tulip. In a speculative sentence however, the predicate does express the essential nature of the subject, such that the subject can no longer be thought of as an inert substance supporting accidents. *This* tulip is essentially red. The subject is no longer a firm point of reference but something now thought in a different way, and of course the same thing is happening to the predicate.[264] But this will only work if there is both a dialectical movement back and forth between the two terms and if the speculative sentence is set within a whole discourse of speculative sentences providing context and meaning to one another. Since speculative sentences articulate the nature of thought, and thought is inherently developmental, the sentences themselves must be part of a whole development of thought and reason, which no single speculative sentence can achieve.[265] The subject of the subject-predicate sentence proceeds by the same self-developing or negative self-articulation as the self-conscious subject;[266] and just this thought undermines the conception of the self-conscious subject as a substance with externally attached accidents.

Rose's use of speculative thinking within social theory is closer to what Surber calls its pre-systematic use than the systematic use in Hegel's *Logic*, since the terms in question are not the fundamental categories necessary for thinking per se but the historically given terms by which we understand our social world. In Rose's view, speculative philosophy is required for understanding the human social world because it dialectically and progressively relates finite and infinite; it knows what Spirit is in and for itself, a matter of "practical self-consciousness."[267] History, reason

263. Ibid. §60.

264. Cf. *DN*, 56–67, and *Hegel's Idealism*, 81.

265. Houlgate, *Opening*, 93–98; Kolb, *Critique*, 74.

266. Surber, "Speculative," 215.

267. Pippin, "Logic of Experience," 227.

and *Geist* cannot properly be understood in "ordinary, finite terms,"[268] which is why positivism does not suffice. Speculative social theory therefore takes less for granted than its transcendental or quasi-transcendental cousins, just as it does in logic. For example, it provides a powerful way of handling contradiction and antimony. Here we may consider a very different kind of sociology from Rose's own writing, in order to see how her social philosophy is equally capable of providing a logic of descriptive/empirical sociology. In 2012 Rebecca Catto and Linda Woodhead published the results of large-scale, multidisciplinary, team research project entitled *Religion and Change in Modern Britain*. Their approach can be read as exemplifying various aspects of Rose's philosophy.[269] They used a combination of methods, including qualitative and quantitative.[270] They bore in mind the position of researcher and theory with respect to society, and approached theories as both *explicans* and *explicandum*: "Far from being neutral voices speaking on the post-war religious condition, these [secularization] theories are integral to it. And, as such, they offer an important route into some of its deepest presuppositions."[271] They emphasize a historical perspective on the multiple levels of mediation of religion and secularism, both of one another and by other social forms such as policy, media and law. They propose a dialectical relation between "religion" and "secular" as mutually determining, since "'secular' gains substance in relation to the kind of 'religion' it rejects."[272] And they offer a speculative conclusion: "Post-war Britain emerges as both religious *and* secular. . . . Neither makes sense without the other, and their shifting meanings must be analysed in relation to their changing linkages, configurations, commitments and mutual hostilities."[273] Here we have an example of some of the best contemporary sociology, combining various forms of empirical data collection and analysis, affirming that sociology needs to think in terms of contradictions and determinate negation, must use increasingly comprehensive levels of explanation and historically in-

268. Houlgate, *Criticism*, 139.

269. For the background to Rose's views on empirical sociology, see also *TMS*, esp. 77–148.

270. *TMS*, 95–108.

271. Woodhead and Catto, *Religion*, 3.

272. Ibid., 4.

273. Ibid., 3–4. One cannot avoid the contradiction by assigning "religious" to some sectors of society and "secular" to others. As the volume shows, secular and religious mediate and so constitute one another in complex and changing ways.

formed analyses, and be aware of its own role within its object of study. Although the empirical and descriptive work in this volume fits the criteria of Rose's social theory, it still leaves open the normative questions that Rose makes clear need to be tackled. Rose's work thus offers significant advantages to social theorizing. It provides a deep methodological basis for social theory in logic itself; and a sophisticated framework for relating the methodological, logical, descriptive, metaphysical and normative moments of social theorizing.[274]

5 Double Critique and Implied Totality

The second main task of this chapter is to show how Rose first used her social philosophy to critique speculatively both society and social theory, and relate that critique to the implied totality it suggested. Rose's first foray in this direction was to critique the bourgeois property form in relation to social contract theory and the subjectivity fostered by both. From a speculative perspective, the implied totality of absolute ethical life then emerged to view.[275] This was Hegel's Absolute and why his philosophy has no social import if it cannot be thought. As noted, Rose knew any totality she posited would be an imperfect grasp of society not only because our knowledge is finite but also because society itself is always dirempted. (I therefore refer to the totalities she proposes as "implied" because they never fully exist.) Hence absolute ethical life is for Rose a facetious term, both necessary and impossible. Rose regarded law as an essential way to gain a provisional yet comprehensive view of the social totality. She explored the connections between legally determined social forms and the forms of consciousness they produced (both existentially lived and philosophically expressed in theory). Law is, for Rose, a privileged view of the totality for several reasons. It is universal (it applies across the whole nation-state, which is primary for Rose) and yet applies to particulars. Individuals must negotiate individual laws and the ethos they create. Law and ethics are both rationalized in modernity but also mediate one another. Mutual recognition is the actuality (i.e., inner normative goal) of law, ethics and politics, though they are all dirempted internally and in relation to one another; thus the totality must always

274. See further Brower Latz, "Gillian Rose," in Bonefeld et al., *Sage Handbook to Frankfurt School Critical Theory*.

275. See *HCS*, 51–63.

be conceptualized through its multiple mediations and diremptions. Throughout her work Rose explores some of the different effects of juridification on philosophical and natural consciousness.

5.1 A simultaneous critique of society and social philosophy

Rose carried out her first critique of society and social theory by repeating Hegel's critique of Kant and Fichte in his essay on natural law.[276] Hegel criticizes the contradictions involved in the ethical, political and legal dimensions of the social contract theories of Kant and Fichte, and proposes an alternative.[277] The crux is the way in which the individual is imagined within the state of nature: it is both a natural condition—what would remain when all society was stripped away—and acknowledged to be a fiction. As a consequence, "although the natural will has the liberty to choose whatever it wishes, it is still always bound to choices that are given to it rather than determined by freedom."[278] The so-called natural will in the state of nature is according to Hegel merely the least developed picture of the will that is still coherent. It is the will at the stage of "abstract right" in *The Philosophy of Right*. It is simply a desiring will, the part of the will essential to private economic transactions and interests, inflated to take the position of the entire will, obscuring its other textures, such as intersubjectivity and universal morality. The result is not only a mistaken political anthropology but a view of the state as subservient to private economic exchange, and so not a sovereign political body at all.

This fiction imports into philosophy certain features from current bourgeois society and treats them as natural, such as the atomized individualism and economic rationality of the private property owner. The philosophy of Kant and Fichte thus reinforces some of the problematic aspects of subjectivity and social forms in their society, as when it treats the atomized individual as a fixed substrate to which can be attached accidental predicates, precisely the form of thinking speculative philosophy is designed to surpass. Hegel's speculative philosophy then enables the individual and the family, or the individual and society, or the society and the state (and so on, through various combinations) to be imagined as mutually defining rather than mutually indifferent terms

276. Ibid., 51–97.

277. Hegel, *Scientific Ways of Treating Natural Law*.

278. Winfield, *Reason and Justice*, 84.

forced into some kind of external connection (such as Fichte's form of social unity [in Hegel's view]). Such triune thinking underlies Hegel's combination of *Moralität* and *Sittlichkeit* in ethical theory.[279] For Rose, speculative philosophy provides the insight that Kant and Fichte have, in effect, taken what is given in their society and justified it (in a transcendental manner) rather than allowing the aporia and contradictions of society to point toward some alternative.[280] The form and content of thinking are very clearly related in this instance.[281] Rose detects a parallel between the Fichtean concept of subjectivity as the absolute positing ego, the legal personality of bourgeois property law, and the moral subject in Kantian *Moralität*, because all exclude some of their determinations *and* the knowledge that they are so excluding portions of actuality.[282] Fichte's concept of the self, the subject of *Moralität* and *Moralität* as a form of ethical life, all repeat and reinforce the structure of the property holder, which itself reflects the Roman legal person's absolute dominion over his property (*res*). Kant explicitly assumed the categories of Roman law in order to give a transcendental deduction of them,[283] whereas Hegel opposed Kant's attempt "to turn Roman civil law categories into a rationally grounded law of nature."[284] This results from inflating the role of property ownership into too dominant a place in society, and from failing sufficiently to see their positing of ethical theory *as* a positing.

Rose would expand on this critique in her next book (see ch. 3), both of Kant and of poststructuralism, as unknowingly relying on and importing features of different legal systems. In the present case, although Rose never defines "bourgeois property form" or "private law," she clearly relies on the general Marxist view of these terms. Private law was a distinctively Roman legal category for property and "the regulation

279. Pippin, *Idealism as Modernism*, 92–128, "Hegel, ethical reasons, Kantian rejoinders."

280. Hegel viewed this as a failure to follow the development of the concept of freedom all the way from abstract right to morality to ethical life. In abstract right, for example, what and how much any person possesses is indifferent, precisely because the ideas here are abstract and one-sided (*PhR* §49).

281. Hegel compares the differences in his and their moral thought to an adolescent who thinks everything is bad, a believer in Providence who accepts the status quo too easily, and an adult who negotiates both limitations and change (*EL* §234 Addition).

282. *HCS*, 187. *PhR*, *passim*, e.g., §4, 8.

283. Kant, *Metaphysical Elements of Justice*.

284. Milbank, "Secular Order," 214–15.

of property would constitute by far the largest part of Rome's civil law."[285] The private-public distinction in Rome was new at the time, different from surrounding societies and generated by the role property had in Roman society. "What set the Romans apart from all other high civilizations was their property-régime, with its distinctive legal conception of property; and with it came a more sharply delineated private sphere in which the individual enjoyed his own exclusive dominion."[286] Whereas "the Greeks had no clear conception of ownership, indeed no abstract word for it at all . . . the distinctively *exclusive* quality of Roman property, [was] the degree to which it belonged to the individual to the exclusion of others."[287] "In this way, the 'Roman citizen asserts a claim against all the world, based on an act of his own will.' The concept of *dominium*, then, marks out the private sphere with an unprecedented clarity, and the private is inseparable from property. . . . The partnership of *dominium* and *imperium*, then, sums up both the distinction between public and private and the alliance of property and state that was so distinctively Roman."[288]

Despite significant differences between the liberalism of Kant and Fichte and Roman *imperium* (such as the desire of liberals to protect the individual from sovereign power), there are important continuities, based on property, which then determine class and class relations, the public-private spheres, and so on. The bourgeois property form should thus be investigated against the background of Roman law. Doing so can highlight, for instance, "an interesting violation of the Lockean view that those who create value by mixing their labor with the land are entitled to private property in that value," namely, that "whatever the laborer produces during the period of the contract belongs to the capitalist, not to the laborer."[289]

The religion-state speculative identity suggests a further link between bourgeois property law as social form on the one hand, and the form of morality and subjectivity in modern society on the other. That is, the legal "person" is the bearer of property rights in abstraction from all other characteristics and relations. "A corollary of defining part of oneself as a legal 'person' in contradistinction to other legal 'persons' is that a

285. Wood, *Meiksins Wood Reader*, 114–15.

286. Ibid., 117.

287. Ibid.

288. Ibid., 117–18.

289. Harvey, *Companion to Marx's* Capital, 119–20.

further dimension of oneself is isolated: subjectivity, the substratum in which the accident of being a bearer of property rights inheres. 'Subjectivity' is thus even more cut off from the totality of social relations which determine it."[290] The legal and political form of property in bourgeois society, combined with a non-speculative way of thinking, expresses and reinforces the mutually constitutive relationship between subjective morality (*Moralität*) and its corresponding form of subjectivity. "'Subjectivity' is the correlate of the legal definition of persons as bearers of private property rights. Misrepresentation of the absolute is the correlate of subjectivity."[291] The subjectivity correlated with legal personality tends to be inwardly hypertrophic, since intentions are the source and content of morality, and outwardly disconnected from others and from the consequences of the subject's actions. This subjectivity often ends up both unworldly because too inward and yet ruthless because it can justify evil.[292] Morality is now thought of as "the autonomous realm of what ought to be," good intentions divorced from consequences. But this quickly degenerates into casuistic self-justification: so long as the agent can present his actions as well intentioned, he is guaranteed to have acted correctly.[293] The absolute as the unity of people, constitution (or law) and custom (or ethics), is then misunderstood in two ways: as an imposed and formal unity (Fichte) or projected into an otherworldly realm by religion. It is in this sense that "the standpoint of subjective morality arises out of bourgeois property relations."[294]

Another example of law providing a view onto the social whole is found in the work of Wayne Martin. In "Antinomies of Autonomy: German Idealism and English Mental Health Law," Martin shows that the antinomy between the duty to care for patients and patients' autonomy cannot be removed from within the liberal political paradigm but it can be mediated through considering what structures should be in place to contextualize it, so that the patient has the opportunity to experience her care as neither alien nor imposed but as open to her recognition and appropriation, even if only retrospectively. (Recognition and appropriation are, as noted above, central to Rose's Hegelianism, in distinction from

290. *HCS*, 92.

291. Ibid., 99.

292. *HCS*, 125–26.

293. This is Hegel's critique of the Romantic debasement of Kantian ethics, not Kantian ethics itself (*PhR* §140–41).

294. *HCS*, 93.

some other Frankfurters.) The doctor-patient relation therefore has to be referred to wider legal, social and professional frameworks. This is the movement familiar from *Philosophy of Right*: a seemingly immediate relation turns out to be comprehensible and actual only through being embedded in and mediated by various facets of state and civil society. These mediations occur over time, partly as a result of past failures. Martin outlines three Hegelian premises he used when considering mental health legislation:[295]

1) "Autonomous determination *can be* determination by another, as long as that other is an other whom I rightly recognize as appropriately not-other." (The speculative combination of freedom and necessity.)
2) Within human society (the realm of *Geist*), dialectic runs all the way down; it is the realm of contradiction.[296]
3) We aim to make the world our own in the sense of being at home in it; the world's rationality and our rationality are congruent.

Martin then discusses the case of a person who took a decision about his medical treatment, which he recognized as his own while simultaneously acknowledging the ways it was influenced by others. This suggests the task of structuring various social forms (family, civil society, laws, professional bodies) as "appropriately not-other," to foster this experience. One of the ways this works is by offering the person different perspectives on themselves—as a sufferer in need of care, as an autonomous rights-bearer, as a biochemical organism—within different time scales. The antinomies will always remain—the problems involved here are objectively difficult choices to which no philosophy can give definitive answers—but the aim is to design institutions (rather than focus on the doctor-patient relationship alone) to enable justice to be done to both sides of the antinomy. Martin suggests the Hegelian approach to the antinomic structure of both reason and society is still more comprehensive than many others. It involves every realm of society, ideas, institutions, and different temporal perspectives.

Using Rose's social philosophy, one can see emerging from this history—immanently, not imposed—an ideal form of subjectivity that knows its determinations as mediations of itself rather than ignoring

295. Martin, "Antinomies," 203–4.

296. Cf. *PhR* §33 Addition.

("dominating" or "suppressing") them and its coherence with the ethical life and laws of its country—in short, absolute ethical life. Recognition and appropriation in Rose obviate the method-system separation, allowing *some* grasp of the social whole through phenomenological reconstruction. The structure of finding the self in the other suggests the ideal of mutual recognition for politics and ethical life rather than the subject-as-lone-property-holder. A different idea of freedom then emerges, one that includes necessity (in the form of social determinations) rather than tries to oppose freedom and necessity (as in Kant and Fichte).[297] The example of Martin's work shows how Rose's social philosophy offers concrete gains not only in conceiving freedom but in practice.[298]

5.2 Absolute ethical life

In *Hegel Contra Sociology*, private law and the bourgeois property form serve as a view of the social whole but the speculative treatment of this whole implies or suggests another social whole: absolute ethical life. Many readers of *Hegel Contra Sociology* came away with the feeling that Rose is undecided between absolute ethical life as "a merely heuristic, negative function" or as something more substantial.[299] Indeed, some commentators did not think she had explained what the Absolute (her shorthand for absolute ethical life) was at all.[300] This is because on the one hand Rose insists on mutual recognition as the form of absolute ethical life, while on the other she refuses to specify, on principle, what that would look like in detail. Here I summarize the picture of the Absolute in *Hegel Contra Sociology*; expand on it through a 1987 paper by Bernstein expressing his and Rose's shared views; and then highlight some of the problems in this early formation.

Arguing that transcendental sociology cannot properly acknowledge the antinomy of freedom and determination, Rose claims the Absolute can, which gives Rose's version of Hegel's philosophy its social import. She then traces the Absolute in Hegel through the rest of the book to substantiate this. In chapter 2 absolute ethical life is "a critique of

297. *TMS*, 151, describes Adorno's view of *Geist* as "both formed by society and has a partial autonomy."

298. Cf. Pally, *Commonwealth and Covenant*, 46–47.

299. Gorman, "Whither," 53.

300. E.g., Hawthorn, "Ideal Speech," 15–16.

bourgeois property relations"[301] and the indication of a different property relation; but just what that is remains "elusive."[302] In chapter 3 absolute ethical life emerges as a form of life implied by the historical trajectory of forms of freedom from *Sittlichkeit* in Greece, through the subjectivity produced by Roman law and Christianity, to the culture of reflection with its *Moralität* and formal property law. Chapter 4 examines the illusions generated by bourgeois society in relation to work and the appropriation of wealth, linking the deformations of current ethical life to arrangements of property, law, labor and political economy. Chapters 3 and 4 suggest that in modern society philosophy has taken over from religion and art as providing the predominant means of formation of subjectivity (a "culture," "vocation" or *Bildung*). Chapter 5 traces the historical development of forms of ethical life in more detail and suggests philosophy itself has been deformed in its attempts to replace art and religion as the primary culturing source in modern society. Chapter 6 sees Hegel's *Science of Logic* as a speculative rereading of Kant and Fichte to produce an implied unity of theory and practice that enables the Absolute to be thought (but not known in detail). Chapter 7 summarizes what has been learned for sociology and for Marxism.

As the unity of finite and infinite is implied by that very distinction in theoretical reason, the unity of law and morality is implied by that distinction in practical reason. Absolute ethical life is the implied unity of theoretical and practical philosophy, law and morality, finite and infinite. Its content—whatever we can discern thereof—arises from reconstructions of what we have learned about them through phenomenological experience (or experience speculatively exposited). That is the only way the Absolute can be shown in religion, politics, art, labor, and so on. Absolute knowing is this speculative-phenomenological approach to the history of ethical and political life. As noted above, spirit is "the structure of recognition or misrecognition in a society," and absolute spirit is "the meaning of history as a whole,"[303] meaning a phenomenological reconstruction of how we arrived where we are, which Hegel showed was the only adequate form of understanding and justification of beliefs and institutions. Thus, absolute spirit is a position taken on the lessons to be learned from the philosophy of history with a particular view to the different forms of

301. *HCS*, 97.

302. Ibid.

303. Ibid., 44.

recognition and misrecognition involved in individuals' relationships to society. Rose arrives at absolute ethical life by extending existing ethical values and practices, rather than applying a predetermined universal norm,[304] since the content of the norm is filled in over time through different attempts to apply it. This, as we have seen, is how speculative pairs of terms work in Rose, re-cognizing and re-appropriating their meaning. One must therefore distinguish the "1)—not knowing i.e., positing the Absolute—and 2)—the re-cognizing i.e. knowing which is precisely knowing of the history of the formation and deformation of the aporia—which is speculative or absolute."[305] Rose's condensed expression indicates the difference between proposing an ethical or social form without fully taking into account its social (and not only logical origins), and the Hegelian attention to the act of positing as well as what is posited, which includes our inability to know what a moral law is unless we know how to apply it. The history of a concept's application, judgments about good or bad applications, and the difficulties involved therein, are therefore part of the concept itself.[306] "Positing" in the first sense is insufficiently historical, whereas recognition is historically better informed.

The problem with this extension of phenomenologically justified values, however, is the deformation of imagination by current, "relative" ethical life. Rose says absolute ethical life should be viewed as equally "lost" and "not yet attained."[307] For Rose this means absolute ethical life is implied by current ethical life (as its perfection) but not completely known (not "pre-judged"). Hence there is a twofold "necessity" to current ethical life, which is both the rationality discernible in current ethical life and the way that rationality is changed, hidden, distorted (the necessary illusions identified by Frankfurt School ideology critique).[308] Current ethical life can be viewed heuristically as a lost version of its

304. Cf. *PhR* §1–2.

305. Rose, letter to Bernstein, 27 March 1987.

306. *MBL*, 1–14: acknowledging aporia differentiates a comprehensive philosophy from an ideology, it provides it some contact with the difficulty of reality and opens philosophy to correction.

307. *HCS*, 168. Bernstein, *Fate of Art*, 60: "Judgments of beauty are memorial: in making aesthetic judgments we judge things 'as if' from the perspective of our lost common sense, a common sense that may never have existed (evidence for it deriving strictly from the torsions of the analytic articulation of aesthetic experience). This 'remembered' common sense is . . . both presupposed in the judgment of taste and yet to be obtained."

308. *HCS*, 165.

ideal, most rational self to which we strive to attain. Absolute ethical life therefore contains current ethical life because it will sublate it. (This is the logical form of the concept in Hegel: after a sequence of categories has developed we see at the end that each was a partial expression of the full concept.) The Absolute exists between real and logical possibility, as Bernstein suggests:

> The *imaginary* space between logical and real possibility which the critique of the "Postulates" elaborates is precisely the space of modernist art practices . . . some empirical events themselves can have an equivalent status, possessing a kind of unreal reality, or, more exactly, as making a promise about what is empirically possible as a form of life which is implied by their mere existence but which cannot be further specified or justified. Certain empirical events have the status of both actualizing a possibility and in so doing making a promise about the future; it is this notion of an event that is a *promise* that I want to claim as filling the space between logical and actual possibility.[309]

In one sense, the Absolute is "actuality": "If actuality is not thought, then thinking has no social import."[310] Actuality (*Wirklichkeit*) is Hegel's way of talking about what things really are and should be. For instance, when we ask, "is that really art?" we are asking about the actuality of a putative artwork. Or if we ask whether pot smoking is actually religious we are enquiring after what religion essentially is. When Hegel says the concept drives actuality he means, for example, that insofar as a phenomenon is really religious then it actualizes the concept of religion.

Beyond this, Hegel also attended to two things: how the determination of individuals is also a determination of ethical life; and how those determinations are often either ignored or misrecognized. These two observations have important structural consequences for the account. Rose's social theory is interested in the actuality and concepts recognized and misrecognized in ordinary ethical life. "Phenomenology acknowledges the actuality which determines the formation of consciousness. The recognition of actuality takes the form of a presentation of the various attempts at reform and revolution which displace the real determinants of consciousness and action and therefore do not effectively change

309. Bernstein, *Adorno*, 419.

310. *HCS*, 229. The similarity between this sentence and the refrain of "Hegel's philosophy has no social import if the absolute cannot be thought" brings out the point.

those determinants but reinforce them."[311] When the social influences on subjectivity are misrecognized they tend to be reinforced. Throughout her work Rose thus attempted to reveal some of the unrecognized or misrecognized social influences on social philosophy, and to provide a logic for thinking about the relationship between subjectivity and society that acknowledges both the givenness of social reality and the contribution of social actors.[312]

Rose aimed to show her readers socially generated illusions to help them see through them to some extent. For instance, the commodity form influences the way people relate to their own labor and themselves (as commodities): this is a real experience and yet a certain illusion, caused by the economic organization of society rather than being a fundamental necessity. Stepping back from this illusion and thinking differently is not yet a solution, since new insights are not yet new social forms. The current, overall, organizing social form can therefore be critiqued by reference to another, implied totality—absolute ethical life. This also acts as a criticism of some postmodern philosophy since the current totality is not "Western metaphysics" as a whole but a particular historical form—capital. "Instead of working with the general question of the dominance of Western metaphysics, the dilemma of addressing modern ethics and politics without arrogating the authority under question is seen as the ineluctable difficulty in Hegel, Nietzsche and Kierkegaard's engagement with modernity."[313] Unlike some postmodern social theory, by naming the reigning universal "capital" Rose directs attention to the need for sociological explorations in place of condemnations of "metaphysics." Rose wrote: "Speculative thinking transforms the critique of epistemology and the critique of morality into recognition of what the theoretical and practical concept has suppressed—historically and politically—its absolute is therefore intrinsically aporetic—both 'absolute' knowledge and 'absolute' ethical life."[314] Like Adorno's negative dialectics, Rose's Absolute tries to discover what the current form of ethics and epistemology hides from view, but unlike negative dialectics (in her opinion) it offers a universal, a version of the infinite it knows to be imperfect but knows it cannot do

311. Ibid., 232.

312. Ibid., 227–29.

313. Ibid., preface.

314. Letter, 27 March 1987. Bernstein interpolated many of these points into the second draft of "Speculation."

without: absolute spirit. And it is more willing to justify some aspects of society, to acknowledge the development of the concept in history.

Rose's Absolute is a form of ideology critique. "It is only by acknowledging the lack of identity as the historical *fate* (*Bestimmung*) of a different property structure that absolute ethical life can be conceived. This ethical life includes relations (lack of identity), but these relations do not give rise to the illusion that they afford the immediate and absolute basis for the 'moral' freedom of the individual."[315] That is, the perspective of absolute ethical life shows current ethical life and its forms of recognition as always a mixture of recognition and misrecognition, since the ideal is full mutual recognition, which is never attained. The absolute—in its different forms as knowing, ethical life and subjectivity—depends on a "*triune* relating . . . [this is] where recognition/master-slave/the Christian Trinity/the concept of law, come together in Hegel: to recognize another there must be a third."[316] The mediation between two terms by a third is a key component of triune rationality. Absolute ethical life would be the unity between individual will (including disposition: *subjektive Gesinnung*) and the general will (expressed in laws), and the *Sittlichkeiten* of civil society groups.[317] It would be a society explicitly and intentionally organized to bring about this harmony. Rose, like Hegel, believed the threefold structure of modern society (individual/family, civil society, state) provided the best opportunity for such harmony thus far in history, not least because mutual recognition was immanent to it. She thought too that such harmony was impossible to achieve but did not rule out improvements in its realization (nor has she any grounds to rule out further rational "surprises" in terms of major social change). All of this comes from her speculative (historical-phenomenological) approach, whereas non-speculative approaches delivered individualist social contract theories (and, later, denials of metaphysics vulnerable to dialectical reversal, ontological violence [see ch. 3], over-moralized politics, triumphalist and hasty theoretical mending of diremptions [see ch. 4] [and we could perhaps add: amoral systems theory]).

315. *HCS*, 62.

316. Letter to Bernstein, 27 March 1987. Cf. *PhSp* §50.

317. Cf. Neuhouser, *Foundations*, *passim*.

6 Objections

Aside from the problems considered earlier, two main objections would be raised against Rose's work from this point onward. The first, made by Peter Osborne and Tony Gorman, is that she abandons a Marxist critique of political economy and as a result is unable to move beyond immanent phenomenology to anything more substantive. The second, put most forcefully by John Milbank, is that she refused to entertain the possibilities of improvement and the partial repair of dirempted social life, leaving absolute ethical life too vague to be helpful.

6.1 Political economy and substantive theory

As we have seen, Rose makes private property central to her notion of bourgeois society, and an alternative property form central to Hegel's notion of the Absolute. "By acknowledging the contradictions of bourgeois enterprise and private property, Hegel hoped to surmount and contain them."[318]

> Throughout all Hegel's writings reference is made to a series of property forms. Out of these distinct historical "types," Hegel tried, time and time again, to compound an alternative. . . . This alternative is never definitively explicated. The fundamental paradox of Hegel's thought is that he was a critic of *all* property forms, but his central notion of a free and equal political relationship is inexplicable without concepts of property . . . and hence incomplete without the elaboration of an alternative property relation.[319]

Real recognition can "only be achieved in a just society,"[320] which is to say it "requires different property relations."[321] Rose's tone gives the impression that Hegel believed private property to be wrong, though she briefly acknowledges that in fact Hegel thought private property was

318. *HCS*, 74–75.

319. *HCS*, 86. MacGregor, *Hegel, Marx, and the English State*, argues Hegel did have a coherent and radical view of property and a "structural solution to poverty: worker ownership of the means of production" (156n15). Part of his case is made by using Hegel's Heidelberg lectures, which only became available in 1983, two years after Rose's book was published.

320. *HCS*, 74.

321. Ibid., 83–84.

necessary but should not be inflated into such a prominent position in society, and that formal property law is better than the arbitrariness of feudalism.[322] She nevertheless underplays Hegel's view that private property is necessary to the realization of freedom and subjectivity.[323]

Rose thus announced at the end of *Hegel Contra Sociology* the project of a "critical Marxism" that would combine Marx's analysis of capital with analysis of capitalism as a culture (in Hegel's sense: a form of life that indirectly shapes subjectivity and consciousness in both good and bad ways).[324] Her main criticism of the Marxist tradition was not "Marx's analysis of *Capital*, but . . . any presentation of that analysis as a comprehensive account of *capitalism*, and in any pre-judged, imposed 'realization' of that theory, any using it *as a theory*, *as Marxism*."[325] Yet critical Marxism never fully arrived. Osborne and Gorman noted the disappearance of full-blooded Marxism from *The Broken Middle* and later works, attributing it to her absorption of Kierkegaard's Christian influence. In my view, her commitment to a "critical Marxism" announced at the end of *Hegel Contra Sociology* had already ceased by *Dialectic of Nihilism* three years later. The connection between property, law and subjectivity is still there and is still seen as the commonality between Hegel and Marx, but the insistence on the need for different property relations is absent in this and all her other books, while her emphasis on law and jurisprudence remains. Critical Marxism was replaced by jurisprudential wisdom, itself sublated into the broken middle. Thus the analysis of "the contradictory relations between Capital and culture"[326] focuses on antinomies of law and diremptions between state and society (both in modern, capitalist societies) but is not aimed at "revolutionary practice" nor linked to "analysis of the economy."[327]

A more important question, at least from a position sympathetic to Marxist critique of political economy, is whether Rose's work is compatible with such critique. It seems to me it is. Robert Bernasconi declared, "I find her reading of Hegel much closer to other Marxist theories than

322. Ibid., 181.

323. *PhR* §41; Speight, "Hegel's Critique," 389–90. Minogue picked up this problem in his review. Perhaps, however, she later remedied this, since *BM*, 229, is skeptical of Arendt's going to "great length to disqualify private property."

324. Cf. *HCS*, 231.

325. Ibid., 235.

326. Ibid.

327. Ibid.

she would have us believe."[328] In the 1987 paper "Speculation and Aporia," capital rather than "Western metaphysics" was the focus of attention. This may explain her later attacks on Derrida's version of Marxism as lacking any connection to institutions or property relations: such a hollowed out Marxism is no Marxism at all.[329] Yet as Osborne notes, Rose discusses Marx only occasionally and not at length and her view of Marx must be surmised from these different treatments.[330] The fact is Rose did not address such questions in enough detail to be put on one side of the debate or the other, though her emphasis did shift away from private property toward other diremptions in her later work. Thus Rose's work also seems compatible with those like Habermas and Honneth who accept capitalism for the time being and seek to ameliorate it.

Nevertheless, it is not the case that Rose's work is incompatible with theory or specific analyses of determination per se, as Osborne and Gorman charge. She uses phenomenology not to oppose substantive positions but to lead to them, improve them and justify or critique them. The philosopher does not abandon or disown "the edifice" of her civilization but inspects it.[331] Having said that, Rose only forwards her own substantive positions in tandem with the critique of others, which makes them difficult to discern and not as fulsome as one may wish, though this may be a consequence of her shortened career.

6.2 Vagueness

The Absolute is implied but not known. Since it never fully exists it cannot fully be known but only imagined. Hence Rose insists "there are no statements about the absolute in Hegel—there are speculative propositions about experience. This recognition is developed speculatively and without positing an absolute."[332] This means there are no straightforward descriptions about absolute ethical life, but the speculative exposition of dirempted experience to bring out suggestions of the lost and impossible unity such diremptions can be made to reveal. Yet what good is an

328. Bernasconi, review of *HCS*, 43.
329. Rose, "Ghost in His Own Machine," 32.
330. Osborne, "Gillian Rose and Marxism."
331. *BM*, 286.
332. Letter to Bernstein, 27 March 1987.

Absolute that remains elusive and "an unspecific unity of concept and intuition"?[333] Does it not thereby lose all its social import?

> Rose so emphasises Hegel's anxiety that determinate negation appears to have slipped out of sight, and one is left to puzzle about her attitude to Hegel's "speculative" anticipation of a resolved social future. It is clear that she wishes to stress our confinement to the "logic of illusory being," yet Hegel does not present his account of the absolute "Notion" as something abstractly known outside of historical purpose. On the contrary, it is only unfolded—as both presupposed and anticipated—by way of the historical passage through illusory being. And for precisely this reason, Hegel never denies us access to anticipation of the resolved future, and indeed gives some description of it in terms of a market economy mitigated by local corporations and centralized state. No equivalent vision is provided by Rose. Nor does she comment on such a crucial question as her attitude to the capitalist market.[334]

It appears the Absolute retains the structure of a regulative ideal, a contradictory ought, the same structure Hegel criticized in Kant. Or does Rose's Absolute turn out to be a Kantian transcendental object—thinkable in some way but not knowable? A difference between Kant and Hegel on Rose's reading is that Hegel fully embraces the antinomic structure of the "ought" and has arrived there on a phenomenological, speculative basis, which changes its function somewhat.[335] The Kantian ought "does not deny the whole world, but acknowledges part of it, the partial or formal law of private property relations. It thus *looks as if* it recognizes the universal or ethical,"[336] but the moral law is not complete as it claims. "The law defines *actuality* as an infinite task and thus draws attention away from the real significance of the *acts* of the moral subject."[337] The problem with the Kantian ought—on Rose's somewhat one-sided reading—is its inability properly to actualize itself, its tendency to remain implicit rather than realized in individual character and group ethos. Whereas:

333. *HCS*, 83.

334. Milbank, "Living in Anxiety," 22.

335. I owe this point to Peter Osborne in comments made during the "Thinking in the Severe Style" symposium.

336. *HCS*, 187.

337. Ibid.

> The absolute is the comprehensive thinking which transcends the dichotomies between concept and intuition, theoretical and practical reason. It cannot be thought (realized) because these dichotomies and their determinations are not transcended. . . . Once we realize this we can think the absolute by acknowledging the element of *Sollen* in such a thinking, by acknowledging the subjective element, the limits on our thinking the absolute. This is to think the absolute and to fail to think it quite differently from Kant and Fichte's thinking and failing to think it. . . . Thinking the absolute means recognizing actuality as *determinans* of our acting by recognizing it in our acts. Thus recognizing our transformative or productive activity has a special claim as a mode of acknowledging actuality which transcends the dichotomies between theoretical and practical reason, between positing and posited.[338]

For Rose, by the end of the *Phenomenology*, philosophical consciousness realizes the inevitability of antinomies and diremptions, and Hegel offers an elaboration of, not escape from, that situation. For instance, rather than seeing ethical and juridical antinomies as an illusion (Kant thinks there cannot be a clash of duties in an ultimate sense), they are regarded as intrinsic to ethical life and thought. The Absolute remains as a form of ideology critique—current ethical life always retains some form of misrecognition—but does not provide a "how to" for policy or a political program. Despite this, mutual recognition can be a substantive guiding principle (see ch. 4).

Yet there is a tension within the Absolute between its force as a critique and her stress on its unknowability:

> The overall intention of Hegel's thought is to make a different ethical life possible by providing insight into the displacement of actuality in those dominant philosophies which are assimilated to and reinforce bourgeois law and bourgeois property relations. . . . However, as long as these relations and law prevails [*sic*] the absolute can only be thought by an abstract consciousness. . . . This accounts for the difference between the unconvincing nature of Hegel's attempts to state the absolute by comparison with the powerful speculative rereadings of law. . . . Hegel had no "solution" to the contradictions of bourgeois productive and

338. Ibid., 218. Cf. *EL* §234 Addition.

> property relations. He searched for a different concept of law but it could only be explicated abstractly.[339]

The extent to which the Absolute is so different from current political-ethical life that we cannot fully imagine it undermines its role not only as a guide to action but even as ideology critique. Hegel's own view was that philosophy had discerned the essential nature of the state as, roughly speaking, predicated on freedom, self-determination and mutual recognition between citizens and between ruler and ruled, but that within the essential structures entailed by this basis the details of law and policy had latitude based on the needs of the day and ethos of the state and its people.[340] Rose is therefore following the Frankfurt School appropriation of Hegel for the needs of the present, pressing his philosophy into the service of critique, but in this early work she underplays Hegel's appreciation of modernity. Robert Bernasconi identified the problem: the Absolute

> takes account of the fact that it arises in a society governed by the "reality of unfreedom" . . . and is as yet only abstract, a "concept," a "result to be achieved," . . . it is neither predetermined nor imposed, but speculative. Clearly a strong sense of "speculative" is required here. It cannot mean only that the absolute is indeterminate, although her idea of the just society is undoubtedly that. . . . Nor could the speculative simply carry the sense she gives it of a lack of identity between concept and object, in that sense every *Sollen* could be understood as speculative.[341]

It seems Rose underemphasizes the moment of the concept in favor of the moment of social determination. That is, her philosophy has more space to fill in the details of absolute ethical life than she realized at this early stage. Perhaps the best that can be made of Rose's Absolute is to read it as something like Amartya Sen's work on justice, where the focus is less on realizing a fully worked out ideal than on achieving real increments in justice beginning from where we are, in the middle.[342] But if so Sen has the better of Rose in two ways: he provides more detail and substance than Rose, and he writes more accessibly without losing critical or analytical power, giving his work far more reach and influence than Rose's.

339. *HCS*, 223.
340. E.g., *PhR* §214.
341. Review of *HCS*, 43.
342. Sen, *Idea of Justice*.

To echo Pleasants, in these two respects Sen is a better critical theorist than Rose.

One is forced to ask whether Rose overplays the difference between Hegelian speculation and neo-Kantian *Geltungslogik*, especially in the claim to have produced a "wholly different mode of social analysis."[343] Certainly they are different on a formal logical level and this can affect the social analysis itself, but the fact that Rose is close to Habermas, Bourdieu and Giddens in many ways certainly gives one pause. The problem seems more acute for Rose's "broken" Hegel. For example, Hegel criticizes Kant for using the kind of thinking that attempts social explanations by a regressive chain of causation or by reciprocity. Hegel's alternative, the concept or conceptual thinking, is to consider everything as interrelated moments of the whole. But, as finite beings, that is not possible, as Rose herself insists: we have to draw a line somewhere in our analysis of mediations.

The Absolute seems to be a regulative ideal just like Kant's, though with the crucial difference that it includes *Sittlichkeit*. But *Sittlichkeit* in a modern, pluralist nation state is unlikely to be able to do as much work as Hegel imagined it could in his day. Thus either one accepts that Kant's *Rechtslehre* is as good as we can do at the national scale and hope to encourage moral *Sittlichkeit* in small communities (to which Bernstein comes close); or one tries to save some *Sittlichkeit* within national law at the risk of it seeming irrational, overriding pluralism, or imposing a *Sollen*; or one must try to find an ethical culture thin enough not to impose itself unduly but thick enough to act as a *Sittlichkeit* at the national level. Clearly, Rose must attempt the third option, and it is no surprise that when she does so in her later work she is close to Axel Honneth who also turns to mutual recognition to navigate this Scylla and Charybdis, as we will see in chapter 4.

The tightrope Rose is trying to walk is however not of her own making but in the nature of modern societies. Consider a tension in Rose's exposition: the organic unity of (idealized) Greek ethical life simply is not fully compatible with modern self-consciousness. The Absolute therefore cannot be a completely coherent statement of what ought to be; it is a projection of contradictory and yet equally valid social goals; a form of value pluralism that reminds us to question whether the current balance is working. It is a postulate—both necessary to and guiding thought—yet

343. *HCS*, 1.

impossible, and known by Rose to be contradictory. Since the Absolute is a contradictory idea, it cannot be stated, it can only be implied by, or shown through, speculative statements. A speculative statement calls attention to the identity of identity and difference, "A = B and A ≠ B" (e.g., "religion and the state is one and the same thing"). Here the importance of Hegel's speculative logic to the rest of his thought becomes clear. Hegel's concept of "autonomous negation" does not grant ultimacy either to the law of non-contradiction[344] or to the law of the excluded middle.[345] It is precisely in the human, cultural (*geistig*) realm, when trying to think the Absolute and the infinite, that such laws break down. The antinomies encountered suggest the need for a different form of reason. Nevertheless, Hegel developed a substantive, positive political and social philosophy of his own, whereas Rose's work is largely critique of other theories. As many critics have pointed out, Rose's own theory actually depends on there being a substantial, positive theory, which she never offers; put otherwise, her critique is parasitic on the "edifice" of politics and its philosophical justifications. In fact, however, Rose was well aware of this:

> Neither politics nor reason unify or "totalize": they arise out of diremption—out of the diversity of peoples who come together under the aporetic law of the city, and who know that their law is different from the law of other cities. . . . Philosophy issues, too, out of this diremption and its provisional overcoming in the culture of an era—without "disowning" that "edifice," it (philosophy) steps away to inspect its limitations, especially when the diremptions fixated in the edifice have lost their living connections. We should be renewing our thinking on the invention and production of edifices, that is, cities . . . not sublimating those equivocations into holy cities.[346]

344. E.g., *EL* §115: the law is valid for reflective thinking but not *simpliciter* for speculative or conceptual thinking.

345. This logical law says a specific predicate must either be ascribed to a subject or not. The phrase "broken middle" may be an allusion to this. The phrase "broken middle" may also allude to Hegel's remarks in *Faith and Knowledge*: "The most interesting point in the Kantian system . . . [is] the point at which a region is recognized that is a middle between the empirical manifold and the absolute abstract unity. But once again, it is not a region accessible to cognition. . . . It is acknowledged as thought, but with respect to cognition all reality is denied to it. . . . What it lacks is the middle term (*Mittelglied*), which is Reason . . . the middle" (85, 94).

346. *BM*, 286.

Rose thus accepts her works' reliance on and implication in the politics of her context and its philosophical justification and lack thereof. And she does, in her work as a whole, have substantive commitments to mutual recognition as the actuality of ethics and politics; to the problems with the bourgeois property form and its legal enforcement; to proper balance between individual, civil society and state, which involves a commitment to institutions of the middle. That is why she must be read in the synoptic way my reconstruction enables. In contrast to some of her interlocutors, she insists the possibility of legitimate power still exists, and if this possibility is denied then the capacity of critique is diminished. She also insists that theory alone cannot heal diremptions in society and, as a theorist, saw it as one of her main tasks to point out where other theories mistakenly attempted to do so. As we have seen this involves a view of the whole without either totalizing or reductionism. Her work leans toward therapy rather than solution though it is not without substantive commitments, and we will see in chapter 4 that an account of mutual recognition can be fleshed out to provide more of what Rose's theory needs in this respect. Her later work thus improved on the earlier, in a way that responds to these objections.

7 Conclusion

This chapter set out Rose's Hegelian-Frankfurt social philosophy as a way of holding together the methodological, logical, descriptive, metaphysical and normative aspects of social theory. It showed the way she used it to propose absolute ethical life as a social totality implied by the experience of the diremptions of bourgeois property law and their reflection in the antinomies of social contract theories. It has thus shown the basis for the coherence of her social theory and the unity of her trilogy, and the way she used her social philosophy to critique simultaneously society and social theory by relating philosophical and metaphilosophical issues. It supported Rose's claim that her Hegelian speculative philosophy offers a better approach to social theory than the classical and early Frankfurt sociological traditions. Rose's main criticism was of their neo-Kantian or transcendental structure, whereby one term becomes the precondition for all others but thereby remains unknowable and unexplainable, affecting their judgments about society. Transcendental social theory is less able than speculative social theory to account for its own social determinations. Hegel's speculative phenomenology avoids this problem by historical-phenomenological knowing and a logic that articulates the structure of that knowing in a totality. The *Phenomenology* provides the motivation and some justification for the categorial structures explored in the *Logic*; even if the *Logic* fails as a complete system it nevertheless has much to teach us about how reason works. Rose's social philosophy is thus its own metaphilosophy, which incorporates the meta-level into the substantive level of knowing, by considering its own logical and social preconditions. The use of speculative propositions brings into view the diremptions of society and theory so they can be speculatively handled. It relates philosophical claims about the nature of reason, phenomenology and metatheory, with sociological claims about society as permanently dirempted in various fundamental ways. Awareness of these features of philosophy and society are, for Rose, components of practical wisdom in modern society.

Both the critical and constructive sides of Rose's social theory are well-motivated and plausible, contrary to its initial reception. This is evident in that both Biernacki and Pleasants make parallel critiques of social theory, and a range of contemporary Hegel scholars support the broad thrust of Rose's Hegelianism. Nevertheless, the case should not be overstated, as Rose's language sometimes does. Rose's social theory has varying degrees of proximity to other powerful approaches to social theorizing: Weber, Habermas, Adorno, Bhaskar, Bourdieu, Giddens. Her aim to "retrieve Hegelian speculative experience for social theory"[347] does not mean she believed the only worthwhile works in social theory were *The Philosophy of Right* and *Hegel Contra Sociology*. Her "essay" was an attempt to clarify the logical basis of social theory so as to provide a better self-understanding for the discipline to enable it to guard against mistaken methods and conclusions, not to rule out other forms of social theorizing, which she accepted as necessary and valuable. She did not disregard transcendental sociology, but offered a more comprehensive historical-phenomenological basis for social theory. And this has real benefits. Her philosophy alerts social theory to its tendency to slip into neo-Kantianism. Her Hegelian framework, through its historical nature, is able to account for the good practice of empirical sociology, to avoid reducing philosophy and social theory to the sociology of knowledge, and to account for the role of totalities in social theory. Epistemo-

347. *HCS*, 1.

logical totalities are necessary to explanation but only imperfectly and provisionally available. Social totalities are more than the sum of their parts—"organisms" for Hegel, "emergent wholes" for contemporary social theory. Rose places a cautionary mark against all quasi-transcendental theories, including metacritiques, which have usually understood themselves to be as critical as it is possible to be. To an extent, Rose's Hegelian social philosophy equates to the "wary" or alert use of Weber's ideal types, that is, a use in which, heeding Weber's warning, the types are known to be posited even though referring to real structures. Yet Rose is clearer than Weber on our ability to know the truth about reality and moral norms because she draws on Hegel's phenomenology and logic for the structure of social theory. With the appropriate qualifications in place then, one may affirm Rose's claim to find in Hegel a different mode of social analysis from classical sociology, though it is clearly a part of Frankfurt social theory, to which we now turn.

2

Rose's Frankfurt Inheritance

. . . perfect rationality is a self-defeating goal.

—Leszek Kołakowski, *Modernity on Endless Trial*

1 Introduction

WITH SOME DETAILS OF Rose's Hegelian social philosophy in place, the way is open to nuance those ideas while locating Rose more precisely within the Frankfurt and philosophical traditions. The relation between Rose's work and that of Bernstein, Kołakowski, and Henrich is completely unremarked in the secondary literature, but I show in this chapter, based on new archival research, how it adds significant nuance and precision to an understanding of Rose's social philosophy, and allows the synoptic vision necessary to a proper understanding of her mature thought. This chapter also explains the key features of Rose's Frankfurt theory that created a structural openness in her thought to religion: self-limiting rationality and metaphysics as an unsatisfiable yearning, a posing of questions necessary to ask but impossible to answer with any finality. The current chapter thereby prepares for the next stage of the argument, since Rose's view of both reason and metaphysics as limited and necessary plays a decisive role in her notions of jurisprudential wisdom and the broken middle.

In the first part of this chapter I set out the similarities between Rose and Bernstein as a way of further delineating the shape of Rose's social philosophy and her understanding of the nature of philosophy as a modernist enterprise (§2). This clears the way for a discussion of the main feature of philosophy so understood: the search for self-limiting rationality or non-rationalized reason, a wider or more textured reason than the version dominant in society, which admits its reliance on what eludes it (§3). This feeds into Rose's notion of implied totality (§4). Since Rose belonged to the Adorno-Hegel strand of the Frankfurt School, I compare Rose to Adorno in order to bring out useful contrasts between them, but I focus in particular on her distinction between her version of speculative thought and Adorno's negative dialectics (§5). Rose's Adorno-esque modernism involved a different view of philosophy's nature and task from some analytic philosophy, while her view of the social totality provided a sociological element missing from some continental philosophy without succumbing to their critique of "totalizing" systems.

2 Rose and Bernstein: Aporetic Ontology, Philosophical Modernism

Bernstein acknowledges Rose in several books as an intellectual colleague.[1] He wrote, "There is no one to whom I am closer intellectually and spiritually than Gillian Rose; what is best in this work would not have been there without her."[2] Bernstein's arguments that critical theory must work more centrally with Hegel's doctrines of the causality of fate or the dialectic of ethical life were a shared concern.[3] Rose dedicated *Judaism and Modernity* to Bernstein and acknowledges his help in reading drafts and discussing her work in several of her books. She mentions him as one of the few philosophers doing similar work to her in her RTÉ interview. In Bernstein's 1987 conference presentation of their shared Hegelianism he said:

> Gillian and I are Hegelian-Marxists . . . exoterically hegelians and esoterically marxists. . . . What is esoteric for Marx and exoteric for Gillian and I is Hegel's "doctrine," or better, procedure

1. *Recovering Ethical Life*; *Fate of Art*; *Adorno*; introduction to Adorno, *Culture Industry*.

2. *Fate of Art*, vii.

3. Bernstein, *Ethical Life*, 8.

> of developing speculative propositions. . . . That speculative thinking engages and intrigues an aporetic ontology is what, if anything, distinguishes our comprehension of speculative thinking; and has implicitly and explicitly sustained our dialogue with one another over the past decade or so.[4]

The aporetic ontology, explored through speculative propositions, has two consequences relevant here: philosophical modernism and a turn to a modern version of *phronesis*. Bernstein wrote an essay after Rose's death on their shared view of philosophy's vocation as responding to the questions of meaning and justice created by modern disenchantment. It is worth citing at length.[5] For them, much analytic philosophy has "become a series of conceptual puzzles," while "most of what passes for continental philosophy . . . is as academic in its way as the most baroque constructions of analytic philosophy." "The post-modern pragmatist systematically denies the existence of big problems: to insist that society is *suffering* from the destruction of tradition . . . is to be nostalgic for a long lost, never to be recreated unity. Contemporary philosophy not only insists on the absence of big problems; it charges those who think that there are such problems with being unmodern and naïve." The urgency of the philosophical task for Rose and Bernstein lies in its nature as a response to "wounds tearing the flesh of spirit": the pressure put on meaning and truth after the death of God. Bernstein describes this as philosophical modernism or avant-gardism. Hence "the motivation of all philosophical modernism since Kant: to demonstrate the limits of the disenchantment of the world by showing how scientific truth is not the whole truth . . . and thus inscribing a space of *unavoidable* and legitimate anthropomorphism." "This is the *leitmotiv* of Rose's philosophy: there

4. Bernstein, "Speculation and Aporia" (non-capitalization in original). There are two drafts of this paper in the archive, both of which Rose has edited for Bernstein. I have quoted above from the second draft. Cf. Bernstein, *Ethical Life*, 207: "Castoriadis's social ontology is an aporetic ontology; it poses the being of the social-historical as neither act nor product, neither instituting nor instituted, but as the continual passage from one to the other without rest or resolution. At its most extreme point, this is to say that we can attempt to think the being of the social-historical *as* instituting praxis—the perspective of agency and autonomy; or *as* instituted—the third person perspective of the always already produced, and so of heteronomy; what we cannot think through or get behind is the *as* itself that is the place of exchange between instituting and instituted. The instituting/instituted *as*, which cannot be got behind, is what forever, so long as there are social doings at all, prescinds reason from determinacy."

5. Bernstein, "Philosophy among the Ruins," 27–30. Quotations in the rest of this paragraph and the next are from this essay.

is an unavoidable anthropomorphism in every concept; no concept can escape equivocation and complicity." Rose's works

> reveal a wholly modernist sensibility . . . the absence of any certainties, foundations, absolutes. But these skeptical conditions cannot be *dissolved*, only reformed. . . . The key to Rose's philosophical practice was her way of utterly *inhabiting* the gaps and absences of the modernist agenda. As a modernist, she knew that we are unable to re-unite the dualisms between knowledge and truth, unable to provide a conception of virtuous politics or a power wholly drenched in legitimate authority. Perhaps her hardest and most stringent criticisms are addressed to those who seek, through force or fantasy, to deny the brokenness of our condition. . . . For Rose, if the dualisms could not be engineered back together again, neither could they be dismissed or dissolved: we may not possess a conception of truth worthy of its name, but every attempt to dismiss it ends up reducing human knowing to conventionalism or relativism or traditionalism. We may be very unclear about what virtue could be for us . . . but a politics based solely on a conception of humans as utility maximisers or rationally self-interested is quite implausible. . . . [Yet] she never leaves the dualisms of the present as mere abstract concepts. Inhabiting those dualisms means revealing them as human creations inscribing our relations with others and ourselves.

The turn to *phronesis* is related to the theory-praxis question within Frankfurt (and more generally Marxist) thinking. Gorman, a PhD student of Rose's, argues that she and Bernstein had a "shared project" and "common front":

> A commitment to the method of immanent critique, genealogy and phenomenology without historical completion, as a means of rescuing lost forms of knowledge, political wisdom and ethical life . . . to trace the historical roots of the deformation of reason, as it is reflected in modern/postmodern social theory, jurisprudence, politics and aesthetics, in order to open up new ways of resuming the values of classical theory (i.e. the Platonic-Aristotelian *praxis* and *phronesis*) within the present . . . [recognizing that] the deformation of reason renders impossible the direct expression and reinstatement of these values.[6]

6. Gorman, "Nihilism and Faith," 1n8.

Gorman shows their similar analyses of modernity, indebted to Weber, focused around disenchantment and rationalization, nihilism, injustice, the simultaneous gain and loss of freedom, the separation of the three validity spheres of knowledge, morality and art. Both agreed it was impossible simply to think oneself out of modernity's deformations of reason because they were institutionally and culturally produced. Both criticized the two common responses to modernity's malaise of retreating into cynicism, boredom, despair, or into idealized, "other-worldly" communities. The latter will be "corrupted within by their opposition to the overly rationalized world without."[7] In response, an expanded, non-instrumental version of reason is required.[8] Hence, "speculative thinking is, as such, a form of political insight, political wisdom, *phronesis*, theory mediated self-reflection."[9] But any theory centrally based on and promoting *phronesis* cannot be immediately or straightforwardly action-guiding since that would remove the element of judgment and leave easy application of rules. Modern *phronesis* must therefore take central account of social mediation of both the agents' actions and the consequences of her actions.

3 Self-Limiting Reason

A central issue within German Idealism was reason's autonomy, its independence from external authority. Hegel, for Rose, accorded reason a nuanced not absolute autonomy. Reason was based in and reliant on a shape of spirit, its ethical life, its institutions, and so on. Yet reason, via the individual, was able to take some distance from itself and the shape of spirit on which it depended, and thereby gain a certain freedom with respect to what determines it. This achievement is never perfect, such that reason and the subject are always partly free and unfree. Rather than setting these boundaries of reason or the subject once for all, they should be investigated as they change. "Only an expansion of reason, rationality, and cognition will answer the dilemma of disenchantment . . . the direction of expansion will be the inclusion in reasoning of ineliminable moments of dependency and particularity. The depth, pervasiveness, ineliminability, and constitutive role in rationality of dependence on

7. Ibid., 24.

8. *MBL*, 6–7; RTÉ interview; Bernstein, *Adorno*, 4.

9. Bernstein, *Ethical Life*, 158.

sensuous particulars is . . . Adorno's central thought."[10] For Rose, too, reason is grounded not only on itself but also on physical particulars and moments that exceed reason's grasp, such that no perfectly complete or autonomously grounded reason exists.[11] The result is, as Rose put it, "the reassessment of reason, gradually rediscovering its own moveable boundaries as it explores the boundaries of the soul, the city and the sacred";[12] and "a rationalism which constantly explores its own limits without fixing them . . . renegotiat[ing] knowledge and responsibility under their historically and politically changing conditions."[13] Rose believed postmodern versions of this idea had reduced reason's powers and thereby critical purchase on our own lives. The "different ways of severing existential eros from philosophical *logos* amounts to *a trauma within reason itself*."[14] Reality "is *always pervaded with meanings neither party intends*, but which are recoverable by reflection when challenged."[15] Hence it is possible to make progress in finding "the *actuality* of the concept."[16] Rose would come to express this version of self-limiting reason as "aporetic" rather than "deterministic" philosophy. Her view of reason did not carry skeptical or relativistic implications as with some postmodern thinkers.

Self-limiting reason has both existential and cultural-political implications, which are intertwined in Rose's work: she identifies "the existential drama . . . at the heart of Hegelian rationalism."[17] Zygmunt Bauman believed Rose's version of reason "speaks directly to the experience of men and women that happen to live in times of contingency and face the awesome task of patching up meaningful lives out of a world cut to fragments and time sliced into episodes. This is the best reason on offer; a kind of reason we truly need and one we can afford."[18] Like her teacher, Leszek Kołakowski, Rose thought, "We may admit that no traditional metaphysical questions are soluble and still deny that this is a reason to dismiss them or declare them meaningless. . . . There is no absolute

10. Bernstein, *Adorno*, 31.

11. *JAM*, ix–10.

12. *MBL*, 11–12.

13. *JAM*, 17.

14. Ibid., 2.

15. Ibid., 4.

16. Ibid. Once again we see a difference between Hegel and Rose's Hegel. For Hegel, a self-limiting reason sounds contradictory.

17. *HCS*, preface.

18. Review of *JAM*, 576.

beginning in thinking. . . . Inevitably, we start and end in the middle of our itinerary."[19] And "we never start from the beginning. . . . Philosophies voice the aspirations and the choices of civilizations [which] are never perfectly coherent."[20] Hence, "we believe that contradictions which actually exist may well be overcome so that a synthesis is established between them; but we also believe, in accordance with the entire experience of history, that a contradiction which vanishes is merely replaced by a new contradiction, so that no universal synthesis is possible."[21] Shapes of spirit—the social and philosophical arrangements worked out in a particular society—are rational to some extent, though never perfectly so. As such they are available for assessment and comparison, at least in some ways, extremely difficult though the task is. To deny this is to accede to cultural relativism and bar the way to phenomenology. The always-unfinished, existential-cognitive appropriation of a preceding reality forever beyond complete comprehension has parallels to theology. Self-limiting reason, for Rose, could begin to open Frankfurt theory to religion. This remains a suggestion in her work rather than a developed argument however.[22]

Bernstein shows how a self-limiting reason "involves the elaboration of the interconnection of three elements: local reason and rationality, sensuous particularity (nonidentity, alterity, otherness, the body), and judgment."[23] Indeed, "part of the rationality of *ordinary* communicative interaction derives from the fact that in it reflective and determinant judgment remain entwined and mutually dependent."[24] This creates the need for a dialectic between local and universal reason. By contrast,

> the Enlightenment conception of discursive reason, [is] reason as subsumption, entailment, inference, system, and so on; that is, reasoning as governed by forms whose force is indifferent to content. In fact, most concepts we employ are non-topic-neutral (unlike the logical constants and such terms as "several," "most," "although," etc.), and therefore are not and can not be governed by pure (logical) forms. . . . While topic-neutral constraints might be conceived of as providing the outer boundaries of rationality,

19. *Metaphysical Horror*, 8–11.

20. Ibid., 99.

21. Kołakowski, "In Praise of Inconsistency," 206.

22. It is developed by Milbank, *Theology and Social Theory*; Shanks, *Innocence*; Williams, *Edge of Words*.

23. Bernstein, *Ethical Life*, 172.

24. Ibid., 170. The two kinds of judgment refer to Kant's third *Critique*.

> actual inferences, and hence patterns of inference, are dependent on the practices in which concepts are employed.[25]

Reasoning and arguing should therefore involve a dialectic between local and universal reason. Adorno's style is an attempt to perform this, to evidence the fundamental place of particulars and judgment within fully adequate cognition. "His style is thus designed to induce his reader to think in that different way which he believes is desirable and possible. It is an indirect exhortative method."[26] "Adorno's works are exemplars of negative dialectic, that is, they are informed by the idea that concepts, as ordinarily used, are distorting and mask social reality. . . . The question of communicating his ideas becomes the question of what the reader should experience when confronting the text, and Adorno insists that expressing the relation of the thought to its object should be prior to any concern with ease of communicating that thought."[27] Thus, "in the same way in which 'getting' a musical work can require coming to hear in a new way, and this really the only route to it, so for Adorno every significant piece of philosophical writing is soliciting from the reader a 'conversion,' a coming to see/experience/understand the object in a new way."[28] He "explicitly opposes the disavowal of the responsibilities and risks of authorship (authoring belief) implied in the ideal that philosophy should provide demonstrations that no one could rationally deny."[29] Rose's style in *The Broken Middle* (and to some extent in some other works) attempts the same task. It was also intended as a literary equivalent to legitimate authority rather than illegitimate power, because its irony, facetiousness and poeticism (its Kierkegaardian indirect communication) force the reader into doing work, undergoing an experience of thought, rather than providing ready-made propositions.

Her style, however, is not without its difficulties. Gorman proposes a criticism of Rose's conception of style as method, of theory as praxis:

> Rose commits herself to the critique of all forms of universalism, aiming to expose the hidden interests behind their respective claims to disinterestedness. Yet this critique is nonetheless oriented by the goal of universal, mutual recognition. Crucially,

25. Ibid., 168. See ch. 4 for some ethical implications.

26. Rose, review of *Negative Dialectics*, 599.

27. *TMS*, 11–12.

28. Bernstein, *Adorno*, 360.

29. Ibid., 132.

> however, Rose no longer identifies this goal with the realisation of a future form of society. Now, the accomplishment of mutuality resides solely in its *being accomplished* in and through the work of critique and incessant self-relinquishment.[30]

Yet this will not quite work. Rose does not reduce praxis to style and/or theory. On the contrary, Rose was acutely aware of the limits of theory, which drives her critique of theory that would "mend" society's diremptions in thought but not actuality. Indeed, Gorman goes on immediately to quote Rose as characterizing politics as risking action on behalf of all people.[31] The "accomplishment of mutuality" does not result *solely* from intellectual work and self-relinquishment, but these are two important sites for promoting it, especially for the audience of Rose's books. In Kierkegaardian fashion, Rose wants her writing to create existential anxiety within her readers, so as to prompt their transformation. This is an aspect of her modernism, enabling her readers to experience modernity's diremptions and the problems they cause, not merely think about them in a detached manner. She pushes her readers to see the moveable boundaries between the soul and the city, between their subjectivity and their society, perhaps so they may take up political or institutional action. Philosophy in her view should be transformative of the self. She aimed not to present readers with facts about society but to encourage them to question their own relation to and understanding of it. Rose's terms "anxiety of beginning," "equivocation of the ethical," etc., are designed to allude to this dialectical (rather than narrowly logical) situation. Rose used this rationality to unsettle dualisms in order to "make it possible to reconstruct the modern political history of unfreedom—above all, the inversions of morality and legality, autonomy and heteronomy."[32] It is important to emphasize this element of an at least partially adequate learning, of the possibility of rounding on ourselves in order to increase freedom, of the attainment of a defensible view of a concept, because in *The Broken Middle* Rose so warns against premature closure, against fleeing the anxiety of beginning, the equivocations of the ethical and the brokenness of the middle, that she sounds to some as if she is exactly like the postmodern philosophers she criticizes for epistemological and ethical nihilism. As we have seen, however, it is not that Rose refuses the possibility of any (provisional)

30. Gorman, "Critical Marxism," 34.

31. *MBL*, 63.

32. *JAM*, 19.

resolution to philosophical or social problems—phenomenological history is in one sense the history of the series of such solutions—but she is concerned to avoid two errors where such proposals are concerned. First, imposing an alien view on a society; second, any proposed improvement must assess how it will filter though various social and political diremptions and be corrupted by them. Whereas Milbank thinks Rose lacks solutions or imagination, Rose thinks his are too hasty.

Simon Jarvis raised another problem with the style of *The Broken Middle*: "The question of the truth of this work, because it aims at much more than correctness, will not be entirely separable from that of its reception. It must be too early to say yet whether the original rubrics of Rose's work—the triple configuration of 'anxiety of beginning,' 'equivocation of the ethical' and 'agon of authorship'—will remain an idiolect, or whether they can take the critical purchase for which they hope on the ethical and political life which they address."[33] Twenty years on and the critical purchase is yet to emerge, despite signs of increasing interest in Rose's work. This highlights the risk of failing to find an audience inherent in avant-garde style and drawing a different map of the intellectual terrain. This risk seems not to have paid off for Rose. In Bernstein's opinion, Rose's work "failed to find a wider readership" because "she too often focused on easy, fashionable or little known 'continental' targets rather than taking on the more permanent and recalcitrant philosophical mammoths of modernity: Enlightenment rationalism, naturalism, scientism, pragmatism, liberalism."[34] There is a moment of truth here, although with continuing critiques of poststructuralism Rose also seems prescient.

4 Social Totality

The self-limiting nature of reason—its imperfection, its inability to offer mathematical, QED type proofs—and an aporetic ontology feed directly into the imperfect nature of the social totality. Three forms of the totality may be discerned in Rose's work. The most encompassing is absolute ethical life, though it is also the least substantive. There is also the totality as the emergent whole of society as it currently exists; or, in Hegelese, substance is a subject. Then, third, there is the totality of a subsection of society, say the economy, or universities, or the publishing industry.

33. Review of *BM*, 92.

34. "Philosophy among the Ruins," 30.

There are, further, four aspects of the idea of a social totality implicit in Rose's use of the latter two forms. First, there is an epistemological aspect, that a satisfying explanation must be a conceptual one, which grasps the whole by understanding the relations among all the parts. Second, the substantial aspect of the totality is the theorization or depiction of the whole itself. Examples could be: a view of the national and global economy arrived at by the Bank of England in order to set interests rates; the view of Baltimore society conveyed in *The Wire* or of English society in *Our Friends in the North*; Roman Catholic theorizations and enactments of the Eucharist as a kind of concrete universal expressing the heart of Catholicism;[35] or a comprehensive history or biography. Clearly such theorizations are partial and no conceptual grasp of such large totalities will be perfect and should always stand open to revision, which is why for Rose the concept is always a broken circle or a broken middle, yet clearly many disciplines and significant actions depend on conceptual knowing and totalities as wholes. The third aspect of the totality follows: it is interpretative.[36] The totality does not immediately appear but underlies immediate appearance in the way picked out by Hegel's essence/appearance distinction. The two-level structure of transcendental accounts is apparent here but so is the difficulty of judging which essence is most determinative of which appearance (something emphasized by critics of this approach). Critical theory maintains a fruitful tension between "society" as a critical-philosophical idea and the empirical facts that discipline any interpretation.[37] Finally, there is a normative moment, insofar as the unity of law and ethics in absolute ethical life would allow citizens to see the law as expressing their own ethical life; law would be less alienated and less rationalized. The interpretative and normative moments differentiate Rose's social philosophy from some other kinds of sociology. It aims to raise consciousness, critique society, critique theorizations of society, and prompt thought about alternatives. The nature of the prompt is delicate; it must be open enough not to shut down imagination (which is difficult since our ideas of absolute ethical life are tainted by rationalization, the

35. For the idea of rituals and ceremonies as forms of Hegelian concepts, see Han, *Psychopolitik*, 92–96.

36. *TMS*, 79: The philosophical ideas Adorno used to interpret society (such as nature, totality, essence/appearance) "cannot be translated, *tout court*, into empirical terms because . . . they depend on a notion of totality and 'a view of the totality is necessarily philosophical.'"

37. Ibid., 78.

domination of exchange-value, and reification), but it thus risks not giving the imagination enough on which to feed.

Absolute ethical life is thus both the most overarching totality and one aspect of understanding individual phenomena. As a Hegelian, Rose thinks everything is mediated (even the immediate is in fact mediated and its experience as immediate must be understood through *Schein* or semblance: it contains a moment of truth and hides its truth). This mediation leads ultimately to the idea of absolute ethical life as the overarching totality in which alone the individual can be understood. (The fact/value distinction is therefore not ultimate, though of course it has its place in the relative autonomy of some areas of research from normative questions.) This is why Rose, unusually among Frankfurt thinkers, insisted on the social import of the Absolute, on retaining recognition and appropriation, and method and system, from Hegel. Recognition begins with the experience of an initial shock, bumping up against the difference between the object and the subject's idea of it (the possibility of this difference is the basis of Rose's view of experience). To do justice to this experience requires the subject to appropriate the moment of recognition, to work through it, to find its mediations. As Hegel knew, a change in the (subject's view of the) object creates a change in the subject—or it can, *if* it is appropriated. The work of appropriation is never finished, which is why the path of knowing must be continually re-trod, and this is the meaning and unity of method and system in Hegel, and why Rose retained them. This is no epistemological pedantry but has important effects. To take one example, it goes to the heart of Rose's approach to the Holocaust. Rose not only charges much contemporary thought with mystifying the Holocaust, she gambles that it can be appropriated much more significantly than most people are willing to accept, both individually and in cultural, artistic and political realms. Thus, although appropriation is never finished or perfect, individuals and cultures reach resting places for thought (with varying degrees of adequacy), which are available for later revision. A view of the totality, properly understood, is thus not "totalizing" as poststructuralists (and Adorno) feared.[38]

Rose refused "the super-eminence conferred on 'the Holocaust' as the logical outcome of Western metaphysical reason."[39] She noted the

38. On appropriation, cf. Jaeggi, *Alienation*. On the possibility of speech about traumatic events including the Holocaust, see Brower Latz, "More Sayable than You Think."

39. *MBL*, 11.

dialectical reversal that frequently occurred in works on the Holocaust, in which philosophy, history and sociology are used to explore it, and then at the end of the work the very tools that have enabled the exploration are indicted for contributing to the Holocaust and then abandoned. Rose insisted on the continuities between our reason, philosophy and society and those of Nazi Germany; like Adorno's verdict on culture, they are indicted and still necessary. Rose objects to the abandonment of reason, truth and justice, and the rescinding from any involvement in power and complicity in its violence (in short, the rejection of metaphysics and politics), as a response to the Holocaust. "The possibility of structural analysis and of political action are equally undermined by the evasion of the anxiety and ambivalence inherent in power and knowledge."[40] That is why Rose argues for shifting the balance from regarding the Holocaust as ineffable to analyzing its historical and political causes, because it operates as an evasion of the continuity between our own thinking and acting, our own society and politics, and those represented by Auschwitz. She sums it up as a shift from "Holocaust piety" to "Holocaust ethnography."[41] Rose opposes two responses to disappointment in reason's role in abetting domination and genocide: mourning and melancholia, a distinction she took from Freud.[42] In mourning, the subject works through her grief to appropriate her loss and be able to move on. In melancholia this work is not performed, the grief becomes permanent, distorting perceptions of self and world; it is "a refusal to let go."[43] She argues postmodernism responds to the Holocaust with melancholia rather than mourning. Hence Rose's alternative—*Mourning Becomes the Law*—means that the slow, gradual work of reassessing reason and its moveable boundaries "can complete its mourning" and return to the creative, active nature of law and power.[44]

Rose regarded Adorno as an ally on this front. Adorno's aphorisms "to write poetry after Auschwitz is barbaric" and "the metaphysical capacity is paralysed" are cited by Rose as "dramatic irony in the major, sustained, philosophical reflection of an authorship devoted to defending comprehension against fundamental ontology in the wake

40. *MBL*, 36.

41. Ibid., ch. 2, "Beginnings of the Day: Fascism and Representation," 41–62.

42. Rose also uses the terms "aberrated" and "inaugurated" mourning.

43. *MBL*, 11.

44. Ibid., 12.

of 'Auschwitz.'"[45] Further, neither wished to abandon metaphysics or transcendence but to develop an immanent transcendence that would reform the metaphysical tradition. Adorno criticized any transcendence that could remain untouched by history. For Rose, a rational account of ethical and political action must be corrigible and so responsive to historical experience. Metaphysics in Rose means, "speaking with generality about the real or actual";[46] "an overall proposal concerning the character of reality as known by agents."[47] Metaphysics cannot be "settled by appeal to a tangible state of affairs or set of facts, yet at the same time [it is] not a question that can be relegated to a matter of taste or private judgment."[48] It concerns "the classical preoccupations of philosophy . . . eternity, reason, truth, representation, justice, freedom, beauty and the Good."[49] Furthermore, ethics and metaphysics are connected, so that to separate them is to undermine both.[50] "Ethics and metaphysics are torn halves of an integral freedom to which they have *never* added up."[51]

Metaphysics involves putting the concepts of truth, goodness, justice, and so on, into some kind of connection, but in a way that acknowledges the imperfection and failure of the account.[52] Like her teacher Dieter Henrich, Rose thinks metaphysics is unavoidable because reason seeks totality and "thoughts of closure," and impossible, because these can never be settled or completely successful. Dieter Freundlich's summary of Henrich's view expresses central parts of Rose's own:[53] refus-

45. *BM*, 288. My interpretation relies on: Adorno, *Metaphysics*; Adorno, *Negative Dialectics*; Adorno, *Kant's* Critique; Bernstein, *Adorno*, 371–456; Thornhill, "Adorno Reading Kant," 98–110; O'Connor, *Adorno*, 86–109; Sachs, "Acknowledgement of Transcendence," 273–94; Williams, *Lost Icons*, 122–29.

46. Williams, "Between," 3.

47. Ibid., 7.

48. Ibid., 5.

49. *MBL*, 1.

50. Ibid., 2.

51. Ibid., 9.

52. Given this view it seems odd Rose did not engage more with normative political philosophy from Rawls onward. It may be simply that her field of philosophy was continental. There are brief remarks in *MBL*'s introduction about communitarianism and libertarianism, which she charges with being inattentive to equivocation and unifying metaphysics and ethics too closely, as if there can be a fully rational-political whole. While suggestive, these remarks are hardly satisfying.

53. Quotations in the rest of the paragraph come from Freundlich, *Dieter Henrich and Contemporary Philosophy*, 167. Henrich has Habermas in his sights here.

als of metaphysics and "detranscendentalized" social philosophy avoid whatever cannot be subject to "methodologically controlled procedures of reasoning." The "relative epistemic certainty attainable through methods modeled on the sciences is bought at too high a cost." Important questions are no longer asked. Henrich implies "the turn away from the metaphysical tradition from Plato to Leibniz that was brought about by the rise of empiricism and its aftermath has meant the loss of a whole dimension of human understanding and experience, a dimension that may be worth exploring again, especially in the light of the way in which it was rediscovered and kept alive for some decades by German Idealists from Kant to Hegel."[54] Adorno saw in Kant a yearning for transcendence and metaphysics, despite the strictures he placed on both. The theological resonances are clear.

There are, however, differences too. It is telling that Adorno glosses "aporia" as "however you do it, it's wrong," whereas Rose glosses it as exploring a way through to find "good enough justice."[55] Metaphysics for Rose is an attempt to navigate the aporia between the law or universal and the particular;[56] ethics is its development: "being at a loss yet exploring various routes, different ways toward the good enough justice, which recognizes the intrinsic and the contingent limitations in its exercise."[57]

Despite her unique emphasis on appropriation, Rose is clearly influenced by Adorno, who also used the concept of the totality in his social philosophizing in a nuanced way.[58] On the one hand, his "analysis of the underlying processes of society is not based on any notion of society 'as a whole.' The emphasis on commodity exchange means that the 'whole' of society cannot be the object of analysis."[59] Adorno rejected the "illusion" "that the power of thought is sufficient to grasp the totality of the real."[60] Here, Adorno denies the adequacy of philosophy to grasp the whole from

54. Freundlich, *Henrich*, viii.

55. Adorno, *Metaphysics*, 137, and Rose, *LW*, 116.

56. *LW*, 115.

57. Ibid., 116.

58. See, e.g., Adorno, *Hegel: Three Studies*, *passim*, but, e.g., "If Hegel's whole exists at all it is only as the quintessence of the partial moments, which always point beyond themselves and are generated from one another; it does not exists as something beyond them. This is what his category of totality is intended to convey. It is incompatible with any kind of tendency to harmony."

59. *TMS*, 143.

60. Adorno, "Actuality of Philosophy," 120.

pure reason alone (of course, Rose did not believe Hegel had tried to do so). On the other hand, Adorno believed it was possible to obtain a grasp of the whole society in a particular if one sufficiently attended to it in its mediations by means of a constellation.[61] "In sociology, *interpretation* acquires its force both from the fact that without reference to totality—to the real total system, untranslatable into any solid immediacy—nothing societal can be conceptualized, and from that fact that it can, however, only be recognized in the extent to which it is apprehended in the factual and the individual. It is the societal physiognomy of appearance. The primary meaning of 'interpret' is to perceive something in the features of totality's social givenness."[62] It seems the whole, like universal history, must be construed and denied. For both Adorno and Rose, philosophy provides critical concepts (totality, essence/appearance, etc.), while sociology provides empirical discipline. Philosophy without sociology may wander into wild supposition; sociology without philosophy may be swamped in detail. Martin Jay comments: "as Gillian Rose has perceptively noted, Adorno's use of totality must be taken as an example of his general anti-realist use of concepts. The inevitable gap between concept and object . . . meant that Adorno's own concepts were themselves not to be taken as perfectly true to reality."[63] Thus Rose and Adorno are able to deal with the objection raised by Hans Albert against the use of totality within social philosophy, namely that it is unverifiable, because they refuse the positivist metaphilosophy on which the objection rests. Adorno replied it was not a fact available to be verified but was nevertheless real.[64]

In the previous chapter we saw Hegelian conceptual thought does not think in terms of efficient causes all the way down. Adorno developed an implication of this because he "specifically rejects the notion that social influence can be understood as some kind of *causality*."[65] As a consequence of the increased complexity of society, there is no social center, no simple causality. Instead there is "integration—where the universal dependence of all moments on all other moments makes the talk of causality obsolete."[66] Dialectics immerses itself in the object, hence the

61. In the words of Horkheimer, "Each individual inquiry should have a certain character as key to the total situation" (Wheatland, "Debate about Methods," 128).

62. Adorno, introduction to *Positivist Dispute*, 32.

63. *Marxism and Totality*, 265.

64. Adorno, introduction to *Positivist Dispute*, 32–33.

65. O'Connor, *Adorno*, 28.

66. Ibid., 29, citing Adorno, *Negative Dialectics*, 267.

importance of empirical sociology,[67] yet it "does not possess a canon of thought which might regulate it."[68] This highlights the risk of knowing and theorizing, attention to which, as we have seen, is the only way to maintain epistemological discipline (not a predetermined method). This produces a view of society as "full of contradictions and yet determinable; rational and irrational in one, a system and yet fragmented";[69] a fine gloss on the broken middle *avant la lettre*. Yet the dialectical approach to society does not lack mooring points. For Adorno, exchange value within capitalism was the single most important key to the social whole (exchange value is the only way in which the commodity can appear).[70] The danger is this becomes reductive, and Rose thought Adorno gave insufficient weight to human praxis, the state, power and social class.[71] Rose identifies the diremptions between law and ethics, and between state and society, as two other crucial keys to the social whole. She was adding to the list of important social determinations not replacing exchange or commodities as central to society.[72]

5 "From Speculative to Dialectical Thinking"

Rose wrote an essay characterizing Adorno's negative dialectics as a regression from Hegelian speculation.[73] This was an obvious provocation, since Adorno designed negative dialectics to improve upon Hegel's speculative thought, and Rose's version of speculation is obviously very close to Adorno's negative dialectics.[74] Some commentators have even identified them: Stewart Martin believes her "anti-metaphysical account of Hegelian speculation secretly elaborates Adorno's negative dialectics."[75] One

67. Adorno, "Free Time," in *Culture Industry*, 96, discusses interviews carried out by the Institute, which provided "a virtually text book example of how critical-theoretical thought can both learn from and be corrected by empirical social research."

68. Adorno, introduction to *Positivist Dispute*, 9 (cf. 43).

69. Adorno, "On the Logic of the Social Sciences," in *Positivist Dispute*, 106.

70. *TMS*, 27.

71. E.g., *TMS*, 28, 37.

72. Hence, Gorman, "Critical Marxism," 26: "Rose agrees with both Lukács and Adorno that Marx's analysis of the commodity form is the necessary point of departure for the speculative critique of culture and society."

73. *JAM*, 53–63.

74. Cf. Walsh, *Skepticism, Modernity and Critical Theory*, esp. 94–98, 137–40.

75. Martin, *Adorno and the Problem of Philosophy*, 189.

suspects facetiousness at work here, aimed less at Adorno than postmodern uses of Adorno prevalent at the time Rose wrote the paper.[76] Nevertheless despite the similarity, as Nigel Tubbs has argued, Rose thought the essential difference between her and Adorno was that Adorno did not sufficiently allow for development, learning or growth (personal or sociohistorical), thereby undermining critical consciousness and the possibilities of experience generating critical thought.[77] There are two main aspects to this.

The first aspect is the relation of critique to social change. Hegel claims a negation of the negation is positive because it retains the moment or memory of what was negated and part of the character of the result comes from that moment. Adorno denies this: negation does not lead to an affirmative or positive result. The whole may be critiqued but the whole remains despite the critique.[78] Critique is thus of limited potency in contemporary society.[79] Adorno thinks contradictions persist until society changes. Critique can only point them out, "it cannot go with Hegel in thinking that critique is already a step beyond the state of affairs criticized."[80] We have seen Rose handled this problem by reference to the kind of *Sollen* found in Hegel's thinking: recognizing the *Sollen* as such allows for the role critique can play (which varies between contexts) while giving primacy to changes in social form above intellectual critique. Rose thinks the critique is a partial step beyond the current situation for those who appropriate the critique if they are able use it to gain some freedom from social determination. It may make a difference to the subjectivity of the individual. For Rose, Adorno underestimates *praxis* and *phronesis*. Adorno arguably "lost hope of discovering behind present social facts dynamic objective possibilities,"[81] he believed in late capitalism there is only "the antinomic alternatives of critical thought, illusionless but impotent, and mere reduplication in consciousness of the world of administered controls."[82] For Rose, Adorno had regressed from

76. The essay was first presented at a conference on critical theory in 1987.

77. Tubbs, *Contradiction of Enlightenment*, 134–46.

78. Adorno, *Negative Dialectics*, 158–60.

79. Rose, "How Is Critical Theory Possible?," 69–85.

80. O'Connor, *Adorno*, 49.

81. Jay, *Totality*, 202.

82. Arato, introduction to "Esthetic Theory and Cultural Criticism," in *Essential Frankfurt School Reader*, 201.

speculative to dialectic thinking because his thinking had at that point become fixed and ahistorical.

The second aspect is the possibility of progress in thought. Adorno differentiates his constellations from Hegel's concepts because in constellations "there is no step-by-step progression from the concepts to a more general cover concept."[83] Adorno's constellations "are not progressive but combinative: a nonprogressive combination. . . . The configuration of concepts therefore does not present itself as a progressively sufficient identification of the object."[84] In Hegel's logic there are different forms of movement: in the Essence section the movement is diversity or reflection, whereby new forms are accumulated without being either lost or unified; in the Concept section the movement is development, in which new terms develop by incorporating previous terms.[85]

> Rose notes the way in which Adorno misses the ironic dimension in Hegel's system and accordingly remains at the level of a dialectic that fails to think itself consistently. Adorno appears as the apostle of irreconcilable non-identity, the renunciation of comprehensive theory; but to arrest the dialectic *as* dialectic is to leave the terms of the contradictions of dialectic untouched. By contrast, Hegel's thinking insists not on a return to identity but on the "speculative" projection of a continually self-adjusting, self-criticising corporate practice.[86]

Yet these differences should not be overstated. Adorno insists the concept wishes to be identical with its object, though it never can, and constellations provide "emphatic" and "definite" knowledge.[87] He remarks his real difference from Hegel is not to be found in individual distinctions but the intent of their work: Hegel wished to affirm unity, Adorno wishes to oppose identity in his attempt to resist the "universal coercive mechanism" of society (but found too in traditional philosophical systems).[88] Rose is thus somewhere between Adorno and Hegel. She has clearly found (or imported, or both) much of Adorno's critique of Hegel already

83. Adorno, *Negative Dialectics*, 162.

84. Ibid., 162–66; cf. Martin, "Adorno's Conception of the Form of Philosophy," 55.

85. E.g., *EL*, §79–89, 161; *PhR*, 31.

86. Williams, "Between," 14.

87. Adorno, *Negative Dialectics*, 159. These terms come from a footnote in *Negative Dialectics*, almost as if Adorno wishes to sneak back in what he is at pains to deny in the main text.

88. Ibid., 145.

in Hegel; she insists on diremptions, the historicality and sociality of self-limiting reason, the imperfection of any knowledge; yet she is more insistent on the possibility of definite and emphatic knowledge than Adorno, she stresses the possibility of appropriation, which entails some kind of synthesis and totality, to which Adorno was averse (and which remain unfashionable).[89] Yet the synthesis entailed is a broken one.

Another way to approach the difference here is between determinate critique (*bestimmte Kritik*) in Adorno and determinate negation (*bestimmte Negation*) in Hegel. Adorno critiques forms of life to find a counter-image, but will not be drawn on what the good life is. The good is not what we have now, and is extremely underdetermined by our negative knowledge of it. Attempts to imagine the good life will almost certainly reinstate current damaged life, since our thinking is so dominated by reification. For example, according to Rahel Jaeggi[90] Adorno thinks gift-giving as currently practiced is deformed because it does not treat the other as a subject, but Adorno will not conclude that some other version of gift giving is part of the good life and can be used as a means to measure or critique society. Rose's historical phenomenology could argue, however, that gift-giving is so universal we can be reasonably certain it is part of the good life. Adorno thus refuses too much knowledge: "The dilemma of enlightenment and domination has priority over presenting speculative exposition or *Bildung*—the relation of universal and particularity as it is actually and potentially negotiated by the singular."[91] This stems from Adorno's ethical negativism.[92] Adorno accepts individuals can attain to some moral good, but he thinks this happens rarely, fleetingly, and does not "add up to either a good life or to knowledge of what the good life would consist in"; that it is not obvious which are genuine goods, and to tell ourselves otherwise is an illusion.[93] Even a decent life is not right but only amounts to resisting wrong, because we will have largely left in place the social conditions that produce poverty for half the globe,

89. Analogously, Bernstein argues in *Adorno* that Adorno unnecessarily restricted the possibilities for ethical and metaphysical experience to modernist art, when they can be found in everyday life, instances of individual moral courage and social movements.

90. Jaeggi, "No Individual Can Resist," 65–82.

91. *JAM*, 59. In partial defense of Adorno, see Adorno and Becke, "Education or Maturity and Responsibility," 21–34.

92. Here I follow Freyenhagen's account in *Adorno's Practical Philosophy*.

93. Freyenhagen, *Adorno's Practical Philosophy*, 226.

grave environmental pollution, and the possibility of more large scale violence. One of Adorno's examples of a moral good is a good family life that creates individuals with robust egos who will not be so easily prey to propaganda and social pressure. Yet notice that family life is not rare but common; not fleeting but lifelong; and known as such; and is most likely one component of the good life. It therefore runs against Adorno's views of what we know about goods. Likewise, Adorno risks making family life instrumental—it is good only because it helps people resist society—but the burden of proof surely lies with his view. Thus once Adorno opens the door to let in some positive goods he cannot shut it quickly enough to keep out the normative force of those goods. And that means there is more to normativity than the negative, than avoiding the bad. Even granting the negativist thesis that the imperative to avoid extreme bads carries enough normative force to generate much of ethics without the need to invoke any good, most of life is not occupied with avoiding extreme bads, which implies some positive values, duties, virtues, or ends are required to shape and guide behavior beyond knowledge of what bads to avoid. Rose believed Adorno could not bridge his moral and political philosophies and that his ethics remained individual rather than social.[94]

These reflections suggest Rose's essay opposing Hegelian speculation and Adorno's dialectics is best seen as a way of registering differences over moral and political thinking and the nature of critique. Indeed, before Rose had produced her interpretation of Hegel she had already written, the "idea that Adorno is an Hegelian Marxist is a misleading oversimplification. . . . In this general sense of 'sublating' the tradition, not rescinding it, Adorno betrays an Hegelian inspiration, but his conceptual apparatus, such as the criticism of identity thinking, negative dialectic, reification, is never Hegelian in origin."[95]

6 Conclusion

The archival research behind this chapter revealed significant aspects of Rose's work hitherto unrecognized in the secondary literature and provides crucial steps toward three aspects of my argument: setting out important features of Rose's social philosophy, revealing the synoptic

94. *TMS*, 76. A similar charge is made by Zuidervaart, *Social Philosophy After Adorno*, 157–81.

95. *TMS*, 142.

vision necessary to appreciate the broken middle, and the determining relation between Rose's work and religion. Rose was a critical theorist in the Hegel-Adorno tradition with strong similarities to J. M. Bernstein. As such her thought includes a Weberian analysis of modernity, a combination of sociology and philosophy, a realist-idealist epistemology rather than positivism or relativism, and immanent critique aiming at emancipation and reflexive self-knowledge. Her speculative philosophy involves an aporetic ontology; a vision of philosophy as a modernist cultural practice opening the way to modern forms of *phronesis* and *praxis*; and a self-limiting rationality acknowledging its inability fully to grasp reality (which she thought paralleled the theological admission of mystery in reality). Failure to acknowledge this has led to a mischaracterization of her work as overly theological and a mistaken view of her epistemology as non-realist. Appreciating her work as Frankfurt critical theory explains Rose's hesitation about normative solutions as downplaying the deformation of reason and institutions, the rationalizing fate awaiting ethical action. Her Adornian heritage also explains her concern with style, though Kierkegaard was important here too. Rose's speculative philosophy has a great deal in common with Adorno's negative dialectics, but is more insistent on and optimistic about the possibilities for learning, justice and transformation on both individual and cultural-political levels. This was driven partly by the place she accorded recognition and appropriation in speculative thinking, and was apparent in her treatment of metaphysics and ethics in light of the Holocaust.

3

Jurisprudential Wisdom

Even now there are places where a thought might grow . . .

—Derek Mahon, "A Disused Shed in Co. Wexford"

1 Introduction

THUS FAR I HAVE shown Rose's social philosophy as a Hegelian-Frankfurt enterprise, incorporating its own social and logical preconditions to achieve maximal metaphilosophical awareness. I have shown Rose held a sophisticated idea of a social totality as a necessary normative and theoretical ideal, a view she had in common with Hegel, Marx and first-generation Frankfurt thinkers. Since Rose's work is a simultaneous critique of society and social theory, in this chapter I focus on Rose's critique of social philosophy in *The Dialectic of Nihilism*, and show how it contains, though partly implicitly, elements of her critique of society and further elements of her own constructive position. This furthers my claim about the integrated nature of Rose's work as a whole, and addresses the second part of her trilogy to show the latter's unity. I reconstruct a significant feature Rose's social philosophy—ideology critique via jurisprudence—that is unknown in the secondary literature.[1]

1. Excerpt, Brower Latz, "Ideology Critique via Jurisprudence," 80–95.

I show how her ideas of self-limiting reason and of metaphysics led into a view of social philosophy as "jurisprudential wisdom" in contrast to narrow forms of legal positivism. These elements are essential for having a non-reductive view of Rose's mature social philosophy of the broken middle, which I address in the next chapter.

In *The Dialectic of Nihilism*, the "antinomy of law" names the speculative unity of law and ethics in absolute ethical life, which, we have seen, is an extrapolation from the ever-shifting diremptions between law and ethics. Rose used the perdurance of this antinomy to perform an ideology critique of social philosophy in Kant and the post-Kantian tradition. She developed the argument broached in *Hegel Contra Sociology* that Kant reflects the bourgeois property form, itself similar to Roman law, by examining the Roman legal influence on Kant's form of rationality as a whole. She critiqued the post-Kantians by the second main form of Frankfurt School ideology critique, which is to discern where theorists mistake "theory for reality."[2] She charged certain neo-Kantians of thinking to remove antinomies and metaphysics from jurisprudence, but only by unintentionally transferring them onto their conception of society; she accused prominent poststructuralists of ontologically ossifying social diremptions, or ahistoricising them, and so precluding the possibilities of critique, change and justice. The critique of society thus receded into the background in this work, though by reading Rose's work as a whole, and especially her trilogy of works as constituted around the speculative handling of diremptions and absolute ethical life, we can nevertheless see accruing to Rose's social philosophy further constructive components, which she called "jurisprudential wisdom." Jurisprudential wisdom is social philosophy able properly to handle the antinomy of law and discern its effects on both society and social theorizing.

In order to exposit this jurisprudential wisdom, once again some ground clearing is in order. First I clarify Rose's term of art "antinomy of law" (§2.1); then I outline Rose's argument in *Dialectic of Nihilism* (§2.2); and sketch her view of the state-society relation as influencing philosophy (§2.3), to which we return in more detail in the next chapter. I am then able to assess Rose's argument about Roman law and the form of rationality in Kant, as a test case of her ideology critique via jurisprudence (§3). This reveals the continuity between her previous and subsequent books and substantiates my claim that Rose had a coherent, though developing,

2. Arato, introduction to "Esthetic Theory and Cultural Criticism," in *Essential Frankfurt School Reader*, 201.

social theory underlying and unifying her different publications; brings out further what she regarded as important within her theory of modernity; and shows some of its key developments. I find Rose's remarks about Kant ultimately untenable but the broader position from which she makes those remarks still valuable. In §4 I show some of the implications of the constructive elements of her philosophy in relation to political philosophy and jurisprudence; namely, support for a social and political philosophy inspired by Hegel's *Philosophy of Right*, the use of law to gain a view of the social totality, and an expansive view of jurisprudence as examining the links between the metaphysical, ethical and legal.

2 The "Speculative Identity of Form and History"

2.1 The antinomy of law

The term antinomy of law is "the dual implication of rule and regularity, of force and generality, known to the tradition as *regulae iuris* and to us as 'diachrony' and 'synchrony.'"[3] The *regulae iuris* means the unwritten but generally practiced principles of interpretation of written laws;[4] they contain a tension, present as far back as Justinian's *Digest*, between describing existing practice and stipulating normative conditions for law. The antinomy of law, in short, names the tensions between law and ethics and the hovering between description and prescription. "The connection and the conflict of law [*des Rechts*] with ethics presents the fundamental problem of the entirety of law in its entire history."[5] She associates this with the "mystery of the categorical imperative: inconceivable but absolute."[6] In her next book, *The Broken Middle*, Rose called the antinomy of law "the dual implication of law and ethics."[7] It is "the 'juridical' and 'litigious' in law, for both of these terms carry impositional and ethical connotations."[8] This distinction connects to several aspects of law, seen in the explicit glosses on the "antinomy of law" in *Dialectic of Nihilism*:

3. *DN*, 2.
4. Ibid., 18.
5. Ibid., 45, citing Hermann Cohen, Rose's square brackets.
6. Ibid., 2.
7. *BM*, xiv–xv.
8. Ibid., xv (referring to *DN*, 2, 17n30).

a) The "characteristic compound in modern states of individual freedom with individual depoliticization."[9] For instance, modern individuals are both legal "persons" (they have rights) and "things" (they are the commodity labor-power).[10] In this sense, the antinomy of law is one way of thinking about what we may call "actually existing autonomy."

b) Universality/particularity:[11] law, like metaphysical and linguistic terms, must be universal and yet apply to particulars.

c) Freedom/necessity:[12] law as coercive yet enabling freedom (rather than the question of free will versus determinism), with the focus on how the tension is worked out in different contexts.

d) Agents' activity and passivity in law, agents as both actors in and subject to law; both judges of and judged by other judged judges.[13] (In the background is the Kantian trial of reason by reason, culminating in Nietzsche's notion of nihilism as a normal condition, in which all values are undermined by valuing objective truth [the sociological dimensions of which were pursued by Weber]).

e) The relation between political structures and ideology,[14] state and religion, rules and ethos.

f) Von Ihering's positing of egoism and altruism as human motivation.[15]

Each of these is surely difficult, but are they strictly speaking antinomic? This depends on whether antinomy is equated with contradiction. Rose differentiated the two. "An antinomy is a conflict of two arguments or doctrines, each of which taken in itself is cogent, but they cannot both be valid, and one cannot establish superiority over the other."[16] In her later work, Rose equated antinomy with aporia and preferred aporia to contradiction because, "while 'contradiction' is a logical term, which, applied to social structure, implies possible resolution, 'aporia' is prelogical,

9. *DN*, 3.
10. Ibid.
11. Ibid., 15.
12. Ibid., 18.
13. Ibid., 65.
14. Ibid., 5.
15. Ibid., 38.
16. *TMS*, 54; cf. 149–50.

it refers to lack of way, and implies no exit from its condition."[17] Rose's view is that the internal structure of law and its metaphysical correlates and the social outworking of both are internally in tension and produce dilemmas and paradoxes (e.g., the well known legal problems associated with tolerance, equality, free speech, and the antinomies listed above). The historical fact that no finally satisfactory answer has been attained to these questions supports the characterization of law and metaphysics as antinomic and attests to the wisdom of Rose's aporetic rather than deterministic mind-set in philosophy.

Others take a similar view. As H. L. A. Hart argued in response to the perennial difficulties in conceiving law, the "price of uniformity" is distortion.[18] The contemporary Hartian John Gardner writes, "There is no bigger picture. I don't have a theory of law, let alone . . . a . . . comprehensive theoretical position."[19] Neither does Rose present a comprehensive theory of law. She does present mutual recognition as the actuality of law but she does not work out many details of this view. She uses the historically shifting form of the antinomy to discover latent problems in other social philosophies. Once again Rose's works are best construed as therapeutic interventions concerned to oppose the reduction of rationality and philosophical resources of critique; they do not aim to solve narrowly defined technical problems but to aid theorizing by locating metatheoretical problems and their theoretical counterparts. The important and damaging reductions at work in poststructuralism included abandoning the self-legislating, or autonomous, self; ignoring the mutual mediation of law, politics and ethics; and downplaying the centrality of law for politics, ethics and social theory.

17. *BM*, 206n217. Cf. "Dispute over Marx and Weber," in which she contrasts contradiction (in Marx) with paradox (in Weber) in much the same way. "A paradox is repeated and cannot be transcended or resolved." The connections with her later use of Kierkegaardian repetition are striking, but see also "Antinomy," in *TMS*, 149–50.

18. Hart, *Concept of Law*, 38–42.

19. Gardner, *Law as a Leap of Faith*, v. Nevertheless, Gardner thinks the tension between law's rightness and positedness may be resolved in an analogous way to resolutions of the Euthyphro dilemma.

2.2 The argument of *Dialectic of Nihilism*

The context for Rose's book on poststructuralism and law is "the difficulty in the conceiving of law since Kant."[20] Poststructuralist reception of Nietzsche and Heidegger "has taken them to overcome legality" in a "reconstruction of the history of law which blinds us to the very tradition which it disowns and repeats."[21] The wider context is, as Darrow Schechter writes, the post-Kantian "crisis of legal anthropology."[22] The legal subject was, like the Kantian moral subject, rational and self-legislating. The correlative view of anthropology, ethics, jurisprudence and reason was put under pressure by the post-Kantian tradition and Rose wrote to avoid having the baby thrown out with the bathwater. Since the Roman period, juridical thinking posited person, thing and obligation as a fundamental, trifold distinction, and Rose believed this was a true and useful distinction, which could adequately respond to the criticisms made of juridical rationality and the legal person by using a sufficiently textured view of reason and self-rule, including one attending to the inner life of the individual. Like Hegel, she believed that in politics "law itself is a legitimate means . . . there is no legitimacy or legitimate ends without law."[23] She presupposes, in common again with several Frankfurt thinkers, that

> the emergence of modern reason is inextricable from the emergence of modern law: that rationality acts as a means of maintaining temporally and locally overarching sequences of predictability, calculability and organisation—that is, of securing conditions of *legal regularity* through society. Modern rationality, on this account, is co-genetic with the construction of the thinking person as a universally identifiable centre of imputation, and as a legislatively empowered agent, capable of ordering its social and cognitive relations in accordance with generalised conceptions of validity.[24]

Rose introduces *Dialectic of Nihilism* as part of "a larger endeavor to retrieve the speculative identity of form and history."[25] Rose is again

20. *BM*, xiv.

21. *DN*, 1.

22. *Critique of Instrumental Reason*, 7. For an excellent survey of this crisis in post-Kantian German thought, see Thornhill, "Law and Religion."

23. Schechter, *Instrumental Reason*, 14.

24. Thornhill, "Law and Religion," 103–4.

25. *DN*, 5. Cf. above, ch. 1, §4.1.

probing an aspect of what Hegel called a "shape of spirit," the identities and differences between a form of life and a form of consciousness. Here, the issue is to examine "the historical connection between psychology and objective spirit. In this way its law may become knowable."[26] We will return to this claim in the next section, but for now it is best explained by an abstract for a paper entitled "Legalism and Nihilism," in which Rose wrote,

> The various "ends" of metaphysics [attempts to show metaphysics is finished], sociological as well as philosophical, always appear in historically-specific jurisprudential forms; and . . . it is these jurisprudential traditions which themselves found and recapitulate metaphysical categories. This paradox is presented [by Rose] neither as an hermeneutical circle nor as the convention of discourse but as a speculative identity: an interlocking of form and history to which only jurisprudential wisdom can do justice.[27]

Rose proposes the speculative identity and difference between law and metaphysics (broadly construed), insofar as each confronts similar problems (such as agency, ethics, will, subjectivity) and uses related categories (such as person, thing, action, power, property, possession, validity, cause and effect). The speculative identity of form and history is, in this case, her way of showing "the discovery of the concepts and institutions of Greek, Roman and German law at every level of philosophical and sociological thinking—methodological, formal and substantive."[28] She shows the influence of Roman law on Kant,[29] Homeric law on Heidegger, feudal law on Foucault,[30] modern private (property) law on

26. Ibid., 124. By contrast, 83: "Heidegger takes us so far away from the antinomy of law, of theoretical and practical reason, of knowledge and ethics, that this 'place' in which we are de-posited is irrelevant to a life which is lived, understood and transformed in and through that antinomy."

27. "Legalism and Nihilism," unpublished abstract, no date, box 47.

28. Rose, "Parts and Wholes," 99.

29. Kant of course did not try to end metaphysics but establish it as a "science" (*Wissenschaft*), but Rose includes him in this list as the starting point of examining the link between philosophy, sociology and law in the post-Kantian tradition. Kant, however, also argues in *Metaphysical Elements of Justice*, preface, 205 (Ladd, 3) (the translation used by Rose) that no complete system of justice is possible because justice (despite being a pure concept) is applied in "empirical diversity and manifoldness."

30. For a sympathetic and critical discussion of Rose's criticisms of Foucault, see Cutrofello, *Discipline and Critique*.

structuralism and poststructuralism. The earlier philosophical tradition faced up to these problems, the poststructuralists presented their work as a departure from law's categories and the problems associated with them; but since they cannot escape either, the result is to fail both to tackle the problems fully and to use the accumulated wisdom of the tradition in dealing with them.[31] Poststructural antinomianism is thus "expounded as a series of regresses to identifiable types or epochs of legal form. . . . Post-structuralist nihilism completes itself as law—unreflected but always historically identifiable."[32] This reversal is the titular dialectic of nihilism—one to which it is subject rather than intentionally performs.

The neo-Kantian attempts of Cohen, Lask, Stammler and von Ihering to simplify law to one principle (in order to remove its antinomies and aporias) went hand-in-hand with their attempts to eliminate metaphysics from Kantian philosophy. But the antinomies returned in different forms, usually transferred to their conceptions of society.[33] Rose's critique thus echoes Ernst Cassirer's, who "in contrast to neo-Kantian jurisprudence . . . maintained that the dichotomy between positive law and legal values, ideals, or principles . . . could not be brought to a conclusion, not even through the transcendental method. . . . For Cassirer the antithesis rather epitomizes the infinite task of jurisprudence."[34] Derrida, following Benjamin and paradigmatically for poststructuralism, regards law as ultimately unjust.[35] Rose sees the poststructuralist version of law as an inverted natural law: the given law that all human law merely interprets is now irrational and violent rather than rational and beneficent, an "ontological injustice" rather than original justice.[36] Rose instead treats law through *Schein*. Law appeals to ethical and anthropological principles that have some validity and yet can also be abused by power unguided by those principles. Hence, whereas Hegel showed "the antinomy of law as the speculative identity *and* non-identity of the state and religion—of 'politics' and 'ideology' . . . —so I read the antinomy in the work of our contemporaries as presenting us with a pale cousin: the nihilistic identity

31. Cutrofello, *Discipline and Critique*, also frames poststructuralism as an attempt to escape from "juridical" thinking.

32. *BM*, xiv–xv.

33. *DN*, 4, and, e.g., 36–40.

34. Coskun, *Law as Symbolic Form*, 329. Coskun's "dichotomy" equates to Rose's "antinomy."

35. *DN*, 169.

36. Ibid., 99.

and non-identity of law and metaphysics."[37] Poststructuralism extracts from Nietzsche an "*unhealthy* scepticism toward all human, social and political values, assimilates all signification to a general sociology of control, and then yearns for the raptus of a Singularity which cannot be named, known, or negotiated."[38] A healthy skepticism accompanies a speculative philosophy, whereas an unhealthy skepticism colludes with an ossified and unproductive dialectic. Too much or too little emphasis on aporia is a problem for thought.

If law and metaphysics are always speculatively identified, always antinomic and necessary, the poststructuralist attempt to escape metaphysics and law is a mistake, and fails to learn sufficiently from the tradition it claims to have surpassed; whereas the neo-Kantian attempt to eliminate law's antinomy mistakes the nature of law.[39] Rose's strategy for substantiating this is to show the form of Kant's theoretical and practical philosophy as under the influence of Roman law; show the difficulties of the jurisprudence of four neo-Kantians as they eliminate the antinomy of law; and immanently critique some poststructuralists to show their failures to theorize law, ethics and society and their unwitting reliance on various legal forms. The claim to have finished with all the difficulties entailed by theorizing subjectivity, representation, law, metaphysics and values turns out to land these theorists back in the middle of all the difficulties, but with less awareness of what determines their thought. They are thus subject to a dialectic. Just as Adorno and Horkheimer argued enlightenment and myth, as two forms of reason, are always entwined, so Rose argues there is no escaping from metaphysics and law or their entanglement. She agrees with Nietzsche that nihilism is now a normal condition, since values always threaten to undermine themselves (or, dialectally reverse themselves), but Rose denies anti-ethical or antinomian consequences follow from this, as found in Weber or poststructuralism (but not in Nietzsche in her view). Antinomian poststructuralism attempts to evade law (both as a form of reason and laws in society) yet relies on legal forms: this is its dialectic. Its refusal of law and metaphysical-ethical reasoning is its nihilism. (Rose confusingly operates with two meanings of nihilism without spelling them out: a "neutral" version in

37. Ibid., 5. Cutrofello, *Discipline and Critique*, 132, also concludes that Foucault and Derrida lack a sustainable ethics.

38. *JAM*, 19.

39. Cf. Thornhill, *Political Philosophy*, esp. 239–60.

her interpretation of nihilism as a normal condition, and a "bad" version in the poststructuralist refusal of knowledge, ethics and reason.)

Much of post-Kantian philosophy comprises each generation accusing its predecessor of failing to complete the task of overcoming metaphysics, so it is plausible for Rose to say attempts to overcome metaphysics end up recapitulating it. This could support Rose's view that metaphysics is ineliminable or it could mean success still awaits. More important here is Rose's idea that legal concepts fill the vacuum left by the banished metaphysics. She traces the antinomies of metaphysics as they migrate from law to society (neo-Kantians) to language (poststructuralists), without accomplishing their alleged solutions (supporting her view that antinomies are permanent).[40] Raising awareness of the social and intellectual factors determining consciousness was one of Hegel's aims, as a condition for responding with freedom to those determinations. Poststructural unawareness of the role of law and jurisprudence in social philosophy therefore undermines its ability to negotiate its determinations. Its (and so our) relation to law and legal ideas remains hidden, incubating the social pathologies resulting from over-reliance on one or another competing tendency in society.

Dialectic of Nihilism is therefore Rose's contribution to ideology critique. The archives at Warwick contain a planned table of contents for an earlier incarnation of *Dialectic of Nihilism* entitled *Essays in Speculative Jurisprudence*. On March 17, 1982, Rose wrote (in a letter to the publisher Blackwell who had given her a contract for it), that the book

> seeks to expose the dependence of theoretical philosophical and sociological thinking on unexamined and historically specific legal concepts. In the first part I show that recent linguistic theory has reverted from a civil law to a natural law framework. In the second part I show that the transition from moral and legal philosophy to sociological and historicist approaches continued to rely on juridical thinking. The argument in these two parts is a recasting of the question of ideology . . . a new way of posing the problem of ideology, a way which acknowledges the dependence of theory on historically specific legal concepts . . . my work is more an essay in the philosophy of consciousness:

40. For arguments that metaphysics and its aporias are inescapable, see Kołakowski, *Horror*; *Modernity on Endless Trial*; *Is God Happy?*; "In Praise of Inconsistency."

> it seeks to expose the juridical and litigious presuppositions of our formation.[41]

This is not the usual Marxist approach to law and ideology, in which law is regarded as ideologically shaped by capitalist economic and political forms. Part of her contribution in this regard is to produce a "different map"[42] of the terrain of social philosophy: "The book is an attempt to reconstruct the philosophy of law since Kant"[43] (within, it should be added, the continental rather than Anglophone tradition). We return to this in §3.

Throughout the book she continues to forward her own social philosophy in three important ways. (Many reviewers of *Dialectic of Nihilism* were unsure about her own position but it is much clearer when connected with her earlier and later work, revealing once again the importance of a synoptic view of her work as an interconnected whole.) First, she uses the Frankfurt combination of philosophy and sociology to examine the connection between formal reasoning and forms of social rationality (here, as influenced by legal forms). Second, she uses the speculative logic she took from Hegel to think about freedom and law. The speculative identity and non-identity of freedom and unfreedom, and the antinomy of law, are approached through historical-philosophical phenomenology. Whereas Kant offers a somewhat ahistorical contrast between inclination and reverence for the law, Hegel, Marx and Nietzsche look at various ways in which this inner split is socially and historically conditioned and played out. This is not a rejection of Kant but a sublation.[44] Third, developing themes from *Hegel Contra Sociology*, law is a central category of social philosophy and should be recognized as such (contra the antinomianism of postmodern thought). Social philosophy emerges from the "middle" of "civil society and civil law" and should recognize its context.[45] In her next book, Rose would expand on these themes as the "broken middle," the dirempted relations between state and civil society and between law and

41. The letter and the plan are in box 47. The introduction to the earlier version was headed "Roman Civil Law and the Problem of Ideology." We may note Rose's focus on theories rather than general consciousness, or what Hegel called "philosophical consciousness" rather than "natural consciousness."

42. Written on a plan for *Dialectic of Nihilism*, 2 February 1984, box 20. Repeated in notes for a paper she was due to give later that year called "The Dialectics of Nihilisms."

43. Letter, 13 January 1992, box 24.

44. *DN*, 4.

45. Ibid., 212.

ethics. Already in 1984 she wanted to approach in an "aporetic way" the "antinomy of culture" and "the tradition which holds us."[46]

Such is the broad architecture of the argument of Rose's third book. It is an argument for the antinomic and aporetic nature of metaphysics and law, their speculative identity, the importance of both in social philosophy, and performs an ideology critique by uncovering the jurisprudential presuppositions behind various social philosophies. It leads into a Hegelian political philosophy, an expansive jurisprudence, and the use of law to gain a view of the social totality.

2.3 The post-Kantian condition

The antinomy of law is thus one part of the speculative identity of form and history, the relation between philosophy and its context in the state-society relation (the middle), or the influence of objective spirit on philosophical consciousness. "The separation in modern states of public from private law, of the realm of needs or economic life from the realm of politics and citizenship, arises from specifically modern forms of private property and formal equality. This separation gives rise to the illusion of sovereign individuality which is represented in the absolute demands of morality and religion, and reproduced and justified in Kant's critical philosophy."[47] Notice Kant expresses the *modern form* of the antinomy of law: law and metaphysics have always been antinomic but the form of those antinomies changes with legal-social-political regimes. We have come to expect this from Rose's historical version of speculation (cf. the subtitle of *The Broken Middle: Out of Our Ancient Society*). The speculative handling of these oppositions displays the phenomenological perspective Rose took from Hegel on the combination of freedom and unfreedom in modern subjects. Speculation "reduces the paradox" of law but does not eliminate it.[48]

> Hegel's *Phenomenology of Spirit* shows how the confrontation between master and slave becomes internalized in the "person" as the struggle between the good will and natural desire and inclination. Opening up an historical perspective on the development of the idea of "persons" as the bearers of equal

46. Ibid.

47. Ibid., 2.

48. The phrase comes from the plan of the book's outline, 2 February 1984.

> rights and the hypertrophy of their inner life, Hegel expounds the antinomy of law as the characteristic compound in modern states of individual freedom with individual depoliticization. In the *Grundrisse* Marx examines how Capital posits individuals as "persons," the bearers of rights, and as "things," the commodity "labor-power." The theory of commodity fetishism subsequently developed in the first volume of *Capital* is not simply an account of how material relations between "persons" are transformed into social relations between "things." It is an account of the "personification" *and* "reification" intrinsic to the juridical categories of "commodity," "capital," and "money." Emphasis on the differences between Marx's and Hegel's thinking has obscured the continuity of their preoccupation with the antinomy of law. The juridical opposition of free subjects and subjected things, which characterizes not only relations between different classes but the relation of the individual to itself in modern states, forms the speculative core of Hegel's and of Marx's thinking.[49]

Rose argues her preferred speculative thinkers express the fluidity between the two sides of the various antinomies thrown up by this legal-political structure better than Kant. Rose's rationale for starting with Kant is twofold. First, the antinomy of law in Kant itself reflects the paradox of state and civil society; thus her claims intersect: law and metaphysics are speculatively identified, internally aporetic, and both reflect their social context. Second, Kant's critical philosophy expresses in a powerful and sophisticated way the relationship between social philosophy and the state-society structure, which still conditions modernity, and it provides the starting point for future approaches to metaphysics within the philosophical tradition. We are all post-Kantians now. Thus Rose: "I think you can only be a serious student of post-Kantian philosophy if you understand that the relationship between Kant and Hegel is fundamental. And that means you include not just the argument about metaphysics but social and political philosophy."[50] More specifically, most poststructuralists were, in Rose's eyes, neo-Kantians, where to be neo-Kantian is to be trapped in thought, unable to render objective the subjective mediations of thought. From a Hegelian point of view, the poststructuralists have thus no more escaped the problem of skepticism and the objectivity of knowledge than had Kant's transcendental idealism. The argument about the influence of Roman law on Kant begins the book because he be-

49. *DN*, 3.

50. "Keep Your Mind in Hell," interview with Elaine Williams.

queaths the modern form of the antinomy of law with which philosophy still wrestles, and hence is the context the poststructuralists want to escape (via Nietzsche's reaction to Kant). It is therefore this argument I assess below to display her notion of jurisprudential wisdom as an ideology critique and a mode of social philosophy.

3 Ideology Critique via Jurisprudence: Kant and Roman Law

3.1 An elective affinity

Rose's argument about Kant can be parsed into three connected claims:

(1) Kant's form of rationality as a whole is shaped by Roman legal thought: "In Kant's concept of pure reason, in the familiar opposition between persons and things I find litigation, contract and property."[51] That is, the Roman legal distinction between persons and things does much work not only in his political and ethical philosophy[52] but in generating the form of rationality that uses the "interlocking set of oppositions: ends/means, persons/things; absolute/relative; subjective/objective."[53] This is *not* the usual Hegelian gravamen that Kant smuggles content into the form of the categorical imperative;[54] it is a much more far-reaching claim about the whole shape of his thought: "the split between the ideal and the real itself depends on importing features of the real into the very *form* of the ideal."[55] Notice it is not, as it stands, a criticism; it is simply an observation.

(2) Kant's argument for freedom is based on a *usucapio* defense, that is, "ownership granted by law which suffices to transfer the *dominium* after a specific period of possession, even though the original acquisition did not take place according to the fully legal form of *mancipatio* (sale)."[56] Contra Kant, our possession of freedom is not by the equity of natural justice but homologous to a "right of necessity" (permitted in cases of necessity but not a moral or legal right and so not extendable to other

51. Rose, "Parts and Wholes," 99.

52. *DN*, 21.

53. Ibid., 20.

54. Ibid.

55. Ibid., 19.

56. Ibid., 13, referring to Justinian's *Institutes*, II.VI.

cases).[57] This is a criticism of Kant's self-understanding of his practical defense of human freedom and of the defense itself.

(3) In Kant "the form of freedom is the form of private law."[58] Private law is law governing property possession. Human freedom theorized as noumenal freedom ends up subservient to guaranteeing legal personality and property: "The transformation of philosophy and science into critical jurisdiction draws attention to its basis in absolute property or *dominium*, which is unjustifiable and ultimately shored up by a categorical imperative, an unconditioned *imperium* which cannot be called to account."[59] This is a criticism.

Each of these claims will take some unpacking, beginning with the aims of the argument itself. As with her remarks about neo-Kantian social theory in her previous book, the tone and substance of her claims are unevenly matched. The argument is not that the Roman legal influence on the form of Kant's philosophy invalidates his entire thought; the argument is that Roman attitudes to property skew Kant's picture of freedom, the self, and social and political philosophy, because he freezes the property/thing distinction and inflates the role of property. Nor does she argue social philosophy should escape legal influence; it should instead consciously negotiate its relation to law and theorize law itself as a topic of social philosophy. Beyond such critical aims, Rose is supporting the Hegelian view that freedom is compatible with external influence, and that freedom can be actual and be theoretically known as such (whereas for Kant freedom remains transcendental and so beyond both theoretical knowledge and appearance within the phenomenal realm; it can only be warranted by practical reason [I will come back to this]). Nor need Rose be read as denying the importance of Hume, Newton or theological influences on Kant's theoretical and practical philosophy; she is adding to the list of influences on Kant's thought, though implicitly claiming Roman law as a dominant influence.

Even with the aims of the argument in mind, it is not easy to assess the three claims. Some reviewers believed Rose's claims could only be substantiated by showing direct historical influence on Kant,[60] which Rose does not do. I submit this is the wrong thing to look for because

57. Kant, *Metaphysical Elements of Justice*, 233 (Ladd, 39).

58. *DN*, 20.

59. Ibid., 24.

60. Lash, review of *DN*, 305–9; Murphy, "Memorising Politics of Ancient History," 384–405. No reviewer sets out Rose's argument as I do here.

Rose's argument is best construed as discerning a Weberian elective affinity between the form of Kant's philosophy and Roman legal thinking, and referring his philosophy back to a structure of state and civil society.[61] This of course must be historically mediated, but how exactly Kant comes by his Roman influence is not the key issue.[62] The issue is the relationship between Kant's thought and Roman law (not Kant's view of that relation). It is ideology critique as revealing necessary illusions. Her reading is similar to a hermeneutic of suspicion therefore, but in a way that wishes to sublate Kant's work not reject it.[63] Weber never defined elective affinity, but its meaning was reconstructed by Richard Herbert Howe.[64] The basic idea concerns "interrelationships of networks of meanings,"[65] "whether and how strongly they [two phenomena] mutually favor one another's continuance, or, conversely, hinder or exclude one another."[66] Weber acquired the term via Goethe's novel (*Die Wahlverwandtschaften*), itself named after a term from chemistry. The chemists of the period discussed the process in which substances A and B are joined, but uncouple in the presence of substance C, and A now joins with C. A and C then have a stronger chemical affinity than A and B. Sociological judgments of elective affinity look for shared characteristics; they are portrayals of ideal types not foundations for syllogisms; likenesses not logically necessary deductions.[67] "The greater the number of positive inner affinities between two elements vis-à-vis the total possible number, the more strongly are the elements joined. That is their 'degree' of elective affinity."[68] Rose's main evidence for discerning an elective affinity between the form of Kant's philosophy and Roman law are the three above claims: interlocking oppositions connected to the person/thing distinction, how Kant's defense of freedom actually works (contrary to his own view), and the parallels be-

61. *DN*, 50n2: "In this context 'to sublate,' the standard translation of Hegel's *aufheben*, implies to carry an opposition back to its source."

62. Kelley, "*Gaius Noster*," 619–48; Henrich, "Kant's Notion of a Deduction," 29–46; Conklin, *Hegel's Laws*, 48–52.

63. Cf. *BM*, 283.

64. "Max Weber's Elective Affinities," 366–85.

65. Ibid., 382.

66. Max Weber, *Economy and Society*, 341, where the two phenomena in question are "concrete structures of social action and concrete forms of economic organization." Protestantism and capitalism is his most famous example.

67. Howe, "Elective Affinities," 378–79.

68. Ibid., 381–82.

tween Roman private law and freedom in Kant. These elements of Kant's thought also take in his picture of the subject, state and law. This is Rose's way of pursuing the Frankfurt School theme of the various connections between rationality in the social sense and the more narrowly logical use of reason.[69] Finally, there is no contradiction between ideology critique and discerning an elective affinity, because affinities need not be obvious and once seen may reveal problematic features otherwise unnoticed. In this light, (1) becomes a criticism when it supports problematic features such as (2) and (3). I now assess each of Rose's claims.

3.2 Kantian rationality and the person/thing distinction

Rose argues (1) by reading Kant's critical writings, especially the first *Critique*, through the definitions of property and possession in the *Metaphysical Elements of Justice*. She proceeds as follows.[70] Kant is concerned with both the canon of reason (its proper use in limiting knowledge to the combination of sense experience and concepts) and our "possession" of freedom. Kant's first *Critique* uses "*practical* [my emphasis] ideas of *de jure*, property, possession, justification" to "expound" the transcendental deduction of theoretical knowledge. Here she cites *The Critique of Pure Reason* A84–5/B116–17, which is entitled "On the principles of a transcendental deduction in general," where these "practical" terms are found. She references Schopenhauer's observation that Roman legal terminology is used so much, especially in this section, it appears essential, not accidental, to Kant's thought.[71] (Rose's additional references to Kant are to: B, xiii and A, xx in the first *Critique*; the third *Critique*; the *Groundwork of the Metaphysics of Morals*; *The Metaphysical Elements of Justice* [which is the first part of *The Metaphysics of Morals*]). Given the technical nature of Kant's vocabulary however, it begs the question somewhat to call these concepts in this context "practical." Further, Schopenhauer, in the passage Rose cites, goes on to say that although the impression Kant gives is that moral thinking is specifically Roman legal in character, it is not; it is merely a form of judging like any other.[72] On the one hand, this

69. Cf. Adorno, *Negative Dialectics*, 53–55, and Bernstein, *Adorno*, 140.

70. *DN*, 12–16. All quotations in this paragraph are from this section of the text unless otherwise stated.

71. *DN*, 11n1. The text is "On the Basis of Morality" from 1841.

72. Schopenhauer, *The Two Fundamental Problems of Ethics*, 169–72.

could imply that Kant's thought really was influenced by Roman thought, because he construed all thought as Roman legal trial; on the other hand, it could imply that Kant's metaphor is a metaphor that can apply to any kind of weighing up of reasons.[73] So far, so inconclusive.

Rose's argument is further put into doubt if we turn to the work of Dieter Henrich[74] and Ian Proops[75] (building on Henrich) who have shown that the form of argument used in the Transcendental Deduction is based on a form of legal argument called a deduction, which traces a legal claim (usually to land) back to its source in order to prove its legitimacy. Legal deductions came into existence in Europe in the fourteenth century, "a time when the tradition of Roman law was not yet revitalized and the modern theory of law had not yet been founded."[76] Indeed, Roman law did not make significant inroads into the German-speaking principalities until the end of the fifteenth century.[77] This supports Rose's view of the influence of *some* legal thinking on the whole of Kant's thought—Proops discusses deductions in the first two *Critiques*, Henrich in all three—but not *Roman* law.[78] Henrich notes "the idea of an acquisition of legal titles does not necessarily presuppose a particular legal system with reference to which the entitlement becomes decidable. The Natural Right Kant uses as his paradigm recognizes an original acquisition. The conditions of its rightfulness can be determined prior to any particular legal system."[79] In short, Kant's deductions are not Roman.

After highlighting the legal vocabulary in the Transcendental Deduction, Rose's next move is to read the "critical writings"[80] through the 1797 *Metaphysical Elements of Justice* because that is where Kant defines the terms "possession" and "property," and how they may be held lawfully (*de jure*) (i.e., even without physical proximity). This is a clever idea but has problems. There appears to be slippage in Rose's argument between

73. Wood, *Kant's Ethical Thought*, 176: "The capacity we ascribe to ourselves in regarding ourselves as subject to moral obligation is of exactly the same *kind* as that we ascribe to ourselves in thinking of ourselves as judging according to rational norms."

74. "Kant's Notion of a Deduction," 29–46.

75. "Kant's Legal Metaphor and the Nature of a Deduction," 209–29.

76. Henrich, "Notion of a Deduction," 33.

77. Kelly, *Short History of Western Legal Theory*, 180–81.

78. "Deduction" in the sense identified by Henrich does not occur in Justinian's *Institutes* nor in Hunter, *Systematic and Historical Exposition of Roman Law*.

79. Henrich, "Notion of a Deduction," 36.

80. *DN*, 13n8.

Kant's theoretical and practical philosophy.[81] Rose thinks Kant is pursuing both the canon of reason and freedom in terms of the *de jure* possession of property, but that when Kant explains, in *Elements of Justice*, what he thinks *de jure* possession entails, it rests on a claim of "natural justice,"[82] which is a kind of "given."[83] Rose thinks the "meaning of deduction and justification has shifted at this point" because the "complex machinery of justification rests on a simple appeal to natural justice."[84] Let us accept, in the mode of discerning elective affinities, that ideas from the 1797 text may be used to exposit those from 1781,[85] we must still register the fact that the context of the quotations Rose gives from *Elements of Justice* is Kant's argument for the possibility of *de jure* (noumenal) possession of a physical object, whereas freedom for Kant is explicitly not a physical object, so this sort of argument would not apply to it, nor does Kant imagine it does.[86] In the case of discerning an affinity, however, this is not decisive. Rose could respond that the *de jure* possession needed by Kant to make sense of possession of objects is paralleled by the transcendental nature of freedom, which exempts it from ever being experienced. Perhaps Kant does think of freedom as a property we possess, despite lacking entirely convincing proof of its legitimacy. "Property" and "possess" here are ambiguous between physical objects and predicates/characteristics, which may be part of Rose's point. Yet Kant can reply that his noumenal/phenomenal distinction is transforming Roman private law, rather than vice versa. Nor is it fair to Kant to imply that because we lack theoretical knowledge of noumenal freedom we thereby lack any legitimate way to regard ourselves as free and must treat the idea as a given.[87] Quite the contrary, Kant thinks we have solid practical reasons to regard ourselves as free, such that freedom is fundamental to being a person, as we shall now see.[88]

81. Noted by Lash, review of *DN*, 305.

82. Kant, *Metaphysical Elements of Justice*, 251 (Ladd, 59).

83. Rose is just wrong here—see the discussion of the derivation of property as an acquired right via reference to the will of all in Guyer, *Kant on Freedom, Law and Happiness*, 235–61.

84. *DN*, 13–14.

85. The relevant legal terms are present in the first edition of the first *Critique*.

86. Kant, *Critique of Practical Reason*, 5:29; Ward, *Kant*, 141–66.

87. *DN*, 24.

88. Ward, *Kant*, 141: freedom "is *proved* by our moral experience." See also Guyer, *Kant on Freedom*.

3.3 The *usucapio* defense of freedom

The idea of a canon of reason in the first *Critique* is raised by Rose but immediately dropped and her discussion focuses entirely on "a specific case of unlawful possession: the defense of the 'usurpatory concept' of freedom"[89] (claim 2). Rose's reference is again to A84–5/B116–17, but Kant there writes: "Concepts that have been usurped, such as *fortune* and *fate*," have no "clear legal ground for an entitlement to their use either from experience or from reason." This passage sets up Kant's demonstration of the legitimacy of the twelve categories because they are limited to making experience possible, in contrast to the illegitimate metaphysical use of notions such as fortune or fate. Thus, either Kant does not have in mind here that our freedom is usurped, because he is discussing the theoretical concepts of the categories; or, if he does (after all, the second edition of the first *Critique* was published in 1787, only one year before the second *Critique*), then he will go on to show, in the second *Critique*, that freedom does indeed have legitimacy and is not usurped. The characterization of the human claim to freedom as "usurpatory" tilts the scales too hastily in favor of Rose's affinity claim, as did calling the legal vocabulary "practical."

Kant's view of freedom is admittedly a moving target.[90] Nevertheless it is problematic that Rose discusses only the *Groundwork* and not the *Critique of Practical Reason* because Kant defends human freedom in the latter. Kant offers what is now called (after Henry E. Allison) the Reciprocity Thesis: "freedom and unconditional practical law reciprocally imply each other."[91] In this section Kant considers two problems. In problem 1 he starts by assuming that a moral will is only determined by the form of the moral law (not any material content), and ends up finding that such a will must be transcendentally free, because it is not determined by any material and so natural causal factors, but only by the rational form of a law, which is an intelligible idea and so transcendental. In problem 2 he starts by assuming a will is free, and discovers that it must be determined by the form of law, since it cannot be determined by anything material, but only the intelligibility of a rational law's form. Hence, unconditional moral law and transcendental freedom imply one another.[92] Now, in the

89. *DN*, 12.

90. Wood, *Kantian Ethics* and *Kant's Ethical Thought*.

91. Kant, *Critique of Practical Reason*, 5:29.

92. The Reciprocity Thesis is common to both the *Groundwork* and the second

Groundwork, Kant freely admits there is circularity here.[93] Yet, as Ian Proops has shown, the treatment of the moral law as a "fact of reason" (in the later second *Critique*) does *not* mean it is insusceptible of any proof, contrary to the Hegelian objection, because philosophical proof for Kant is probative, not demonstrative as in mathematics.[94] A legal deduction was a two-step proof, in which a fact was established and then its force for the legitimacy of a *juris* question displayed. Precisely because the fact is legally relevant, its legitimacy for the court's consideration must be established. Hence the fact of reason also needs a proof. Kant's proof for the fact of the moral law (at least in the second *Critique*)[95] is our experience of obligation. We first experience moral obligation and infer from there to our transcendental freedom.[96]

Rose never refers to the second *Critique* in her argument, which is odd, not least because it is the deduction there that most parallels the *usucapio*. The parallel is between taking the moral law as a fact of reason and inferring freedom from it, and the *usucapio* that takes as given a long-term possession and shows the innocent (if unusual) means of acquiring the possession. Yet, even if Rose had registered the parallel, what would it illuminate? The implication seems to be that Kant's defense of freedom ultimately takes freedom for granted rather than proving it, and that freedom, as a given, is of dubious provenance. Yet Kant already admits the impenetrability of freedom to theoretical reason, and he is explicit that refusing to presuppose freedom undermines practical judgments, hence the very need for a defense of our freedom. In neither case does the criticism find any purchase on Kant.

Unsatisfied with the idea of *de jure* property in Kant's political philosophy as (what she takes to be) a foundation for our freedom, and ignoring the second *Critique*, Rose moves straight on to the third *Critique*'s idea of purposiveness without purpose as a way of expositing the kingdom of ends as finally lacking proper coherence, as a kingdom of "righteousness without a right."[97] The kingdom of ends depends, she says, on "a life lived in one reality 'as if' it were proceeding in a different reality,"

Critique; see Allison, "Justification and Freedom."

93. 4:450.

94. Proops, "Legal metaphor."

95. 5:30.

96. Kant's theory is thus partly phenomenological (in the Husserlian sense), contra one strand of the formalism charge.

97. *DN*, 17.

since the way in which Kant separates ideal from real employs features of the real in the form of the ideal. Yet the "as if" characterization of the kingdom of ends is not accurate because the kingdom of ends is for Kant a postulate, which is something we *must* believe if we are to make sense of our reason and moral life.[98] Further, freedom and autonomy for Kant are intrinsically communal, albeit in the noumenal realm outside of time and space, due to their reference to the kingdom of ends.[99] Kant could then be read as providing these ideals as the immanent development of the mores of his society, in which case he should be praised for avoiding imposing an external *Sollen* on his society.[100]

In sum, Rose's view of the *usucapio* does not seem to bring out any features of Kant's views of freedom not already apparent from Kant himself, even if there is some parallel between Roman *usucapio* and the proof of freedom via the Reciprocity Thesis. Kant's deductions, however, are alien to Roman law. Thus far it appears the affinity is weak. Further, Rose's other charge—that freedom in Kant is akin to a right of necessity—conflicts with her *usucapio* analogy. A *usucapio* is fully provided for within the law,[101] whereas the right of necessity is a case on which no law can be made.[102] Given Rose's failure so far to pin her charges on Kant, it seems the contradiction belongs to her not him.

3.4 Freedom and private law

Rose has a series of suggestions to support claim (3), that Kant's form of freedom is that of private law (a mixture of Roman and modern). Discussing Kant's idea that persons have dignity because no price can be set on them, she cites Bucklan on Roman law: "The topic of *Res* or things may be roughly described as the main body of the law: the discussion of all those rights which have a money value, to the exclusion of such rights as liberty, and *patria potestas* which cannot be expressed in terms of money."[103] Private right is commonly acknowledged as the largest part

98. Ibid., 19. Against "as if" readings of Kant, see Ward, *Kant*, 141–66, and Insole, *Kant*, 135–71.

99. See Guyer, *Kant on Freedom*.

100. Contra *DN*, 20, with its bald assertion of an "insidious *Sollen*" in Kant's view of persons as ends in themselves.

101. E.g., Justinian, *Institutes*, II, VI.

102. Kant, *Metaphysical Elements of Justice*, 235–36 (Ladd, 41–42).

103. *DN*, 22, citing Bucklan, *Manual of Roman Private Law*, 31.

of Kant's philosophy of law too. According to Manfred Kuehn the difference between physical and intelligible possession is "almost absent" in common law but central to Roman law; and Kant made intelligible possession a postulate of pure practical reason, such that intelligible ownership is necessitated by reason.[104] As such, intelligible possession always exists, it precedes the state and the state is required not least to secure peaceful ownership of property. Rose's critique of Kant's view of property and freedom is echoed in Marx's critique of Savigny. Marx believed Savigny simply treated Roman contingency as justice, not questioning private property or the original seizure it may involve: "private property . . . arose out of the simple act of prehension, or willful seizure, and then somehow was given legal status by receiving customary acceptance and general social formulation. Out of *factum*, in juridical terms, came *jus*."[105] Similarly, Eduard Gans's critique of Savigny was to state the latter's positions thus: "Possession is a fact, a natural condition and not a right . . . but nonetheless the possessor has rights because of his possession."[106] Rose is here on firmer ground. There are even affinities, unmentioned by Rose, that support her case. Stoic philosophy suited the Roman temperament and there are some affinities perhaps between Kant and Stoic outlooks.[107] Kant's view of freedom as independence is similar to the neo-Roman tradition of Renaissance republicanism. Kant extends this idea: not only the sovereign but no private citizen should have power of interference over another.[108]

One could, as Rose appears to do, also view Kant's systematic approach to law as more akin to the Roman civil tradition than to common law, since Kant's prioritizing of ahistorical normativity is an exception to the usual German interpretive and historical legal tradition.[109] Against the background of the historical debate in the middle ages between codified Roman (civil law) and geographically variable Germanic (common law) traditions,[110] Kant could appear as siding with the former. Further, Kant's practical philosophy shares certain characteristics with natural

104. *Kant*, 397–98.

105. Kelley, "Metaphysics and Law," 357.

106. Ibid.

107. Kelly, *Short History*, 48.

108. Ripstein, *Force and Freedom*, 42–43.

109. Thornhill, *Political Philosophy*, 3. For the necessary qualifications to this characterization, see Ameriks, *Kant and the Historical Turn*.

110. Ozment, *Mighty Fortress*, 35–105.

law, which was an important element in Roman law. Yet when one recalls that the Roman tradition stemming from Gaius (which Justinian's *Institutes* transmitted) emphasized the practical, conventional and historical above the purely rational, natural and timeless, Kant in fact seems closer to the natural law tradition than to Roman law. Friedrich Carl von Savigny took the Roman law as the paradigmatic foundation of his historical legal school precisely because of its preference for the concrete and historical. Indeed, in Donald Kelley's lengthy article on the career of Roman law throughout Western thought, Savigny is the modern Roman and Kant is simply not on the scene.[111] It appears, then, that Hastie was correct to say Kant's practical philosophy "corrected and modernized" Roman law according to "rational and universal principles," such that the influence within Kant's philosophy runs the opposite way to Rose's suggestion, namely, from his own transcendental philosophy to his Roman-influenced philosophy of law.[112]

Rose asserts that the various connected twofold distinctions in Kant's work can be traced back to the Roman person/thing distinction as a hidden influence, organizing their logic. At first sight this seems unlikely since Kant's major, driving division is always between the empirical and *a priori*, or phenomenal and noumenal. Ideology critique, however, must find what is not obvious. Perhaps Kant's unusual (for the German tradition) valorization of private law and property vindicates Rose's suggestion. Thus: "persons and things, conditioned by each other" cannot coherently be made into "unconditioned values," they cannot become "an Ideal of Reason, or the form of the intelligible, since the basic opposition which is thereby formalized is that of the bearers of the substance of Roman private law."[113] Idealizing and reifying Roman categories, in other words, leads to a contradiction. If so, Kant's picture of freedom is one of the Roman absolute property owner combined with the modern view of atomized subjectivity. In "the sphere of private law . . . Kant's doctrine of legal order most closely reflected early liberal ideas,"[114] by giving property and possession a central place in any legitimate *Rechtsstaat*; indeed, it is the peaceful acquisition and transfer of property that dis-

111. Kelley, "Gaius," mentions Kant once in passing as a variety of natural law (634). Likewise Kelly, *Short History*, does not connect Kant with Roman law.

112. Hastie, translator's preface to *The Philosophy of Law* (usually translated *The Metaphysical Elements of Justice*).

113. *DN*, 23.

114. Thornhill, *Political Philosophy*, 110.

tinguishes the *Rechtsstaat* from the state of nature. To Kant's mind, the thought of an object that no one could possess was incoherent,[115] in contrast to traditions of the commons or sacred objects, which allowed for communal use without ownership. Property, for Kant, is *required* by pure practical reason. This leads, for example, to his view that active citizens may only be "persons of independent economic substance";[116] and to his innovation of rights *in rem* over a person, that is, the possession of persons in a thing-like fashion. This applies in the case of spouses (who mutually possess one another), children and servants (the latter two in asymmetric relations to parents and masters). Rose, however, pushes her argument too far. Not only is the category of rights *in rem* restricted to a few cases, it creates greater equality for women and protects the rights of children and servants: a progressive view for eighteenth-century Prussia.[117] It also makes slavery impossible.[118] Most importantly, freedom in Kant is centrally about performing the self-legislated, universal moral law, something she underplays.[119]

Rose points out that Kant wanted to use "for the present age" Ulpian's "three famous maxims . . . live honestly, hurt no-one, give each his due."[120] Yet as Arthur Ripstein notes, Ulpian's comment was regularly used at the time, so there is nothing particularly affine between Kant and Roman law on that score; Kant even admitted to putting content into the phrase rather than merely following it.[121] Indeed, the rationalization and codification of law was a normal practice from the fourteenth century and continuing into the time of Kant and his contemporaries Johann Gottlieb Heineccius and A. F. J. Thibaut.[122] Here again, then, the influence runs from Kant to Rome. Furthermore, why not see Kant as idealizing persons and obligations, rather than persons and things? Or, since

115. Kant, *Metaphysical Elements of Justice*, 52–53 (§2, "Juridical Postulate of Practical Reason").

116. Kelly, *Short History*, 258.

117. Kuehn, *Kant*, 398–99.

118. *DN*, 21: Rose opposes this as an idealization, preferring the speculative view that we are always both master and slave, both internally and in social relations.

119. Ameriks, "Vindicating Autonomy."

120. *DN*, 20; *Metaphysical Elements of Justice*, 42–43.

121. Ripstein, *Force and Freedom*, 37n14; Kant writes, "We give them a meaning that he himself indeed may not have had in mind" (*Metaphysical Elements of Justice*, 42).

122. Kelley, "Metaphysics of Law."

the fundamental Roman legal division is between three terms not two (persons, things and obligations), idealizing all three (which may put him closer to Hegelian triune logic)? Or, why not see the Roman distinction as neutral enough to be common to any number of ways of thinking?[123] For J. M. Kelly, the "Greek inspiration of these [Ulpian's] maxims seems unmistakable";[124] they are not uniquely Roman.

It could be objected against my foregoing treatment that I miss the mode of Rose's handling of Kant's texts, by being too wooden and literal. Clearly there is an echo in Rose's argument of Adorno's approach, based on the view that when texts are read only to divine the author's intentions, whole swathes of thought are ignored, such as the general climate of their thinking and its relation to their own society.[125] I do not think this objection, holds, however, as I have tried to read Kant's texts in relation to their social and historical background as Rose presents it. Her argument is that Kant's rationality reflects Roman law, which is similar to the bourgeois property form and the public-private split it creates, and that Kant's version of autonomy supports *dominium* over property. I have argued her charge does not stick even with this wider context in mind. Where Rose's charges are on target, she picks up where Kant does express elements of bourgeois society (as we will see in §4.1); where she is not, she blames Kant for bowdlerized uses of his thought. Indeed, although Rose opposed the Hegel myth prevalent at the time, she accepted a caricatured picture of Kant overturned by later scholarship. Furthermore, Rose should have known better, as she had written of Adorno's criticisms of philosophy:

> It is difficult . . . to judge the move from revealing irreconcilable antinomies in central concepts to establishing the social origins of those antinomies. This is partly because the move is always accomplished by means of chiasmus and analogy, and partly because there are no criteria by which to judge that this move is the only one which can account for the antinomies discerned, nor any reason why the subject/object relation should be considered uniquely as a social relationship. The only partial criterion is the internal cogency of the analogy.[126]

123. "This presumably exhaustive classification represents, in effect, one enduring expression of the metaphysical foundations of social thought" (Kelley, "Gaius," 621).

124. Kelly, *Short History*, 67.

125. Adorno, *Kant's* Critique, 161–62.

126. *TMS*, 76.

If "autonomy is the supreme concept in Kant's moral philosophy, and by implication also of Kant's theory of knowledge,"[127] and Rose is interested in how such autonomy really exists and functions in modern societies, it would be no surprise she would welcome a reading like Adorno's, which connects Kant's view of autonomy to the coercive nature of the law on the statute books. Yet, Rose did not regard law as merely "the foundation of the coercive character of society";[128] law for her was also enabling—socially by granting rights and psychologically by affecting the inner life of individuals (enlarging it, to the extent of hypertrophy). Nor does she undialectically oppose autonomy to mutual dependency. Thus, her reading differs somewhat from Adorno's, though it highlights the precarious nature of Rose's Adornian interpretative social philosophy and ideology critique (the fact of which both Rose and Adorno were well aware[129]).

To summarize: Rose developed a form of ideology critique aimed at revealing determinations of the formation of philosophical consciousness by different epochs of jurisprudence. She compares affinities between patterns of thinking and judging within a historical legal form and those within a social philosophy, to discern problems in the latter. With regards to Kant, she claims that bourgeois property law, as a form of objective spirit in his society, influenced his philosophy, which expresses it without being as critical of it as it should be. The similarities between property in Kant, Roman law and his society provide the springboard from which Rose investigates this link. I argued in the case of Kant the ideology critique does not quite work because there is not enough affinity between the form of Kant's philosophy in general and the form of Roman law to support Rose's claims. The recourse to Roman law as ideology critique does, however, highlight problems with Kant's practical philosophy, and suggests his application of freedom was more dominated by property than his statements on freedom as the dignity of autonomy imply. Although it is a far-reaching criticism it does not quite fit the bill of the form of Kant's rationality as a whole. Her critique does reveal problems with legal formalism in general, which beset current legal and political forms. Since she takes Kant's philosophy as in some ways expressing current social forms, this is no accident. Her critique

127. Adorno, *Kant's* Critique, 54.

128. Ibid., 55.

129. O'Connor, *Adorno*, 23–52.

seems to work better on the poststructuralists than on Kant,[130] but its concatenated form leaves some ambiguities in place. If Rose is arguing there are forms of objective spirit bodying forth feudal and Homeric legal forms still operative in contemporary society and influencing unduly the work of Foucault and Heidegger, she is not clear about where these forms of objective spirit are located (which is not to say they do not exist). If, conversely, she is arguing simply that their models of power and politics are somewhat defective because they rely too much on earlier models of power fully to address contemporary questions of legitimacy, then she is not making an argument about the influence of objective spirit on consciousness as she believed, but an argument about more straightforward theoretical inadequacy (following perhaps from an insufficient appreciation of the intellectual tradition, which certainly is part of her argument in any case). This seems more like a Nietzschean genealogical critique, discerning sedimented remnants of past legal epochs pushing to the surface in different thinkers. This ambiguity is somewhat resolved in her later work, when she criticizes poststructural/postmodern philosophy for an inadequate response to rationalization in the Weberian sense. We return to this in the next chapter.

4 Jurisprudential Wisdom

I have spent some time on Rose's argument about the form of Kant's philosophy despite judging it a failure because the opening of *Dialectic of Nihilism* is instructive in three ways. First, it shows how Rose's ideology critique via law is supposed to work: a social philosophy and legal epoch are expounded and compared for affinities and illuminations. Second, despite Rose's misfire against Kant, she fleshes out the charge of legal formalism in Kant's philosophy. Rose's argument is more successful when redirected as a criticism of elements of Kant's practical philosophy than against the whole form of his thinking. It serves to support a social and political philosophy inspired by Hegel's *Philosophy of Right*. Third, it begins to reveal her concept of jurisprudential wisdom as the use of law to gain a view of the social totality, and an expansive view of jurisprudence as examining the links between the metaphysical, ethical and legal. It also shows Rose's integration of the jurisprudential tradition with her

130. For dissenting views, see the reviews of *DN* by Bennington, Murphy, and Lash; in support of Rose, see those by Norris, Grier, Beck and Raffel.

Hegelian and Frankfurt sources. Having discussed the first, I turn now to the other two.

4.1 The legal formalism charge

If Rose fails to show Roman legal influence on the form of Kant's thought as a whole, she succeeds in providing greater background and substance to *Hegel Contra Sociology*'s critique of the bourgeois property form shaping Kant's practical philosophy, including his view of subjectivity, the state, property, and the relation between public and private law. Kant's use of Roman categories in his legal, social and political philosophy can be criticized for being too thin, excluding *Sittlichkeit*. If Rose had pitched her argument against elements of Kant's practical philosophy, rather than the form of his philosophy as a whole, she would have been on much firmer ground. Her argument could then be read as supporting Hegel's critique of Kant's philosophy of right. "Hegel draws from Roman law throughout his works,"[131] writes William Conklin, and Hegel developed two ideas in so doing. First, the person in Roman law is not the subject. A subject has interiority into which s/he can withdraw when faced with externality, but "the Roman subject was only recognized as an abstract legal person emptied of intentionality."[132] Second, this abstractness means Roman law "defined the subject to the point that the social relationships, with which Hegel is concerned, were a forgotten remainder."[133] That is why Hegel says Rome had an abstract existence. "Ethical life is sundered without end into the extremes of the private self-consciousness of *persons* . . . and *abstract universality*,"[134] a bad logical conclusion of differentiation: "all individuals [*Einzelnen*] are degraded to the level of private persons equal with one another, possessed of formal rights, and the only bond left to hold them together is an abstract, monstrously insatiable self-will."[135]

Rose's critique thereby provides reason to reconsider a more Hegelian approach to social and political philosophy.[136] Hegel believed in three

131. Conklin, *Hegel's Laws*, 48.

132. Ibid., 50.

133. Ibid.

134. *PhR*, §357.

135. Ibid. Rose is beginning to broach the problem of juridification, that is, laws protect individuals but can also hollow out the ethical life of the social spheres they regulate. See Loick, "Juridification and Politics," 757–78.

136. Cf. Neuhouser, *Foundations*. Rose has much in common here with Honneth,

levels of freedom with corresponding forms of law and reasoning. The first and crudest was abstract right, in which humans are legal persons. The picture is of atomized individuals asserting their will over possessions in pursuing particular purposes. This gives individuals actuality, self-ownership and freedom (i.e., neither slavery nor serfdom) and is therefore "epoch-making and deeply liberating" but it cannot generate any substantial political or legal universality.[137] The second level regards humans as subjects: "that is, where they recognize that their wills are restricted by those of other persons, who have equally legitimate legal claims, and that the realm of human freedom must be regulated by universal moral standards and duties."[138] This is expressed as morality: using reason to determine duties and rights. Kant's philosophy is its highest expression. The third level is the substantial unity-in-difference of a state that allows for civil society and the economy as distinguishable arenas. Hegel's three levels of right and society become part of Rose's broken middle. As we saw in the first chapter, Rose does not think antinomies would be resolved even in the highest level of a state embodying absolute ethical life because tragic conflict and structural illusions always remain, but the more a state embodies absolute ethical life the more it "reduces the paradox" of political aporias by mediating between them. Rose's position attempts to incorporate Hegel's belief in the state as the legitimate, rational framing of modern life, and the Weberian-Marxist-Nietzschean pessimism about the state as a monopoly of violence and coercion, which, *qua* monopoly, is frequently irrational and unjust. The broken middle recognizes the perdurance of both moments in modern politics.

4.2 Jurisprudential wisdom and social philosophy

At the end of *Dialectic of Nihilism*, Rose names her approach "jurisprudential wisdom."[139] We can discern within it two tasks for social philosophy. The first, as we have seen, is a form of ideology critique uncovering the connected legal and metaphysical categories at work in social philosophy. This in itself implies a view of social philosophy as involving metaphysical, legal and ethical connections. The second is to use law and

---

Freedom's Right, on which see the next chapter.

137. Thornhill, *Political Philosophy*, 119.

138. Ibid., 120.

139. *DN*, 212.

jurisprudence to gain a view of the social totality in both senses noted in chapter 2: an overall view of society leading into absolute ethical life. Rose's reaction against poststructuralism was based on its "displacing or rejection of social and political theory and a return to a less sociological position."[140] This stems from responses to Kant, whose "Copernican revolution in philosophy left us with no legitimate theoretical knowledge of the whole, the infinite, things in themselves, the totality."[141] The neo-Kantian *Geltungslogik* (including metacritique) kept the form of condition/precondition but not the unknowability of noumena because it dropped the phenomena/noumena distinction. It then became "an inquiry into the constitution of scientific object domains rather than into the conditions of experience as such. *Geltungslogik* describes the unknowable but productive principles of these scientific regional ontologies."[142] Derrida's *différance* is an example of an unknowable but productive principle. Deconstruction is neo-Kantian in its logical basis, but suffers in comparison to the original neo-Kantians such as Weber, Durkheim, Marx, Ihering and Cohen, because it is not as sociologically moored. It also relies on an opposition between force and expression, which is a metaphysical distinction, just as Comte's attempt to reject metaphysics rested on the (metaphysical) appeal to natural and social "forces."[143] On the one hand, then, the loss of confidence in a view of the totality as a legitimate aim for social philosophy fragmented epistemology and ontology, as well as various areas of enquiry from one another—not least sociology from philosophy. On the other hand, Rose is arguing that, approached phenomenologically (and so historically), law provides a necessary view of the totality; a way to view what social philosophies may otherwise exclude. The view of the totality afforded is not perfect, but the inevitable imperfection does not justify giving up on attempts at comprehensive views. Within discourses—competing academic discourses, for instance—one can keep provisionality, ambiguity and agnosticism in play; but, when it comes to law or policy, definitions are enacted, the stipulated essences imposed. This is unavoidable, but postmodern aversion to the possibility of legitimate coercion led many to seek to avoid it. The substitution of the free-floating nature of academic disputes, in which definitions can re-

140. Rose, "Parts and Wholes," 96–97.

141. Ibid., 97.

142. Ibid., 98.

143. Ibid.

main in dispute, for the decisionism necessary for power to operate—and to judge whether power is operating legitimately or illegitimately—was a major failure of poststructuralism in Rose's view.[144] Law is a *sine qua non* of social philosophy.

Rose's discussion of the similarities between Marx's analysis of commodity fetishism and Weber's examination of legal-rational authority is a useful example of the way law enables a view onto the social totality. As she put it in a lecture, "Marx and Weber were very well aware that the distinction between persons and things is a distinction from Roman law."[145] Marx describes money, *qua* commodity, as universal, impersonal and rational. These are the features by which Weber describes legal-rational authority, so that money can be seen as an example of legal-rational authority. Money is a thing, but things are defined in opposition to persons: as Marx and Weber knew, in and since Roman law they have been mutually defining terms. As Marx notes, *qua* thing, money relies on persons to operate: commodities cannot take themselves off to market.[146] This introduces a series of paradoxes into the form of commodities and the social life pervaded by them, which are the sites of inversions of intention and dialectical reversals. These paradoxes are the focus of Lukács's analysis of capitalism as a culture, of a society pervaded by the commodity form.[147] These paradoxes are, that money *qua* formal standard is universal, but is also particular as arising out of concrete activity. It is impersonal in the way it mediates exchanges between people; but insofar as it mediates between people it thus requires persons. Third, money is rational as the basis of calculations, but it is irrational in the way it differentiates people through the contingencies of distribution, market fluctuations, etc. The three features of the commodity form of universality, impersonality and rationality equally imply the three features of particularity, personality and irrationality; and these cannot be strictly demarcated but dialectically flow into and out of one another. Commodities rely on the legal distinction between persons and things and thereby involve a mixture of rationality and irrationality. Viewing commodities as a form of legal-rational authority can then reveal the mixture of person/thing and rationality/irrationality at the heart of legal-rational authority, and thereby its pres-

144. *MBL*, 77–100.

145. "Simmel, Lukács and German Critical Theory," from the course "Sociological Theory and Methodology II," Sussex University. This paragraph follows the lecture.

146. Ch. 2 of *Capital*, vol. 1.

147. *JAM*, 57–59.

ence in other forms such as bureaucracy.[148] Rose's analysis goes further in seeing the person-thing distinction transposed into persons and things themselves. The most famous aspect of commodity fetishism is the way persons are treated as things and things as persons,[149] but Rose points out that both persons and things are treated as both persons and things. Things (commodities) are of course treated as things, yet insofar as they are reified (and Rose accepts reification as a central category of capitalist society)[150] they begin to govern human life, to exert control over humans, and so in a sense become persons while persons become things before them. Persons too are both personified and "thingified."[151] "A person is a legal term for the bearer of rights and duties, including the ownership of labor power, and labor power, which is part of the individual, becomes the thing which can be bought and sold."[152] Here, then, an originally Roman legal distinction between persons and things is seen to structure, in various permutations, the commodity form, and so society as a whole and the people within it; and to provide a perspective on the dominant form of rationality in modern society.

The historicality of Rose's approach and its "failing toward" totality thus follows Marx and Weber in providing a way to theorize substantively about society, but it also follows Hegel in bringing both elements into the logic of social theory itself. In chapter 1 we saw Hegel's logic was a theory of logical categories that was its own metatheory because it included its own logical possibility within itself by developing the logical categories we use to think. Hegel's phenomenology and logic show our current categories are historically attained but nevertheless some are *a priori* necessary. Rose's social philosophy is its own metatheory because it includes within itself both its logical and its sociohistorical preconditions, by learning from phenomenology the historically developed nature of moral and epistemological categories, some of which gain in reliability as

148. Weber of course spoke of three kinds of rationality—traditional, charismatic and legal-rational; but from the point of view of the latter, which dominates modern society, the other two appear increasingly irrational.

149. Cf. the famous passage from *Capital*, vol. 1, ch. 1, sect. 4.

150. The discussion of Lukács in *JAM*, 57–59, offers a very condensed example of Rose's speculative method at work. Cf. *DN*, 2.

151. *JAM*, 58n16: "Although Marx does not use the word *Verdinglichung* (reification) in the *Grundrisse* or in the first vol. of *Capital*, he does employ *als Personifikationen*."

152. "Simmel, Lukács and German Critical Theory," from the course "Sociological Theory and Methodology II," Sussex University.

they survive the phenomenological testing process. Rather than a theory of ideal conditions, which produces an abstract model of society that can never be attained, "better to include the pre-conditions in the notion of the desired order, and operate with something realistic": a social theory should "include . . . its own conditions, rather than taking them for granted and then declaring itself unavailable for most of mankind through the absence of suitable pre-conditions."[153] Of course social philosophy lacks the *a priori* necessity to be found in pure logic. It is impossible to think without using the categories of cause and effect, but people and societies can get along without recourse to mutual recognition. In that sense, it will be a social philosophy "for us," for those already committed to certain values; yet it does not eschew attempts at a certain universalism and completeness. The fact that choosers of fundamental values are always culturally formed does not render value choice arbitrary, and phenomenology provides a way to show the logical testing of various forms of value. Phenomenology scrutinizes the rationality of its preconditions so it need neither rubber-stamp current historical forms with a rational imprimatur nor be viciously circular. Such phenomenology explains the Frankfurt School commitment, shared by Rose, to "rational reconstruction," a hybrid between normative and descriptive theory.[154] Asking where we stand in relation to the Hegelian dialectic is thus to

> investigate the possibility of an ethics which does not remain naive [*sic*] and ignorant of its historical and political presuppositions and hence of its likely outcomes. Such an ethics requires a comprehensive account of substance and subject, of modernity and subjectivity; an account, that is, of the modern fate of ethical life: of the institutional and individual inversions of meaning in the modern state and society, where increase in subjective freedom is accompanied by decrease in objective freedom, where the discourses of individual rights distract from the actualities of power and domination.[155]

Having a view of the totality also requires having a view of theory's relation to that totality, since the two are internally related. Absolute ethical life then emerges from the speculative reading of the social totality. It is an unattainable goal but nevertheless held up as a model for society. A

153. Both quotations from Gellner, *Conditions of Liberty*, 189.

154. See ch. 4 §3.1.

155. *MBL*, 70–71.

full depiction of it is deliberately kept vague, so as not to impose an unacceptable morality or political culture on a population. On the other hand, mutual recognition is seen as both immanent to modern society—so not imposed—and capable of providing a robust enough picture to help society move toward absolute ethical life, of which it is a major part—so answering some of the vagueness problem raised against Rose.

Rose argues social philosophy cannot be fully performed without a jurisprudential perspective. She reads Hegel, Marx and Nietzsche as early sociopolitical philosophers aware of how legal conceptions and forms filter through into social philosophy. Ignorance on this score prevents social philosophy from full self-comprehension and leaves it more exposed to the inversions of its proposals. Here again, Rose's Frankfurt anti-positivism is important. In 1981 Rose argued that speculative logic better described the best practice of social theorists and that explicit awareness of it could prevent substantive errors. George Steinmetz's 2005 edited volume makes a complementary argument: although many humanities scholars oppose the *theory* of positivism, in *practice* it frequently remains the "epistemological unconscious of the contemporary social sciences."[156] Despite having been "declared anachronistic" in the 1900s (Lenin), 1930s (Parsons), 1960s–70s (Adorno, Gouldner, Giddens), "positivism's uncanny persistence in the human sciences up to the present moment"[157] endures. Rose's argument therefore remains contemporary. The broken middle is not an ideal theory never finding perfect expression in real conditions. Rose does not develop a universal concept of law or democracy or society or community and then lament its imperfect realization in various places and times. She neither gives up on rationality and universality nor expects the complete kind of universality that some philosophical approaches do. The subtle differences at the metatheoretical level, in what is expected and demanded from theory and reason, and the differences between what people believe they are doing and what they actually do, have effects at the substantive level.

Rose's view may be a minority but it is not a lone voice. Sean Coyle, for example, argues many of the same points as Rose: "From the earliest times, philosophical texts on politics put law at the centre of their reflections upon the character of the 'City.'"[158] Since H. L. A. Hart's legal positiv-

156. Keane, "Estrangement, Intimacy, and the Objects of Anthropology," 59.

157. Steinmetz, introduction to *Politics of Method*, 2.

158. "Legality and the Liberal Order," 401. Cf. Rose, "Dispute over Marx and Weber."

ism, however, there has been among some a narrowing of jurisprudence, separating it from any metaphysical, social or moral ideas, relying on "facts" and philosophers' "intuitions." "This separation was not simply a dogma . . . but a determination of the field of inquiry itself."[159] Some legal philosophers in this mold would claim that their "characterisation of legal order applies to law in all its manifestations, not simply that of the liberal order. . . . But many of the assumptions involved . . . indicate a specifically liberal vision of legal order . . . the modern liberal order is the immediate context to which, for better or worse, jurisprudential understandings must be directed. It is this 'City' that the jurist's explanations must elucidate."[160] Theory and society are reciprocally conceptualized, whether intentionally or not. Whereas Rose's implied totality of the unity of law and ethics concerns what it would be like for *us* to embody our shared ethos and normative commitments in law, and thereby explicitly foregrounds its beginning in the middle, the "veil of ignorance" approach has led some liberal thinkers to conflate the universal and particular in the wrong way.

We can thus take the work of Sean Coyle as an example of the Rosean approach,[161] with the following caveat. Coyle's criticisms of legal positivism apply only to some of the field. Hart himself, for instance, was very alert to the antinomy of law: "Many such assertions either fail to make clear the sense in which the connection between law and morals is alleged to be necessary; or upon examination they turn out to mean something which is both true and important, but which it is most confusing to present as a necessary connection between law and morals."[162] One of the advantages of Hart's positivism as a theory of law is its ability to say, "This is law but iniquitous,"[163] and thus to identify laws before an answer to normative questions is settled. As with Rose's critique of sociology, then, Coyle's critique of legal positivism should not be taken as condemning jurisprudence as a whole.

159. Coyle, "Legality and the Liberal Order," 402.

160. Ibid.

161. *From Positivism to Idealism*. Coyle cites *DN* on p. 17 but is not heavily reliant on her work.

162. Hart, *Concept*, 202. As Gardner notes (*Law as a Leap*, 48–49), legal positivism is a thesis about legal validity not a whole theory of law, so it is compatible with various views of law-ethics relations. Rose's point is the focus on validity can distract attention from metaphysical issues.

163. Hart, *Concept*, 210–11.

Coyle shows the effects of expecting the wrong kind of universality from philosophy of law. Within some strands of legal positivism the "status of the philosopher's 'necessary conditions' thus hovers uneasily between a stipulative definition and a sociological claim that a certain form of regulatory framework is *in fact* most prevalent among existing forms of social order."[164] This wavers between the attempt to define the concept of law universally in abstraction from all its manifestations, yet also the assumption that something like the current English or American system is close to the real nature of law, which fits exactly Rose's description of the quasi-transcendental form of metacritiques as vacillating between transcendental and empirical in the wrong way. Where this happens, legal positivism tries "to ascertain the necessary or 'essential' conditions for the existence of a legal system; but . . . the identification of *those* conditions (in place of some other list) serves to articulate a sociological judgment about the instances of legal order that actually exist."[165] Choices about central cases are already based on conceptions of law, and central cases are taken as illuminating the nature of law. Thus there is a fundamental methodological unclarity within this kind of legal positivism between describing actual practice and making universal claims, precisely because it is neo-Kantian (in Rose's terms). Once again we meet the circularity of socio-logic in which thought and reality, subject and object, are internally related, because the way the object is conceptualized partially constructs the object itself (and the subject in relation to it). The difference between neo-Kantian and speculative circularity is again a crucial issue.

Phenomenology as Rose practices it also wishes to achieve something close to universality, it does not wish to confine itself to the parochial or particular, but it is more aware *in practice* that such universal forms are never attained. The legal positivism Coyle identifies may even acknowledge this in theory but its way of going on does not reflect it. The theory is not consistently its own metatheory, and so (unconscious) metatheoretical errors create theoretical errors. "The possibility of fruitful inquiry into the moral nature of law is therefore obscured by the prevalence of disputes about the characteristics of the 'concept' of law, so that jurisprudential argument consists largely in advancing rival and incompatible versions of this concept, which jurists then assert and oppose

164. Coyle, *Positivism to Idealism*, 3.

165. Ibid., 2.

to each other. . . . [They] have largely abandoned the traditional attempt to comprehend the ethical nature of that experience."[166] The same pattern sometimes repeats itself in the circularity and non-neutrality of political theories grounded in the state of nature.[167] Such theory assumes that in the state of nature a collection of individuals will want to decide their situation through equal discussion to reach a consensus—an already liberal impulse thus begging the question. Likewise, the narrow analytic jurisprudence criticized by Coyle eschews metaphysical elaborations of law and wishes to reach reflective equilibrium between rational clarification and "intuitions." As Coyle points out, the danger is always that intuitions and common sense have been smuggled in rather than transformed. The testing of intuitions against reason is inevitable, but the question is how that process is thought of and carried out. If the process is described as rational clarification to reach reflective equilibrium there can be no objection. It is the wider set of expectations and ways of going on that determine just what these mean; and this is where problems arise.[168] Legal positivist "conceptual analysis" does help clarify to a great extent but it can also mistake the nature of its enquiries and goals due to its overambitious hope and metatheoretical inaccuracies.

Even if these methodological (in the loose sense of the word) cautions against reductionism and metatheoretical ambiguity are accepted, it may still be objected that jurisprudential wisdom fails to provide satisfaction if it does not forward any specific theses or positions. Even if one accepted Hart and Kant had made metatheoretical and substantive errors, their work remains extremely powerful and generative for contemporary thinking. Rose's own work risks lapsing into unfairness without recognizing these real achievements. Yet since Rose accepts the need for different sociological viewpoints her account is structurally open to the insights of jurisprudes too.

166. Coyle, *Positivism to Idealism*, 3–4.

167. "Legality and the Liberal Order"; cf. the discussion in ch. 1 of Hegel's critique of natural law.

168. Cf. Kamenka and Erh-Soon Tay, "Beyond Bourgeois Individualism"; cited in *DN*, 176–77.

5 Conclusion

Jurisprudential wisdom was a development of Rose's social philosophy in several ways. It continued the critique of society and social philosophy on the basis of a Hegelian philosophy and metaphilosophy that speculatively posited absolute ethical life as a social totality. It used law as a way to view the social totality and argued explicit knowledge of law was necessary to social philosophy and must be pursued in connection with its ethical and metaphysical entanglements. Law is a condition of possibility of ethics and politics, and of social philosophy, and a privileged place for observing the speculative identity of metaphysical ideas and their social manifestations and inversions. Indeed, one of social philosophy's tasks is to bring to explicit awareness the tensions and aporias in a culture or form of *Geist*, to make them exist for and not just in philosophical consciousness, to make them *an und für sich*. Shifting law within philosophical consciousness from *an sich* to *an und für sich* is Rose's unique form of ideology critique of philosophical consciousness and its formation. The increasing distance between the disciplines of philosophy and sociology created distortions in the theorizing of law and ethics, including their abstraction from one another. The "speculative identity of form and history" nevertheless reveals the interlinking of legal and metaphysical categories and forms of thinking in social philosophies. Jurisprudential wisdom aims to reveal these connections and separations in order to enable a better assessment of their role within theory and society, to assist philosophical consciousness in self-comprehension by revealing law as one crucial condition of its formation. In this way Rose integrated jurisprudence into her Hegelian and Frankfurt sources.

Jurisprudential wisdom also provided support for a Hegelian political philosophy in which theories reflect their social context and therefore should do so as thoroughly and knowingly as possible by incorporating their own social and logical preconditions into their theorizing. Thus, rather than grounding a theory on some allegedly universal and given starting point, constructive and critical theories should deliberately and reflexively "begin in the middle" by taking a phenomenological view of their own history. It follows that a theory should begin by assessing what "we" do and think in order to clarify and criticize it to reach out toward something more comprehensive (more universal), but not in the hope of removing all ambiguity or settling on complete universality. This leads Rose to share Hegel's view of individual, civil society and state as fundamental to modern society yet in tension, and his attempt to sublate not abandon the rationally self-legislating legal and moral person into a thicker concept of the subject. It also follows that theory and metatheory must be kept in constant interaction. The recurrence of positivism in social, political, ethical and legal theories shows how difficult it is to maintain these deceptively simple requirements. The combination of descriptive and normative moments in Frankfurt theories alerted Rose to the sensitivity of theory to metatheoretical commitments, and we saw that jurisprudence has the same sensitivity, insofar as it often involves both moments. Social philosophy should not expect to eliminate the antinomies of law, especially the tensions between law and ethics and between facts and norms, but to provide a workable mediation of them, which can contribute to a "good enough justice." At the same time, social philosophy must be critical rather than affirming injustice, oppression, or social pathologies. Legal formalism can become one such pathology, antinomianism another. Mutual recognition may be capable of avoiding both such mistakes, or at least revealing them as mistakes. These themes were developed in Rose's later work.

4

The Broken Middle

Incremental improvements upon unsatisfactory circumstances are the best we can hope for, and probably all we should seek.

—Tony Judt, *Ill Fares the Land*

1 Introduction

By now we have seen Rose's view of reason as phenomenologically constituted, self-limiting and speculative; her stress on the importance of law for social theorizing; and her opposition to the elimination of metaphysics therefrom. We have seen that absolute ethical life as the implied unity of law and ethics plays both a theoretical and normative role for social theorizing. A false version of the unity of law and ethics imagines their seamless integration, a cozy *Sittlichkeit* expressed unproblematically and without remainder in positive law. An alternative false version entirely separates law and ethics: an ethically pure community opposes a wholly illegitimate and coercive legal and state apparatus. Rose referred to these visions as "community" and opposed them on the basis of her socio-philosophically grounded awareness of the necessary tensions between self, society and state. In this chapter I fill out Rose's picture of these tensions, which provide a critical theory of fundamental features of modern society and at the same time a critique of social philosophies that ignore these features. I show Rose's mature social philosophy, the "idea and analysis"[1] of the broken middle (§2), operating as a phenomenology of modern theory and society (§2.1) via the two main diremptions occupying her attention, namely, between state and civil society (§2.2) and between law and ethics (§2.3). The latter section includes Rose's critique of postmodern ("new") ethics (§2.3.1) and her alternative of "suspended" and "equivocal" ethics (§2.3.2): in ethics as in epistemology theory must reflect the dialectical mediations between subject and object, which means incorporating mediation at the beginning of ethical thinking. I show in §3 how Rose has both a useful balance in intellectual mood in relation to politics, and a normative stratum to her social philosophy insofar as mutual recognition is one of its intrinsic moments. This overcomes the charge that Rose's work lacked the means to ward off the relativism or ethical nihilism she detected in poststructuralism. My exposition continues to trace Rose's chronological and conceptual trajectory, focusing on 1992's *The Broken Middle*, though I refer to her later works as I proceed where they illuminate her thought by application and example. In the previous chapters I clarified key features of Rose's work by using other thinkers, some unknown to Rose, who were nevertheless good examples of her thought at work (Bhaskar, Bourdieu, Catto and Woodhead, Giddens, Habermas, Martin, Coyle). Likewise here I go beyond Rose's own examples of her social philosophy and consider other work that may be taken to exemplify and fill out her thought. I discuss Sara Farris's work on the "Muslim question" to show the enduring relevance of the state-society diremption (§2.2). I refer to other theories of recognition (§3.1), which complement Rose's work insofar as they give further definition to her main normative ideal, and I suggest how her retention of the recognition-appropriation dialectic from Hegel shapes her ethics of recognition in a novel and noteworthy way. This chapter therefore completes my examination of Rose's trilogy, shows its unity as the core of her coherent social philosophy, and how that theory may be used in various fields of social theorizing. It shows how Rose integrated the thought of Marx, Arendt and Weber into her Hegelian-Adornian philosophy, and puts in place the final major pieces of the synoptic vision of her work necessary to a proper appreciation thereof.

1. *MBL*, 38.

2 The Broken Middle

The broken middle was Rose's term for her mature vision of her social philosophy as well as for a characterization of modern society, one she felt often lacking from social philosophies, although its effects were discernible on them. The continuity between *The Broken Middle* and Rose's earlier work thus emerges from the foregoing exposition. As with her earlier books, however, its range and ambition (and in this case, obscurity) repay a prefatory remark about the aims of its argument. The argument has three connected moments: it is, first, an immanent critique of contemporary theory (§2.1); designed, second, to further Rose's meta-philosophical position on philosophy and reason; while, third, developing Rose's social philosophy via an examination of the state-society diremption (§2.2) and the law-ethics diremption (§2.3). Whereas her previous book developed ideology critique of theory by reference to jurisprudence, here the critique is at once immanent and by reference to the failure of theories to give due attention to the nature of society as a broken middle. Rose constantly weaves together the theoretical and metatheoretical dimensions of the broken middle, but for heuristic purposes I discuss her phenomenology of contemporary theory and modernity's fundamental diremptions separately below. *The Broken Middle* further fleshes out Rose's view of philosophy and reason. "The book is about philosophy, its possibilities, objects, burdens and conditions."[2] Hence her book "means to be a configuring and re-configuring of philosophy in its most basic conceptual, existential and historical elements." It is therefore "necessarily meta-philosophical and philosophical at the same time." It "represents Rose's vision of the necessity and nature of a contemporary self-limiting rationalism." She shows that comprehension goes hand in hand with "acknowledging what escapes comprehension, existential pathos or politics." As we have seen, Rose believes her approach enables philosophy to play its role in culture by speaking to the existential and political questions of modern life.

Rose was also again drawing a different map of the theoretical terrain: uniting Hegel and Kierkegaard; arguing for an essential continuity between ostensibly opposed political theology and postmodern philosophy; offering alternative and surprising interpretations of and links between thinkers; offering a set of terms to think through the material

2. This quotation and those in the rest of the paragraph are from J. Bernstein's reader's report on *BM* for the publisher, 18 April 1991, n.p., box 36.

(violence in love and love in violence, agon of authorship, anxiety of beginning, equivocation of the middle, pathos of the concept [terms I will discuss below]). She stated "the general aim and ambition of the work" was "to rewrite/reconceive the map of the intellectual terrain (accepted from Heidegger, Derrida, Foucault, Deleuze—as discussed in the propaedeutic to this work *Dialectic of Nihilism*) in a way that must be the concern of *everyone* engaged in debates across the humanist and social scientific disciplines . . . more specifically, to show that *speculative* exposition . . . can accommodate everything post-modernity is convinced it omits, and still *produce a critical account of modernity*."[3]

These aims explain Rose's "high altitude" style. The worry may arise that her work is too high altitude to be useful, which is why Bernstein, Pippin and others are needed to explain the thinking behind her work. In response, it may be noted that high altitude views have their place. Rose's social philosophy is focused on the macro-picture because it aims to combine both theoretical and practical philosophy; to connect an epistemology with social philosophy, ethics, jurisprudence and politics. Its ambition is unfashionable but not an *a priori* mark against it. Rose's first two books were detailed studies of the whole corpus of Adorno and Hegel, with extensive reference to the relevant literature of critical theory, sociology, German idealism and neo-Kantianism; hence Rose, as it were, earned her high altitude view by the detailed background work. Ambitious, large-scale, high altitude theories gain traction by the compelling and illuminating nature of their vision, but they face a double danger. On one side they are vulnerable to the death of a thousand cuts. As each specialist disagrees with the reading of his or her figure, period or area, the plausibility of the overall scheme is called into doubt. Conversely, they run the risk of reductionism insofar as their single narrative or cluster of central ideas explains everything passing through it. As Edith Wyschogrod remarked about *Judaism and Modernity*, Rose's "major difficulty lies in a lumping together of virtually all the thinkers discussed as having failed in their efforts to comprehend the conceptual underpinning of modernity and as having done so on virtually identical grounds. All are alleged to have denounced or misrepresented reason and to have replaced it with Reason's 'sublime Other,' thus precluding efforts to think the split itself."[4] Yet contra Wyschogrod, Rose's work *as a whole* is in fact

3. Letter to John Milbank, 12 June 1991, box 11.

4. Wyschogrod, review of *JAM*, 268–70.

complex enough to refer to several sources of error—rationalized reason, insufficient awareness of preconditions, inflexible transcendentalism, avoidance of law or metaphysics, mishandling of fundamental diremptions—and is therefore not crudely reductive. This example of distorting Rose's work by reading only one part of it shows the necessity of the comprehensive and synoptic reconstruction I provide. She is perhaps more vulnerable to the first danger, since her readings of individual figures remain controversial (not least because they are unusual), and one can always disagree with her focus on the two diremptions (perhaps one thinks other diremptions are more important, or society is not so dirempted as she thinks, and so on). All large-scale theories face this problem and their success is best measured not by perfection in every detail but how illuminating and generative they are.

2.1 A "phenomenology of modern theory" and society

J. Bernstein describes *The Broken Middle* as a "phenomenology of modern theory that works *within* the dialectic of ethical life rather than being about it."[5] Through this phenomenology Rose brings out the connections between her Hegelian epistemology and social theory. It is speculative thought shown through critique rather than stated abstractly. She also criticizes the sociological failures of her contemporaries' social theory and "the separation of sociological thinking (methodological and substantive) from philosophical thinking which leads to the posing of sociological questions without a sociological culture. In *Dialectic of Nihilism* I examine the systematic destruction of social thought in post-structuralism; in my article on architecture I examine the absence of sociological thinking in post-modernism."[6] Rose shows the ways in which postmodern works explicitly witness to the broken middle and how they fail to do so, yet how that very failure can be read as another witness to the broken middle. This rearticulates Hegel's criticism of theories that fail to take account of their uses in society.[7] When theories propose solutions without considering their mediation through social and political diremptions, their solutions are liable to be subverted and distorted by those diremptions, often producing the very opposite of what was intended.

5. Bernstein, *Ethical Life*, 8.
6. Letter to Warwick Registrar, 26 October 1989.
7. Milbank, "Living in Anxiety," 20.

She saw this phenomenon explored by, for example, Weber's work on Protestantism and capitalism and Goethe's examination of Pietist beautiful soulism, but insufficiently appreciated by postmodern theory and political theology. More generally, the phenomenology of theory repeats the meta-philosophical critique of her earlier work by showing disparities between expressed theoretical commitments and actual theoretical practices. This served as a basis to critique poststructuralism, postmodern political theology, the anthropology and politics of Girard and Mann, architecture, and forms of psychoanalysis. My focus in this chapter, however, is to bring out the constructive side of Rose's social philosophy.

As Bernstein indicates, central to her social theory is Hegel's idea of the dialectic of ethical life (also called the causality of fate [to connote a culture- or society-wide return of the repressed]). The dialectic of ethical life names the contradictory ethical experiences that occur when we try to ground our selves and subjectivity otherwise than on mutual recognition.[8] That is, those parts of ethical life, which mutual recognition nurtures, but which are suppressed or alienated in contemporary society, react negatively back onto individuals, who may either experience them as a hostile fate or alternatively may discern in them their own suppressed ethical life.[9] The diremptions suffered in society—between self and society, general and concrete other, moral and ethical, universal and particular, determinate and reflective judging—cannot be put back together, but may nevertheless be felt as two torn halves of a whole we have never experienced. Speculative thought interprets the experience of them as fragments of a whole. We may then seek some sort of improvement, trying to move toward that ideal but implied whole—absolute ethical life—without imagining we may ever arrive or permanently heal the diremptions. This means recognizing "an always already presupposed alterity which in its alterity conditions the self-possession of the subject."[10] Individual autonomy thus depends on an otherness. Autonomy does not mean complete self-mastery but an appropriate measure of self-possession and appropriation of givenness in dialectical relation to undergoing influence from otherness. (The recognition and appropriation of otherness is an important meaning of *Bildung* in Rose's *oeuvre*.) The subject

8. Bernstein, *Ethical Life*, 185.

9. See ibid., 82–87, 159–96; Habermas, *Philosophical Discourse of Modernity*, 28–29, discussing Hegel's *Spirit of Christianity and Its Fate*.

10. Bernstein, *Ethical Life*, 61.

depends on substance in a "speculative recognition of self in otherness."[11] This doctrine is behind Rose's discussions of the shifting boundaries of reason, the city, the soul and the sacred. As Bernstein summarizes it:

> In the aporia of autonomy modernity attains its limit and refutation. Metaphysically, this aporia concerns the rigid *dualism* of passivity and activity, subject and object (only the purely active belongs to the subjectivity of the subject); formally, this aporia concerns the question of what the *content* of the will is, whether the will can have a content and remain a free will; materially, this aporia concerns the changing, shifting and indeterminate, *boundaries* of the self or subject, where such a being can be said to begin or end. If there can be no essential determination of the self or subject, and if the shifting boundaries of identity—from the extreme of the pure activity of thinking and willing to the extreme of sheer external givenness—are co-extensive with the will, then the hope of instituting a substantial conception of autonomy must collapse.[12]

If the struggle against heteronomy, viewed not only as the wills of others but also the resistance of the self and nature, is pursued as aiming at complete autonomy, it turns out to be a struggle against our own suppressed life. This heteronomy must be recognized for what it is—an essential part of ourselves—and the political and ethical life for which we struggle must include rather than suppress it. Hegel framed this as a critique of Kantian moral formalism (better, thinness), to which he opposed life, love, forgiveness and recognition as necessary components of any ethical theory hoping adequately to represent our ethical lives and experience, in a universality thick enough to be substantive. But these concepts undermine full autonomy in the sense that they show our interdependence and they cannot be demanded of others (in the manner of perfect duties) but must be freely given. Bernstein here provides a way to flesh out Rose's speculative view of activity and passivity, personification and reification.

The internally linked critique of theory and society emerges in another way too, as another form of the critique of rationalized reason. Again Bernstein draws it out from the dialectic of ethical life. From within the diremption of universal and particular, the universal is usually privileged in legal-rational thinking, such that normativity is thought to

11. Ibid., 82.

12. Bernstein, "Autonomy and Solitude," 193–94.

be "the deriving of judgments from universal premises or procedures," whereas from Rose's speculative view that sees universal and particular as pointing to but never actually making a whole, the particular is also given its due such that the "validity of rules and norms that are to protect those injurable particulars must make essential reference to them."[13] This involves freeing "reflective judgment from its confines in aesthetics by showing it as a general ethical and cognitive strategy. . . . For the same reason that we cannot discursively vindicate why the deep luminosity of the blue of the sky in 'this' painting is essential to the beauty of the whole, although we can art-critically point to it, so the injurability of the body (which negatively reveals the body's 'integrity') cannot be wholly vindicated as morally relevant in discursive-subsumptive terms."[14] Hence:

> Belief in moral reason becomes irrational when it excludes either self-reflection or the conditions of its employment [when it ceases to be speculative] but the conditions for the employment of moral reason are not themselves rational in the narrow sense since they must include sustaining belief in reason and morality as life practices; and, tendentially, all object-oriented, heteronomous moral codes and theories undermine belief in valuing since they devalue or suppress the activity of valuing, valuing-giving and creating, itself.[15]

This is a classic case of dialectical inversion. A morality that seeks greater security by basing itself on objective reason, safe from the whims of the subject, ends up undermining itself by cutting away at its own conditions of possibility.

The dialectic of ethical life matters for Rose's social philosophy not only as it relates to subjects' reliance on one another in mutual recognition but also in the way theoretically articulated ideals relate to their social context. As Rose put it, the political ideal of moral autonomy is quite compatible with social and political heteronomous restrictions on freedom:[16]

> "Spirit" in this sense of "spiritual-animal kingdom" pervades Hegel's phenomenology, his exposition of modernity and the paradoxes of subjectivity. Kant's inner, moral autonomy is seen

13. Both quotations from Bernstein, *Ethical Life*, 166.
14. Ibid., 166–67.
15. Bernstein, "Autonomy and Solitude," 199.
16. Evidenced in Jones, *Establishment*.

> to be quite compatible with its purported contrary—outer, legal heteronomy. Viewed dynamically, an increase in subjective freedom and autonomy may mean a *decrease* in objective freedom, that is to say, an increase in heteronomy. It is this dynamic and predicament of modernity according to which social actuality tends to undermine and to invert overt moral and political intentions that post-Kantian philosophy and social theory have sought to expound—without trying to overcome these meanings and their inversions, whether metaphysically or post-metaphysically, as long as they continue to be generated by their legal and political and productive preconditions.[17]

Rose's comment here is directed less at Kant than at the sociological realities of political rhetoric about freedom existing alongside restrictions in freedom, such as income, class and gender inequalities, propaganda, and all those social forces restricting the growth and exercise of genuine autonomy. In the spiritual-animal kingdom, for example, the master-slave relation is internalized within each person, and people treat each other as means while assuming they are treating one another as ends. One temptation of this arrangement is to invest in a fantasized unity, such as race, a community or the state, to lessen the discomfort of the unhappy consciousness. Another temptation is to imagine such inversions can be solved or "overcome" by theory, when in fact they are caused also by political and economic conditions. This situation is created most fundamentally by two structural and mutually reinforcing social and political conditions: the diremptions between state and civil society, and between law and ethics. These diremptions are absorbed into the persons within said society. The former creates people internally divided between a self-regarding economic realm and a universally moral political realm; the latter fosters the illusion of a personal ethic unaffected by social, political, historical conditions (an abstract, unmediated form of ethics).

> Modern politics offers no unified focus of domination: the boundaries which separate the state from civil society and *Innerlichkeit* [inwardness] from the rational, methodical organisation of everyday life are now drawn within each individual, while the non-legitimated boundaries between states still corrupt the inner boundaries, now located within each individual soul producing the modern phantasies of exclusive monopolising of

17. *JAM*, 68.

> the means of violence, which take the shape of racism, fascism, religious and ethnic exclusivity.[18]

These diremptions, their presence in contemporary theory, and the way they are expressed in multiple forms in combination with gender, race, class and religion, are the focus of *The Broken Middle*. Rose nowhere argues that these two diremptions are the only way to understand society (she refers to other diremptions such as formal equality and class inequality), but she does think they are structurally fundamental and as such necessary to any adequate social philosophy of modernity.

2.2 The state-civil society diremption

A central dimension of the broken middle as a theory of modernity is the contradictory core of the modern nation state with its civil society: Rose glosses the middle as "the political diremption of the modern state."[19] She remarked that since 1989 we have been returned more forcefully to the same sorts of questions that occupied Europeans from 1789.[20] As with all sociological terms, the meaning and content of "civil society" is debated.[21] Ernest Gellner pointed out that civil society can be contrasted with, first, small, fragmentary societies lacking in centralized political power but in which people are too tied in to roles to have the kind of freedom in modern civil society (ancient agrarian groups); second, centralized political units in which there is little freedom because political power is fused with moral certitude (Marxism); third, large political units without individualism or countervailing pluralist institutions but which have effective infrastructures and economies (some modern Muslim societies). "The simple formula for Civil Society, then, is political-coercive centralization with accountability, rotation and fairly low rewards for those manning the political apparatus, and economic pluralism."[22] For Rainer Forst, civil society "refers to a collective of free citizens who organize their common life in an autonomous and co-operative way."[23] Its meaning is

18. *MBL*, 97–98.

19. *BM*, 309.

20. Ibid., xi.

21. For a discussion of the difficulties, see Fine, "Civil Society Theory," 7–28; Foley and Edwards, "Paradox of Civil Society," 38–52.

22. Gellner, *Conditions*, 93.

23. Forst, "Civil Society," 452.

triangulated by the ancient Greek notion of a common life governed by self-rule to prevent despotism and ensure the community's interests; the idea in Adam Smith, Hegel and Marx of the differentiation between society, state and economy in modernity, in which the focus is individual freedom and the market; and the response to this in Ferguson and de Tocqueville of a less individualistic realm of freely created associations and intermediary bodies. The classic work by Jean Cohen and Andrew Arato offers the "working definition" of "a sphere of social interaction between economy and state, composed above all of the intimate sphere (especially the family), the sphere of associations (especially voluntary associations), social movements, and forms of public communication . . . institutionalized and generalized through laws, and especially subjective rights, that stabilize social differentiation."[24]

These characterizations should contextualize Rose's use of the concept of civil society. As usual Rose prefers not to offer definitions, partly heeding Nietzsche's dictum "only what has no history is definable";[25] partly because in this case a "grand theoretical explanation . . . would hypostatize the distinction. . . . It would probably result in glib philosophical generalizations, oversimplified sociological observations and misguided or dogmatic political recommendations."[26] Instead the distinction should serve as an "*interpretive standpoint* which can be of utility in historical investigations, sociological inquiry, normative discussions and political action."[27] It will become apparent below that Rose indeed views the diremption as an interpretive standpoint, and offers Arendt as an example of its historical investigation. The broken middle is "a condition and a means of investigating that condition";[28] it is, as any reflexive sociological concept should be, *explicandum* and *explicans*.

Rose's account takes off primarily from Marx's "On the Jewish Question," particularly Marx's observation that state and civil society both presuppose and contradict one another, and that the shift from feudal to modern societies involved depoliticized work and property and a bifurcation within the individual.[29] A "permanent 'mismatch' between

24. *Civil Society and Political Theory*, ix; cf. the fuller definition on p. 346.

25. *Toward a Genealogy of Morals*, bk. 2, §13.

26. Keane, introduction to *Civil Society and the State*, 14 (cited by Rose in *BM*.)

27. Ibid.

28. Gorman, "Wither," 55.

29. Henrich, "Logical Form and Real Totality," 246: "Neither state nor society can be reduced to a function of the other, as if either one represented the original actuality

the economic and political spheres is a defining characteristic of modern capitalist systems of production."[30] As a result, people lead a double life: in political life they regard one another as communal beings, but in economic life, which Marx calls civil society, they act as private individuals, treating others as means rather than ends and being so treated, and thus are not entirely free. Indeed, "political life declares itself to be only a *means*, whose end is the life of civil society."[31] As Rose put it, "Marx argues . . . that the reduction of the modern state to guaranteeing the conditions that secure the competition of civil society has the result of dividing each individual citizen into a competitive, ruthless, natural being and a fantastical being for whom the collective good of the state becomes a focus of his or her fantasy life."[32] The resulting modern legal status then involves "abstract legal personality, private property and decay of public, political life."[33] This interacts with Kantian morality's inner autonomy/outer heteronomy distinctions, providing an example of the way in which philosophical meanings are inverted by their embodiment in society. Rose regards Hegel's figure of the spiritual-animal kingdom as a way of addressing these inversions. The dynamic movement of *Geist* means Hegel can see how the social undermines and inverts political meanings, yet "without trying to overcome these meanings and their inversions . . . as long as they continue to be generated by their legal and political and productive preconditions."[34] That is, insight into these inversions cannot solve them by imposition of a philosophical *Sollen*. Yet people do succumb to the temptation to mend the diremptions by theory alone, usually by appeal to some universal: "Spirit is dirempted by modern legality and tries to mend its diremption: racism, Naziism."[35] The cen-

---

of the other. Conceived together, on the other hand, they serve to constitute a syllogistic totality—and in such a way that both also are organized internally and autonomously through further 'mediations' in each case. If the state itself can be said to emerge from society, it does so precisely as a formal implication and more developed stage of the former in terms of a syllogistic 'conclusion' [*Schluss-Folge*]."

30. Keane, introduction to *Civil Society and the State*, 7.

31. Marx, "On the Jewish Question," 44.

32. Letter to Jacqueline Rose dated 13 December 1994, box 14.

33. Draft of "Derrida, *De l'esprit*—diremption of spirit," Warwick workshops in continental philosophy, 30 November 1990, box 24. The rest of the paragraph and its quotations are from this source.

34. *JAM*, 68.

35. Cf. the abstract for "Social Utopianism and Architectural Illusion" for a conference on postmodernism and the social sciences, St Andrews University, 28–30 August

trality of misrecognition in Rose's account of *Geist* avoids this premature and dangerous pseudo-reconciliation of diremptions. It allows for "this political history of separation and its violent overcoming [to be] reconstructed—not by restricting philosophy to antimetaphysical deconstruction," but by understanding and reconstructing the relationship between metaphysics and its embodiment in politics and law, which Rose calls the "speculative identity of form and history" and a "phenomenology of form."[36] Its advantage over the anti-metaphysical deconstructionist focus on narrative and difference is, as noted earlier, its ability to cope with illusory being (*Schein*). As we have seen, in Marxism and Frankfurt theory, this becomes the idea that a phenomenon is not fully understood unless its connections to the totality are known and grounds the idea of necessary illusions. From Rose's speculative point of view it is "both legitimate and necessary to see the state as emerging from the free activity and the union of human beings as subjects of right" as much as "an organization for satisfying the needs of socialized human beings. . . . The state must be grasped in both ways at once to the extent that the very concept of the state presupposes both these modes of mediation."[37]

Rose does not contradict herself by positing modernity as diremptive without examining her act of positing; her view arises from historical-sociological investigations. Modernity "is discovered to be diremptive and is not defined, *quasi-a priori*, as a 'project'";[38] this discovery occurs by investigating modernity's political history and sociology. As we saw in chapter 1, philosophy and politics, "arise out of . . . diremption and its provisional overcoming in the culture of an era."[39] Diremption does not mean the absence of relation, but the relation of mutual dependence *and* tension. Law and ethics, and state and civil society, both require one another but pull apart.[40] Rose's aporetic universalism is a form of rationality

1989, n.p., box 23: "Architecture becomes social utopianism" and it "thereby" acquires an illusory independence, which means it becomes non-speculative and does not see its place in the whole. The illusion of independence "arises from the split between civil society and the state which continues to generate spurious holisms designed to heal the split, such as 'nation,' 'race,' 'public realm,' and 'community'—the latter with its implications of local, apolitical common-wealth."

36. Letter to Jay Bernstein, 27 March 1987.

37. Henrich, "Logical Form and Real Totality," 248.

38. *BM*, 240.

39. Ibid., 286.

40. Similar findings result from non-Marxist analyses, e.g., Thornhill, "Political Legitimacy," 161–62: "The modern political system cannot uncontrollably inflate or

that explicitly works through this tension. "While arcadian and utopian universalism would reconcile and posit the unity of particular and universal, aporetic universalism explores and experiments with the disunity of singular and universal."[41] Her social theory follows the architectonic of Hegel's *Philosophy of Right*, insofar as both affirm the structure of modern society in terms of the three spheres of individuality, civil society and the state. The shift from feudalism to modernity was marked by the centralization of sovereignty by removing power away from multiple institutions in society, tending toward the lone individual facing the state. Hegel saw civil society as a response to this. For Rose, this is not so much a fix for the problem as a way of living with it: "The mediatory institutions that have been fragmented remain the only context for self-conscious subjects. The task is to find a structure of customs inscribed in the very idea of individual freedom."[42] And this prevents identifying either individual or community as the "solution to the political problem,"[43] which occurs when they become ways of fleeing the reality of the diremption of state and society.[44]

The broken middle is thus phenomenologically "locatable—in history, in polity, in institutions, in *dominium*."[45] Rose notes that one of the meanings of *aufheben* is "to carry an opposition back to its source."[46] Much of the social theory put forward within continental philosophy and political theology was in Rose's view insufficiently sociological. She wished to show its failure properly to grapple with its own sociological preconditions (especially the two fundamental diremptions) causes theoretical problems, which in turn reinforces those diremptions. "It has become easy to describe trade unions, local government, civil service, the learned professions: the arts, law, education, the universities, architecture and medicine as 'powers.' And then renouncing knowledge as power, too, to demand total expiation for domination, without investigation into the

extend its politicality without eroding its own self-construction as constitutively political. It is required reflexively to acknowledge that its legitimacy must admit pluralism as its external factual prerequisite."

41. *BM*, 164.

42. Kerr, review of *BM*, 366.

43. *BM*, 283.

44. See Jarvis's review of *BM*, 91. Cf. Martin's approving comments in *Future of Christianity*, 111.

45. *BM*, 288.

46. *DN*, 50n2.

dynamics of configuration. . . . Because the middle is broken—because these institutions are systematically flawed—does not mean they should be eliminated or mended."[47] Social theory must be able to "acknowledge that it *does not know in advance* whether such institutions are violent or peaceful" but "is able to find out—by reconstructing the changing relation between universal, particular and singular."[48] Rose argues modern society cannot properly be understood without reference to the institutions of civil society mediating between state and individual, hence her criticism of the tendency in politics to reduce their power and in (some) theory to denigrate their legitimacy. Equally, theory cannot understand its own preconditions, or itself, if it ignores the state-civil society diremption.

Rose held up Rahel Varnhagen, Rosa Luxemburg and Hannah Arendt as good examples of her social theory. Each of these women experienced in their own self the failure of society to fulfill its own universalist aims—they were excluded as women and Jews—and were sensitive to the social diremptions they inhabited (they inhabited them emphatically, as it were). This sensitized them to the social precondition of their own thought. "In her own way, each of these women exposed the inequality and insufficiency of the universal political community of her day, but without retreating to any phantasy of the local or exclusive community."[49] They exemplified triune rationality and faced up to the broken middle: "This tension of middlewomanship is sustained in all three authorships: they neither opt to abandon political universality, even though it is demonstrably spurious; nor to resolve its inconsistency and antinomy in any ethical immediacy of love: 'community,' 'nation,' 'race,' 'religion' or 'gender' . . . they cultivate aporetic universalism, restless affirmation and undermining of political form and political action, which never loses sight of the continuing mutual corruption of the state and civil society."[50]

Rose regarded the first two parts of Arendt's *Origins of Totalitarianism* (on anti-Semitism and imperialism) as "the most sustained attempt to develop Marx's account of the split between state and civil society from 'On the Jewish Question' . . . to provide a political and sociological history of the modern 'nation'-state, which . . . demonstrates the impossibility of democratic polity in the modern nation-state, in its birth, development

47. *BM*, 285.
48. Ibid., 264.
49. *MBL*, 39.
50. *BM*, 155.

and disintegration, and which is organized around the changing 'split' and 'tension' between civil society and state as revealed and charted by 'the Jewish Question' and the 'social question.'"[51] Part 1 deals with the splits, tensions and equivocations in the state-society division, as it is revealed in the Dreyfus affair. Part 2 is a kind of "socio-political commentary on Luxemburg's political economy of imperialism."[52] Luxemburg developed the idea that capital will only work if it has new areas on which to feed and this leads to imperialism once the initial economy of a country has entirely gone over to capitalism. The state is opposed to the nation, which produces tension over ethnicity and produces the antinomy that human rights are only protected as national rights. These two contradictions work out in different ways but they are the roots of totalitarianism and make fully democratic politics impossible. Arendt's early work is speculative because it historically traces the equivocations and dialectical reversals of bourgeois emancipation, economic emancipation, and the nation-state. Arendt saw an implied ideal that was never attained but she did not abandon it. This ideal is, for Rose, once again mutual recognition. "The law, therefore, in its actuality means full mutual recognition, 'spirit' or ethical life, but it can only be approached phenomenologically as it appears to us, modern legal persons, by expounding its dualistic reductions, when it is posited as modern legal status—the law of subjective rights separated from the law of the modern state."[53] In keeping with the Frankfurt tradition, Rose would likely agree that mutual recognition is the basis of rights, not vice versa, but such recognition only occurs after a struggle, hence Hegel's analysis of recognition through the master-slave dialectic. "Civil rights are not original natural or metaphysical entities they are the legal-juridical expression of the mutual recognitions that constitute individuals as citizens of a political state. . . . Insofar as legal form is construed as the protection of natural right, the structural and historical conditions of civil society are suppressed."[54] The rights-recognition axis maintains the historical-sociological nature of Rose's phenomenology.

To gain some context for viewing the diremptions as an analysis of society we can turn to Zygmunt Bauman's work on assimilation and

51. Ibid., 217.

52. Ibid., 218.

53. *MBL*, 75.

54. Bernstein, "Right, Revolution and Community," 102–9.

the Jewish Question. In his case study of German Jews in *Modernity and Ambivalence*, he shows the ways in which the process of assimilation was essentially contradictory, though it continued as such for approximately two hundred years. The Jew had to match up to the standards of the cultural elite, and the same cultural elite decided if the Jew had succeeded, which resulted in constantly shifting goalposts. When, for example, Heinrich Heine and others became successful journalists, people began to dismiss journalism as a Jewish profession. Worse, the very attempt to prove oneself German rather than Jewish was often taken as evidence of subversiveness and dishonesty, as if Jewishness was being hidden. The results for the individual were often painful: trapped between two cultures, not entirely at home or accepted in either; and, sometimes worse, not knowing if one was accepted or not. Since some Jews (German born) assimilated much more quickly than others (eastern European immigrants), the pressures of assimilation were felt as well in this differential pace. Assimilated Jews had, on the one hand, to distance themselves from their fellow, more traditional Jews, in order to prove their own cultural fitness for assimilation; while on the other, felt the need to help more traditional Jews assimilate in order to prove assimilation was possible and desirable. These social pressures were often internalized by German Jews as shame, embarrassment and disgust at the Eastern Jews and their traditional ways. Yet people bore these sociopolitical contradictions within themselves because they wanted the rights and acceptance of full citizenship. Bauman shows that assimilation is not a constant throughout human history but emerges from the context of modern nationalization. It depends on the nation-state's claim to shared history, shared customs and a common spirit, and attempts to transcend local differences. The era of nation forming was a time of cultural intolerance of differences as the state sought to consolidate and centralize its power. Cultural conformity was frequently conflated with political loyalty and trustworthiness. The task of assimilation was to acquire the culture of those in power; which entailed the destruction of many old institutions, practices and forms of life. The impossible situation of assimilation was revealed in that its acquired nature meant the assimilant could never fully be accepted because s/he was not naturally of the right ethnicity or nationality. The nation sustained itself through the myth of naturalness, a denial of its artificial nature, in which the assimilant could never share.

Against this background the continuing relevance of Rose's work immediately appears. Muslims, for example, now face many of the same tensions faced by Jews. An editorial from September 2014 in the *Independent*,[55] for example, ran the subheading "British Muslims are under constant pressure to condemn extremism. They deserve credit, not suspicion, for doing so." This shows both the pressures on British Muslims to display loyalty to the nation-state and the suspicion attaching to their accession to this pressure. For Rose, the "politics of the middle" is managing the tension between "national and universal," *Volk* and humanity, local and cosmopolitan.[56] A good social theory must include an account of mediation, to show "how abstract individual rights are internalized so that each individual becomes unequal to him or herself, and . . . how this social insecurity of identity inhibits participation in the state and in politics. It would show how political antagonisms are mediated by social relations; and how crises of individual and class identity are mediated by political impossibilities."[57]

Sara Farris's use of Marx's essay on the Jewish Question as a theoretical springboard to analyze her fieldwork on the current treatment of Muslims in contemporary France, as a focal point for the treatment of Muslims more generally in Europe, exactly fits Rose's desiderata.[58] Farris's work shows that "lack of social, economic and cultural rights prevent Muslim girls from entering the promised land of emancipation and equality in the public sphere, but also . . . reveals the contradictions at the heart of the political universalism of the state whereby religion is a mark of individual identity (or a particularity) that the French state politicizes, whereas social class and poverty are defined at the outset as non-political distinctions which can therefore continue to operate and divide."[59] These are exactly the issues—gender, class, religion—picked out by Rose as following from the state-civil society diremption and most important for guiding social theory and sociological investigation: the "triple diremption of modernity collected up in the overarching predicament of love outside the state: the diremption of civil society and state, of natural right and national sovereignty, of abstract equality and class and gender disparity."[60] We see here Rose does not limit herself to the two

55. "Far-Right and Wrong," *Independent*, 27.

56. *BM*, 123.

57. Ibid., 146.

58. Farris, "From the Jewish Question to the Muslim Question," 296–307.

59. Farris, "Muslim Question," 302.

60. *BM*, 261.

fundamental diremptions but also follows the other diremptions proliferating from them. Further, an allegedly neutral secular state in practice excludes religious people by imposing a specific form of secularism as a *Sollen*.[61] Farris observes the construal of "freedom as the dismissal of religion and, as such, as a given, *a priori* category which does not require mediation . . . refers back to the 'ought.'"[62] Rose too "warns against philosophy's pride of *Sollen*, against any . . . imposition of ideals, [or] imaginary communities,"[63] stemming from a lack of mediation.

Farris's work also provides an excellent example of aporetic universalism at work, because it focuses on the antinomies of the universalism of the secular state. The French doctrine of state secularism, *laïcité*, is supposed to be an emancipatory universalism, yet is enforced on religious people (e.g., the 2004 anti-veiling law). One antinomy here is to require individuals to achieve the so-called emancipation of secularism before they can access what are supposed to be the very means to achieve it—principally schools. Public schools in France are supposed to be the means of education into citizenship and integration into the body politic. Yet to be allowed to attend school, children must give up their religious symbols such as Muslim veils, Sikh turbans, Jewish skullcaps or large Christian crosses. They must already act like secularists before learning how to be true secularists.[64] The "separation and contradiction between the political state and civil society" means individuals can technically participate in the universal state (Marx's "political emancipation") but still lack "human emancipation" because they are stuck in particularities holding them back (religion, class, poverty, lack of property, etc.). Most Muslims can only get lower paid jobs because they are discriminated against on the basis of their religion; they also tend to be poorer and poorer students tend to receive lower grades.[65] Yet such political emancipation without human emancipation is not real political emancipation. Trying to force emancipation is "an expression of the contradictions lying at the heart of the universalism of the political state itself. While envisaging equality and freedom as the *ends* embedded in the very fabric of the universalism of rights, the inequalities of civil society upon which the

61. Farris, "Muslim Question," 301.

62. Ibid., 298.

63. *BM*, xi.

64. Farris, "Muslim Question," 297.

65. Ibid., 302.

state was founded, meant the concrete absence of the *means* to achieve those ends."[66]

Yet, as Rose warned, ignoring the difficulties of the broken middle by an enforced *Sollen* (the hasty unity of *laïcité* in this case) only reinforces the diremptions and makes them worse. Hence Farris: "*Veiling rather than unveiling—religious visibility rather than invisibility—has come to signify emancipation*: namely, emancipation from impositions that are perceived as ultimately imbricated with colonial paternalism and as being fundamentally racist."[67] Now, Rose would likely share the feminist suspicions of requiring women to wear a veil, and think that universal equality puts the requirement to wear one into question (though not necessarily the act of wearing one, which must be decided in relation to context), but attempts to reach the goal of equality by means of a blanket legal ban causes its own problems. Farris notes that up till the end of the 1980s, integration in France was achieved through working class institutions (of the middle, in Rose's terms) such as trade unions, sport clubs, political parties, and the Catholic Church.[68] These have all diminished, leaving only the school or the law as the means for integration, leading to the current problems. Rose's warning (in concert with many other writers) that the institutions of the middle were necessary to mediate between state and individual is thereby supported.

Rose's suggested response to such antinomies is to reform the universal, not retreat into some form of community or to abandon the state. Rose's hesitation about the fashionable concept of "community," whether in political theological ecclesiology or postmodern new ethics, was that when people talk about "community" they "hope for a collective life without inner or outer boundaries, without obstacles, or occlusions, within and between souls and within and between cities, without the perennial work which constantly legitimates and delegitimates the transformation of power into authority of different kinds."[69] "The idea of community depends, however, not only on its contraries . . . but also on the implied opposition of the community to the political and social totality. The inevitable political predicaments of sovereignty and representation have been projected beyond the boundaries of the community onto the pre-

66. Ibid., 299.

67. Ibid., 303.

68. Ibid., 301.

69. *MBL*, 16.

supposed but not thematised environing body-politic."[70] The need then is to examine "the sociological actuality of how domination, including local domination, is to be legitimised as authority."[71] This "configuration and reconfiguration of power . . . is our endless predicament."[72] Gellner's observation about nationalisms summarizes well Rose's point: "The rhetoric of nationalism is inversely related to its social reality: it speaks of *Gemeinschaft*, and is rooted in a semantically and often phonetically standardized *Gesellschaft*."[73] The modern *Gemeinschaft* groups, on which the political solution is to be based, are themselves only possible because of the specific *Gesellschaft* achieved in modernity.

Rose, then, did not expect too much from ethical life or its carriers in contemporary society: another connotation accrues to the broken middle. One of the reasons civil society works is because individuals are distanced from their economic, social and political roles, and as such can move around, be substituted one for another, join and leave associations at will without undue penalty.[74] Recognition of the brokenness of the middle prevents an unrealistic investment in the social and political order—considering it sacred (theocracy) or directly moral (in Marxist fashion)—without denying its normativity. Indeed, although civil society has now become routinized (unlike Marxism, which could not survive routinization),[75] it still needs, and has, values.[76] On the one hand, routinization and modularity are essential to the success of civil society and the values and freedoms it rightly contains. On the other, much of the sociological and philosophical critique of modernity from the Frankfurt School objects to that routinization and modularity as constantly carried too far and producing pathologies. The broken middle names this inescapable predicament, the necessary imperfection of current social forms and any provisionally achieved equipoise.

The capacity of Rose's social theory to do justice to these empirical studies answers two objections to her work. Just as one may wonder how much history is allowed into Rose's phenomenology, so one may

70. Ibid., 19.
71. Ibid.
72. Ibid., 20.
73. Gellner, *Conditions*, 107.
74. Ibid., 99–107.
75. Ibid., 136.
76. Ibid., 143.

wonder how much social information is allowed into her social theory and meta-theory. Does Rose's theoretical work lose touch with the facts on the ground, as Tim Murphy claimed? Is there a sufficient dialectic between empirical and theoretical work? This concern withers once the depths of Rose's work are appreciated. As I have shown, there are references to more empirical studies in Rose's work—Weber, Durkheim, Arendt, Marx, Lukács, etc.—which although not always explicitly mentioned are nevertheless part of the engine of her philosophy. Rose's main inspirations, Hegel and Adorno, built their own social philosophies and epistemologies on detailed social and historical comprehension too. This is why Rose's theory describes so well the logic of sophisticated contemporary empirical sociology as well as the other contemporary examples I introduced.

A second objection could be that my exposition appears as if it merely takes instances of good practice in social philosophy and sociology and labels them "examples of Rose's theory." Yet if there is a fundamental structure to knowing and thinking, and if Hegel uncovered it (or a significant aspect of it), then it should work across a range of studies. Rose is far from alone in believing there is a fundamental socio-logic; Rose looked for it in a reformulated Hegel, others look elsewhere (e.g., to critical realism). Indeed, the premise of critical theory is that Marx and Freud enabled a new epistemology, which could explain things to people and societies about themselves they otherwise missed, which can explain theories better than the theories themselves, and which works across a whole range of fields of thought. Most people would accept at least some version of the possibility of this practice. In principle, then, a refutation of Rose's theory must focus on its details rather than on the possibility of a widely explanatory socio-logic. Likewise Rose's theory can give reasons for criticism of both good and less good theorizing within social philosophy, which is its purpose and proves the selection of good and bad examples is not arbitrary but exemplary of the theory's power.

2.3 The law-ethics diremption

In chapter 1 I showed how absolute ethical life was a necessary but unattainable ideal; in chapter 3 I outlined the various forms of the antinomy of law as variations on the contrast between written and unwritten law, or law and ethics. Rose explicitly connects these ideas in *The Broken Middle*:

"This book develops the work of *Hegel contra Sociology* and *Dialectic of Nihilism* by pursuing the diremption of law and ethics, expounded, in the earlier work, as the ideal law which Hegel was unable to obtain, and, in the later work, as the post-Kantian 'antinomy of law' which resurfaces in latter-day nihilism. . . . What I there called 'the antinomy of law' appears here as the dual implication of law and ethics."[77] It is not sufficient to posit the diremption in general; phenomenological learning comes from the negotiations in specific cases.[78] She thus calls the law-ethics diremption "modernity's ancient predicament."[79] This facetious phrase refers to fact that debates around law and ethics stretch back to Socrates and the Sophists yet have a specific modern form, inflected through the Kantian revision of Roman law in combination with capitalist private property:[80] "With the institutionalization of private property and contractual law, a market economy comes into being whose primary organizational unit, the business firm, disposes over purposive-rational methods of accounting, management, and production in the calculated pursuit of profit."[81] Thus the importance of the modern form of the law-ethics diremption: the "single most decisive event paving the way for modern society was undoubtedly the separation of ethics and law from one another and from religious custom (*Sittlichkeit*)."[82] Where Rose's first fundamental diremption followed Marx, the second accepts Weber's pioneering analysis. Modern subjects, unlike their ancient counterparts, now experience the "paradox of life lived in the two apparently different realms of the social and political when both realms are juridical, equally constituted by the civil law. Unaddressable oppositions between morality and legality, autonomy and heteronomy, the good will and natural desire and inclination, force and generality, can be traced to an historically specific legal

77. *BM*, xiv–v. What Rose calls here "the ideal law which Hegel was unable to obtain" is an extremely abbreviated reference to what I addressed as the unobtainable unity of law and ethics within absolute ethical life.

78. *JAM*, 239. Her own work on the architecture, anthropology, history and sociology of Auschwitz was important to her here.

79. *BM*, xii.

80. *JAM*, 250–51.

81. Ingram, *Habermas and the Dialectic of Reason*, 46, discussing Weber. See, e.g., *Economy and Society*, 585, 636–37.

82. Ingram, *Dialectic of Reason*, 45.

structure which establishes and protects absolute property by means of the juridical fictions of persons, things, and obligations."[83]

Rose pursued her analysis in *Judaism and Modernity*, which she described as speculatively examining the methods and new ethics of various thinkers in order to bring out their connections to "modernity and modern law."[84] Rose shows repeatedly how the theories in question ignore or misconstrue, in a way that undermines their results, the specifically modern diremption of law and ethics. "The modern fate of *Geist*—the law of civil society and state producing its diremption and violent overcomings thereof—will erupt again and again as long as this structure persists. Fear of 'contamination' is just the contamination itself—collusion by not comprehending what *can be* reconstructed."[85] She thus aimed

> to address the great divide which has separated social and political theory from philosophy since Kant. All my work starts from Kant and Hegel and then follows these sundered trajectories through the major post-Kantian German traditions in philosophy, sociological theory, jurisprudence and comparative theology up to the present. I always relate the French thinkers of this period to these German foundations. My recent and special interest is to explore what happens to the conceiving of law and ethics when philosophy and social and political theory become separate disciplines in this way. This divided legacy resurges throughout twentieth century European intellectual history and may be the source of the impasse in so many current debates over post-structuralist philosophy and sociological theory.[86]

Rose's references to Weber throughout her writings, and her lectures on him, show her reliance on his theory of modernity throughout her work. As Bernstein points out, Weber's work is a kind of sociological version of many of Nietzsche's ideas, and Rose viewed Adorno in the same way.[87] "Adorno's philosophy is best seen as an inflection of Weber's analysis of disenchantment and societal rationalization."[88] Once this is recognized, it is clear that the law-ethics diremption also refers to the

83. *DN*, 2–3. The adjective "unaddressable" is unfair. Kant had his rationale for the oppositions, Rose simply preferred their handling by some post-Kantians.

84. *JAM*, xi.

85. Ibid., 78–79.

86. Letter to Robert Darnton, 22 September 1988, box 52.

87. Bernstein, *Adorno*, 7, and *TMS*, 1–26.

88. Bernstein, *Adorno*, 30.

Weberian problem of rationalization. Rationalization is the thread uniting Rose's ideas on the law-ethics diremption, violence, and ethical politics. As David Ingram describes it:

> In his study of modern law, Weber stressed the parallel emancipation of individual moral conscience from ethical custom. For the first time ever, civil law appears as something posited, the legitimacy of which is tied to notions of sovereign consent (the social contract) institutionalized in democratic rules of procedural justice. It no longer requires the adoption of any particular moral or religious attitude, but only outward compliance with respect to behavior. In other words, it procures a realm of individual freedom in which it is permitted to do anything that is compatible with a like freedom for others. . . . Yet Weber's diagnosis of freedom reveals precisely the reverse phenomenon: an ineluctable erosion of freedom and meaning.[89]

Society, law and economy all reflect the loss of meaning flowing from rationalization. Ethical values and ideals seemed increasingly less rational as scientific truth and rationality replaced other forms of reason. "Modern, secular reason is self-undermining."[90] With rationalization, society began to doubt ethical values and ideals (including even reason and truth), which in turn lost their motivating force. Agents' ability to understand and guide their lives with practical reason is then undermined. This begins to threaten "the *ethical meaningfulness* of human existence" and "in so doing, undermine the conditions of *rational agency, of goal-directed meaningful action* as such."[91] In terms of law: "Modern legal practice—thinking, writing, deciding—is presented as a sort of hermetically sealed operation, formal logic without regard to 'substance,' a world of its own entire of itself. And it is the elimination of all concrete determinations from this process which is said to be central—the transformation of a dispute into simply or essentially or foundationally one between abstract (disembodied, anonymous) bearers of rights, legal subjects."[92] And within the economy: "From an ethical viewpoint, this 'masterless slavery' to which capitalism subjects the worker or the mortgagee is questionable only as an institution. However, in principle, the behavior of any individual cannot be so questioned, since it is prescribed in all relevant

89. Ingram, *Dialectic of Reason*, 48.

90. Bernstein, *Adorno*, 5.

91. Ibid., 6.

92. Murphy, *Oldest Social Science?*, 56.

respects by objective situations."[93] The result is the legal subject and "the misrecognitions attendant on abstract legal personality, private property and the decay of public and political life."[94]

Rose's embrace of the rationalization thesis lies behind her disagreements with both postmodern ethics and postmodern political theology. As she puts it, "post-modern antinomianism completes itself as political theology, as new ecclesiology mending the diremption of law and ethics."[95] In terms of the latter, theological critics of modernity such as John Milbank (following MacIntyre) think the state and civil society form a seamless whole without any cracks from which to leverage resistance.[96] Any forms of resistance fail from the outset because they use the same form of reason they oppose, and hence are co-opted by the state for its own ends. A voice somehow external to the state-society duality is therefore required. It will come from "the" (Thomistic) church because it retains and embodies premodern forms of life and thought. The best chance to restore meaning and morality is for churches with substantive stories, goals and virtues to provide an intelligible context for the ethical formation of individuals. Rose is skeptical of this strategy. She thinks it overestimates the difference of such groups from the surrounding society while underestimating the plurality of modern social forms. It also implies some sort of unique status for the church group, as if they alone are somehow exempt from the seamlessly monolithic nature of state and society. Even when individuals from such groups have a set of virtues and an understanding of the world different from their surrounding society, all their actions take place in, and are filtered through Weber's "objective situations," the rationalizing, disenchanting social forms of law, economy and society. Christianity, like Judaism (see below), is "*a modern religion*, practiced according to private inclination and interest by individuals defined as legal persons, bearers of rights and duties (not as members of pre-modern corporations), within the boundaries of civil society separated from the modern state."[97] But "Judaism *as a religion* in civil society is no longer engaged in the unequal sharing (even less the monopoly) of the means of legitimate violence—it is no longer *a community* in the

93. Weber, *Economy and Society*, 1186.

94. *JAM*, 67.

95. *BM*, xv.

96. Milbank, *Theology and Social Theory*.

97. *MBL*, 94.

sense that it no longer possesses any means of coercion."[98] The problem with the "ecclesiology as solution" approach is that in modernity religion is partly privatized and is subject to mediation through multiple social forms and especially the fundamental diremptions of modern society. Rather than facing up to their place in the brokenness of the middle, such approaches use "love" to "overcome the broken conceptuality of the modern state."[99] Much of its "normative thinking is naïve about its collusions in the reconfiguration of relation of power and domination. . . . I argue that all thinking—including utopian thinking—embodies a political history which it either reflects or ignores."[100]

Yet if Rose declared any ethical resistance to rationalized reason and forms of life doomed from the outset because they are filtered through objective social forms, no remedial action would be possible. Once again the importance of the triune nature of Hegelian rationality makes an appearance. The identities between universal, singular and particular are filled with tension and contradiction, and thus can disrupt as well as express one another. There is no seamless web of society and state (though it is true that ostensibly state-independent bodies often express the same rationalized logic as the state and end up as the state's means of governing at arms length, as governmentality studies has made clear). And Rose indeed thinks that various institutions of civil society, such as trade unions, medicine, the arts, universities, local government and religious groups do have the potential to mediate between state and individual in a way that could sustain less rationalized forms of ethical life. (Think, for example, of the ethics and identity associated with being part of the medical profession and the importance thereof for its relation to the government.) And, critiques of modernity notwithstanding, there are times when society attains "good enough justice." Rose therefore has no reason in principle to exclude religious groups from the set of middle institutions; that is not the point. Rather, she thinks the theorizing of much political theology overvalues and overestimates what religious groups are able to achieve, and underestimates how much such groups are affected by their surrounding society. Rose sees such political theology as the mirror image of poststructural social philosophy because it

98. Ibid., 97. Hence Rose's comment that the debate in modern Judaism over whether *halacha* required an ethical supplement "presupposes the politics of modernity," in that it already assumes a law-ethics split.

99. *BM*, 309.

100. Letter to John Milbank, 13 October 1991, box 11.

overestimates our ability to fix the broken middle's diremptions whereas the latter underestimates it.[101]

2.3.1 New ethics and the spirit of postmodernism

Thus postmodern and political theological social theories can both be read as one form of the "flight"[102] from rationalization, rather than fully facing up to the broken middle. Rose terms this "the *pathos of the concept:* the simultaneous denial of comprehension, of any experience of coming to learn the diremption of law and ethics, and reduction of conceptuality."[103] This reveals itself in their eschewal of violence and authority, often linked to the turn to Judaism in continental philosophy as a source of "new ethics," as if it was uncontaminated by the problems of modernity (which had, according to postmodernists, led Western reason and metaphysics to Auschwitz). "I write out of the discovery that both recent philosophy, in its turn to what I name *new ethics*, and modern Jewish philosophy, in its ethical self-presentations, are equally uncomfortable with any specific reflection on modern law and the state, which they assimilate to the untempered domination of Western metaphysics."[104]

> This desire to conceive of coercion and law as absolutely distinct from the good and the community . . . represents one of the main ways in which modern Jewish thought participates in a methodological and substantive divorce which characterises the development of modern philosophy in its separation of ethics from the social analysis of the ways in which authority is legitimised. This epochal difficulty in relating the analysis of the operations of modern power—its techniques and its technologies—to the reflection on the nature and actuality of the good . . . has given rise to the intellectual division of labour between philosophy and political sociology.[105]

Rose believed the disciplinary separation of philosophy from sociology had led, in parts of the academy, to a false bifurcation between

101. For an elaboration of Rose's critique of political theology, see Brower Latz, "Purity in Future Theology."

102. Bernstein, *Adorno*, 19–20.

103. *BM*, 308.

104. *JAM*, x.

105. *MBL*, 86.

ethics and its wider setting in law and politics, and particularly of the crucial question of how state power can be legitimate (which of course provides criteria for where power fails to be legitimate). The sweeping, postmodern condemnations of modernity or metaphysics or reason per se are blunt instruments, hindering not helping the critique of power. Postmodern "thinking holds nature and freedom, ethics and politics so separate that no true mediation is possible."[106] The relation between the legitimation of power and modern forms of reason and Rose's response to the problem of rationalization therefore frames her critique of new ethics and the spirit of postmodernism. This spirit was the "idealising of the interpretive or discursive community . . . which rests its claim to authority by evading the difficulty of authority as such—the legitimation of domination and its coercive means."[107] It entailed a "confusion of [literary] criticism and political philosophy."[108] New ethics is a philosophical form of the beautiful soul, which is, as Drew Milne describes Rose's view,

> a symptom of modernity, the subject of privatized ethics that seek to separate moral thought from the aporia configured and reconfigured in political and legal institutions. Shorn of credible frameworks or institutions of duty, the beautiful soul lives through the aspiration to have an inner beauty of moral feeling without recognizing heteronomous authorities. Attempts to conceptualize such aspirations motivate postmodern ethics.[109]

Rose saw new ethics as based on a mistaken view of reason, metaphysics and Judaism. Rather than a purely ethical or discursive community, Judaism was better conceived as involving "the negotiation and promotion of the good and the legitimation of coercive institutions."[110] Law for Rose is best thought of along the lines of (what she thought of as) Jewish Torah: "commandment as a guideline (not a criterion) . . . the idea of mediation or negotiation."[111] The negotiation she has in mind in this quotation is the premodern Jewish community negotiating its own law in relation to the law of its conquerors, that is, of working to make

106. Bergo, *Levinas Between Ethics and Politics*, 273. See 258–76 for a fine discussion of Rose's criticisms of Levinas.

107. *MBL*, 80.

108. Ibid., 80–81.

109. "Beautiful Soul," 65.

110. *MBL*, 86.

111. *JAM*, 188.

power into legitimate authority. In modernity, however, the "authority in crisis—the crisis which carries over from modernity to Judaism and from Judaism to modernity—requires political risk *greater* than that required in traditional society or traditional Judaism when the source of domination was not dispersed."[112] Rose's view also depends on the Hegelian view of the historically evolving nature of law and its mediations.[113] Jewish law cannot simply be abstracted from its context and (de)posited in ours, because "the meaning of law and ethics is not determined by what is posited or intended, or even how it is posited, but by how positive meaning is *configured* within the prevailing modern diremption of morality and legality, autonomy and heteronomy, civil society and the state."[114] Without sociological attention to the mediation of law and ethics, the new ethics remains unable to address its determination by its preconditions. It separates law and ethics rather than mediates their diremption.

Throughout her work Rose not only relies on Weber's analysis of authority as legitimized domination[115] but also "presupposes the definition of the modern liberal state as *the monopoly of the means of legitimate violence*."[116] His famous typology of the three types of authority—legal-rational, traditional and charismatic—throws up an immediate problem for contemporary thought. In a predominantly post-traditional, post-charismatic society, in which tradition and charisma are culturally and structurally marginalized, the main form of authority is legal-rational. Yet legal-rational authority is rationalized (in the way criticized by the Frankfurt School) and contributed to the problems of the twentieth century.[117] In Rose's view, much continental social theory had, in response to these problems, given up thinking about legitimating power as authority; hence its search for a new ethics, and hence its mirror image in the

112. *MBL*, 83. The dispersal of domination is the Frankfurt notion of the increased subtlety and fragmentation of domination in complex modern societies.

113. See Brooks, "Between Natural Law and Legal Positivism," 513–60, and *Hegel's Political Philosophy*, 82–95; cf. Habermas, *Between Facts and Norms*, 211–22.

114. *JAM*, 22.

115. E.g., Weber, *Economy and Society*, 31–38, 212–16. For Weber, power (*Macht*) is the probability of an actor achieving his will despite resistance, whereas domination (*Herrschaft*) is the acceptance of the actor's goals by others as rational and/or in their own interests. This is legitimation, but legitimation can be false if people wrongly assume power operates in their interests. (Rose uses "authority" rather than "domination" to translate *Herrschaft* and I follow her terminology here.)

116. *MBL*, 59; Weber, *Economy and Society*, 908–9, and "Politics as a Vocation."

117. E.g., Cohen, general editor's foreword, xiii, and Kalberg, "Marx Weber," 2–29.

ecclesiology of postmodern political theologies. The Frankfurt School always accepted the necessity of power's legitimation into authority's valid coercion; it only rejected surplus domination. Part of what Rose means by the phrase "love in violence and violence in love" is that coercion may be legitimate and good.[118] She thought morality is in part an internalizing of law's coercion: as power became more centralized in the state, violence between citizens in society decreased. Yet the legitimation of power is never perfect and our participation in state violence (however exactly this should be understood) prevents us from being morally blameless (the desire for which she detected in the search for new ethics). The internalization of legal coercion and violence, which may be good or bad, ought to be faced squarely and comprehended, in the Hegelian sense of understanding a determination of human action. "Acceptance of this inseparability of love and law, Revelation and coercion, prevents the enshrining of originary and incursive violence. On the contrary, the violence in love is explored."[119] By contrast, "there has been a continuous attempt in modern philosophy to isolate violence, and to find thereby a secure niche for 'pure' morality or politics or knowing. So law, power, reason and love have variously been logically refined until all the violence is removed from them."[120] Indeed, the concept of "violence" on its own is abstract; "mutual violence arises from specific legal forms, [it is] not . . . distinguishable solely in terms of 'increasing' quantity, 'function[ing]' transhistorically, across principles."[121] The attempt to isolate violence per se and create some social system without it is thus mistaken. Political theology often takes its lead here from René Girard, continental social theory often from Walter Benjamin. But Benjamin's view of violence at the heart of law and the state "washes away distinctions between the legitimate exercise of power and coercion and illegitimate violence."[122] This view of violence explains "too much and too little," hence the inability of such views to appreciate fully the value of "liberalism and constitutionalism . . . any Kantian . . . theory of the state as resting on the rule of law, the protection of human rights, the rights of citizens, popular sovereignty

118. Another meaning is highlighted by Rowan Williams, *Lost Icons*, 178: "Love stakes a position and so cannot help risking the displacement or damaging of another. It is never far from violence."

119. *BM*, 171.

120. Bernstein, "Philosophy among the Ruins," 30.

121. *BM*, 146.

122. Benhabib, review of *Violence*, discussing Benjamin's essay on violence.

and the like."[123] Rose lamented the lack in poststructural theory of any "social analysis of why political theory has failed."[124] As a result new ethics "intends a new transcendence, a purified reason, for it proceeds without taking any account of institutions which are extraneous to its idea, that is, without taking any account of mediation."[125] As an example of this failure, Rose refers to the reception of Le Corbusier's architecture. His work is now regarded as too mechanistic and impersonal, but this judgment is made without due consideration of what happened to his intentions by various mediations and institutions, of "how the outcome of the idea and act is effected by the interference of meanings, that is, by institutions, which were not taken into account in the original idea, but which mediate its attempted realization; for example, by changes in the family, the occupational structure, property relations, ratio of public to private space, investment in planning, building and infrastructure."[126] Once again, theory should think through the way its preconditions mediate its effects and intentions.

Modern law is bound up in complicated ways with *Sittlichkeit*.[127] "Law is both a phenomenon brought about through the existence of fragmentation and division in human societies, and a body of ideas which, in some sense, stands apart from, and aims to repair or suppress, instances of fragmentation and division."[128] For Rose, "our responsibility may change the meaning of the law; and the law may change the meaning of our cherished ethics."[129] Indeed "it is 'morality' itself which has corrupted and which continues to corrupt us," because "it is possible to mean well, to be caring and kind, loving one's neighbour as yourself, yet to be complicit in the corruption and violence of social institutions."[130]

123. Ibid.

124. *JAM*, 7.

125. Ibid.

126. Ibid. In Rose's later work (1992 onward) she turned to architecture as another major view on the social totality and a way to show the tendency of theory to attempt to mend too hastily the diremptions of society (*BM*, 296–307; *JAM*, 225–57; *MBL*, 15–39). "She argues that architecture, like law, is the privileged occupier of the moment between, the middle in which is performed the difficult and unending art of educating power and of moderating between particular, singular and universal" (Flessas, "Sacrificial Stone," 76–77n22).

127. *JAM*, 23, 48, 156–62. Cf. Coyle, *Positivism to Idealism*, 127–44, 163–79.

128. Coyle, *Positivism to Idealism*, 177.

129. *BM*, 267.

130. *JAM*, 35.

The issue is morality thought in abstraction from its preconditions and mediated effects, from its "good intentions imbedded in unknowable preconditions and consequences."[131] The "strictly private and intimate relation now called 'love,' becomes opposed to law—the duality of love (particularity) and law (universality) opening up the possibility of morality in its Kantian configuration."[132] There is however no individual ethics in abstraction from politics. When the mediation of ethics by politics is embraced, less abstraction and more comprehension are possible in both. Thus "it is the very opposition between morality and legality—between inner, autonomous 'conscience,' and outer, heteronomous institutions—that depraves us,"[133] because it removes attention from the social determinations of action and so our ability to gain freedom by comprehending them.[134] Hence Hegel

> tries to show how the attempt at self-determination requires . . . an understanding of oneself as occupying a place within a larger whole, except in his view that whole is not nature or the cosmos, but the history of a collectively self-determining subject. More concretely, it means that Hegel thinks he can show that one never determines oneself simply as a person or agent, but always as a member of an historical ethical institution, as a family member, or participant in civil society, or citizen, and that it is only in terms of such concrete institutions that one can formulate some substantive universal end, something concretely relevant to all other such agents.[135]

To address this reality requires the dual-directional pull of speculative thinking. "This 'contradiction,' origin of anxiety, is equally the anxiety of beginning,"[136] it sets off the intellectual and existential working through of dialectics. The phrase "anxiety of beginning" uses the genitive in two ways: it is the anxiety that begins the process (of phenomenology, of seeking truth), and it is the anxiety that attends the beginning, the "way of despair" on which we embark and the difficulty of that embarkation without foundations. Weber's sociology provides an example of such speculative thought at work:

131. *JAM*, 35.

132. Bernstein, "Right, Revolution and Community," 109.

133. *JAM*, 35.

134. Ibid., 36.

135. Pippin, *Philosophical Problem*, 72.

136. *BM*, 56.

> the diremption between the moral discourse of rights and the systematic actualities of power in modern states and societies . . . reappears in modern philosophical reflection as the opposition between morality and legality or between ethics and law. The effective opposition between the discourse of rights and the actualities of state power is explored by classical sociology: the inversion of intended ethical meaning in its social institutionalization, what Max Weber called the "unintended consequences" of social action.[137]

2.3.2 *The equivocation and suspension of the ethical*

Rose's recognition of the mutual mediation of law and ethics, the speculative to-and-fro between them, results in her doctrines of the equivocation and suspension of the ethical. The equivocation of the ethical has two main meanings in her work. First, the Hegelian idea that the full and true meaning of actions are available most fully only retrospectively, through the mediations between individual, groups and social structures. The initial position, the first positing by the agent, is always provisional; the fuller meaning only comes after one's own and others' reactions to the action and its effects occur. Rose like Hegel believes in free, right action as in some way universal, but that we "can formulate the content of such a universal law . . . [only] by reference to the history of ethical institutions, the history of what we have come to regard as counting as universal, as what all others would or could accept as a maxim. Just as when we attempt to 'judge objectively' or 'determine the truth,' we inherit an extensive set of rule-governed, historically concrete practices, so when we attempt to 'act rightly,' and attempt to determine our action spontaneously, we must see ourselves as situated in a complex collective and historical setting."[138] And for both theory and practice "there is no 'outside' or extra-conceptual *explicans*. There is only what we have come to regard as an indispensable *explicans*, and the narrative we need to give concerns that 'coming to regard.'"[139] As Rose put it, there is no "overarching law determining our participation" in ethics and politics.[140] Within phenomenological historical narration, therefore, the equivoca-

137. *JAM*, 21.

138. Pippin, *Philosophical Problem*, 71.

139. Ibid., 72.

140. *MBL*, 35, in italics in original.

tion of the ethical appears as the various inversions of meaning explored by, for example, Hegel in the ideal types of the beautiful soul, the hard-heart and pure culture; by Arendt in her history of totalitarianism; and in the numerous examples in *The Broken Middle* from Weber, Goethe, Durkheim, Kierkegaard and so on. Rose's view of the social totality as a necessary but impossible context for explanation and interpretation, and her view of reason as limited, means any view of an action, including the agent's, is only ever provisional. In this sense, secular meaning and action have the same structure as religious meaning and action: both open onto unknowability. Rose drew on Kierkegaard to make this point.

The second meaning of the equivocation of the ethical is the permanent tensions between values. Rose shares many commonalities with the view known as value pluralism. She does not accept the separation of political philosophy from other areas of philosophy such as ethics.[141] She believes values may vary socially and historically without being relativistic; that evaluative terms are unavoidable (against positivism); and that to instantiate some goods necessarily prevents instantiation of others.[142] There is thus the need for political judgment in face of value pluralism, issuing in "noncomprehensive systematization."[143] Against the background of rationalization and the law-ethics diremption, the equivocation of the ethical can be understood to resist the rationalization of reason because it relies on both reflective judgment and determinant judgment.[144] How best to combine plural, incommensurable values into a single decision cannot be decided by rules or procedures, it is a question of judgment. As Weber put it, "the various value spheres of the world stand in irreconcilable conflict with each other."[145]

Whereas some discussions of value pluralism simply treat it as a given, the law-ethics diremption provides a socio-philosophical, historically reflexive explanation for it, based on Hegel's phenomenological account of the differentiation of the three levels of society. According

141. Galston, *Implications of Value Pluralism.*

142. Raz, *Practice of Value.*

143. Nagel, "Fragmentation of Value."

144. Since value pluralism is neutral with regards to ethical theories, in the sense that one can hold to deontology, consequentialism or virtue ethics as either a value pluralist or monist, it is not subject to Bernstein's criticisms of modern ethical theories as rationalized. Conversely, it does use his reflective/determinant judgment (or universal/particular reason) dialectic.

145. "Science as a Vocation," in *From Max Weber*, 147.

to Axel Honneth, the three structural elements of modern societies (individual, civil society, state) reflect three different forms of mutual recognition (love, esteem, respect).[146] This produces a different form of morality from traditional views because the three modes of recognition are necessary for the moral point of view but cannot be in a harmonious relation since they are in "constant tension."[147] Their competing claims cannot be decided in advance or in the abstract. "Thus the entire domain of the moral is pervaded by a tension that can be resolved only in individual responsibility."[148] This is exactly what Rose means by reference to the "single one" as the individual who must hold together the fractious relation of universal and particular in her own self. It is not a retreat from mutual recognition to individualist existentialism, but bearing the tensions of the broken middle within the self.

These tensions, structurally created yet borne in the individual, lead Rose to the discussion of Kierkegaard's teleological suspension of the ethical.[149] For Rose, to suspend the ethical means to step back from *Sittlichkeit* in order to explore its tensions, to recognize its flaws, perhaps to change it or allow that from time to time exceptions to it are possible and legitimate, and then to reenter it and continue to live within it and perhaps somewhat at odds with it. The reentry into the ethical—the affirmation of the necessity of *Sittlichkeit* notwithstanding reservations about its particular form—distinguishes suspending the ethical from "abolishing" it, where abolishing the ethical gives up on the means of communal ethical life and politics because they are necessarily imperfect.[150] Suspending the ethical requires "repetition," or "movement backwards and forwards," learning from the past before thinking about potential for the present and future.[151] Rose's interpretation of Kierkegaardian repetition in *The Broken Middle* therefore aligns it with her interpretation of Hegelian phenomenology: "The core of the book is chapter five where I try to show (and this is the spirit and endeavour of the whole work) that repetition and critical reconstruction are not incompatible: that it is possible to have faith and knowledge and politics in a way that does not

146. E.g., Honneth, "Between Aristotle and Kant," in *Disrespect*, 129–43.

147. Ibid., 144.

148. Ibid.

149. *BM*, 147–53.

150. Rose's theory is thus alert to the possibility of *Sittlichkeit* being oppressive though she does not discuss the problem.

151. *BM*, 116.

require dogmatic reason or lead to existential scepticism or despair."[152] This matters because some of her critics thought her position in 1992 was no different from the postmodernism she criticized for providing no way out of constant agon.[153] This is clearly not the case as she associates reentry to the ethical with Kierkegaard's figure of the "knight of faith," who lives out the sublime in the pedestrian, and "inherits the world in all its mediation and law."[154] She relates this to the subject's dynamic internalizations of law and violence:

> Kierkegaard's pseudonymous "suspension of the ethical" avoids this sequestering of "violence" while exploring the development of individual faith in its violent encounter with love and law. Hegel's phenomenological master-slave dialectic suspends the ethical—*Sittlichkeit*—in order to explore how the violence between two misrecognizing self-consciousnesses will be settled provisionally by death, enslavement, work or unhappiness; this same dialectic of development is then re-explored as *Antigone* in the restored context of "ethical life." By initially suspending the ethical, both authors are able to bring a formation, an education (*Bildung*), into representation as a *struggle—agon*—in which "violence" is inseparable from staking oneself, from experience as such—the initial yet yielding recalcitrance of action and passion. Without "violence," which is not sacrifice but risk, language, labour, love—life—would not live.[155]

For Rose, violence is involved in the misrecognitions of all our attempts to respond to our environment, in which we partly overcome and partly accommodate ourselves to its initial resistance. The imperfect processes for this—laboring, speaking and thinking, the coercions of politics, the imposing of will in social situations—are a kind of violence because they involve coercion and the imposing of will, and some destruction (whether of possibilities or alternatives, or of the wants or intentions of others). But this violence is necessary—it is present in good ethical and legal systems as well as in good personal relationships. To learn virtue, for example, requires the coercion of discipline. To deny the various textures

152. Letter to Robert Jan van Pelt, 14 August, 1992, box 16. Rose's preservation of interiority distinguishes her position from the lack of critical edge critics discern in Robert Pippin's work: O'Connor, "Concrete Freedom and Other Problems," 753–60, and "Neo-Hegelian Theory of Freedom," 1–24.

153. E.g., Milbank, "Anxiety." Contrast *MBL*, 111.

154. *JAM*, 171.

155. *BM*, 151.

of violence in favor of some allegedly violence-free love, especially as a social or political phenomenon, distorts both theory and reality, and distracts attention away from assessing how adequate the accommodations are. At least one impulse for such theory seems to be the desire to avoid the risks of authority devolving into illegitimate power, and of theoretically justifying that process. Yet the risk is ineliminable, so the promotion of a violent-free community or ethical theory cannot achieve this aim and distracts from the real task of assessing the legitimacy of current power forms.

Rose's mention of labor, language and risk/life/love reveals the proximity of her view to Habermas's, who makes work, language and power central concepts of his own work. In *Knowledge and Human Interests* Habermas posits three interests as necessary preconditions for knowledge, and thus transcendental in the Kantian sense. But they are also empirical because they are a function of the way *homo sapiens* organize social life into work, language and power. The interests are: technical, which produces empirical-analytic knowledge to enable control of the environment in work; practical, which produces mutual understanding via action-guiding norms through discursive language; and emancipatory, which produces freedom and self-transformation (both personal and political) through the self-reflexive analysis of reified powers. These have a quasi-transcendental structure since the necessary preconditions both universally hover above the phenomenal world as its preconditions, and yet emerge from that phenomenal world, since they are a function of humanity's natural being. Habermas does not simply posit their status as functions of humanity's natural being, he arrives at them phenomenologically via Hegel and Marx: these functions are observed over time and it is difficult to imagine going back on this analysis. This fits Rose's criteria for speculative phenomenology, yet she describes Habermas as neo-Kantian in *Hegel Contra Sociology*. Habermas is very close to Rose's own position but there are subtle yet significant differences. "How the empirical and the transcendental, the real and the rational are connected does . . . make a difference."[156] Bernstein's nuanced discussion of the way Habermas concedes the phenomenological position only to retract its force explicates the logic behind Rose's criticisms. "Habermas . . . does conceive of the conditioned and unconditioned, transcendental and empirical, as lying on logically different levels. . . . From the perspective of

156. Bernstein, *Ethical Life*, 188.

discourse ethics 'there are no shared structures preceding the individual except the universals of language use.'"[157] By contrast, for Bernstein and Rose, "moral norms are grounded in the reciprocities of everyday life, which is self-grounding, transcendental and empirical at once."[158]

> What the Hegelian claims is not complete self-knowledge, but that our self-knowledge is non-detachable from the conditions that have made it possible; to affirm itself it must affirm them, and hence negativity (what denies ethical life) in general. This knowledge is "absolute" in Hegel's sense because what is absolute or unconditioned, knowledge of ethical life as ground, includes the conditions that made it possible. Thus there is no logical duality between the empirical (the conditions) and the transcendental (the unconditioned): both are ethical life.[159]

To know ethical life is to know it as ground and grounded, as the ground of itself, a fractured whole. Ethical life therefore makes knowledge of ethical life possible—and speculative knowledge of ethical life knows this. Ethical life, like speculative philosophy, is a virtuous circle and a fissured totality. To know the self is to know what is grounding and shaping the self, which is also ethical life. But to know and affirm the self is to know and affirm the ethical life making possible the self. One of the features of modern ethical life is the negativity of subjectivity, which paradoxically denies and diremptsethical life. This dirempting negativity must be known as a condition and feature of the self too.

Rose also criticizes Habermas for excluding non-discursive reason from practical interest and its expression in language and normativity.[160] Recall that speculative thinking, for Rose, is an addition to, rather than negation of, transcendental philosophy. Every transcendental configuration of necessary conditions excludes something on which it relies.[161] The speculative approach seeks to discern these excluded conditions by attention to what the transcendental frame distorts or hides. Habermas excludes non-discursive rationality, a wider reason, a different form of morality, on which his discursive ethics nevertheless depends.[162] For

157. Ibid.

158. Ibid.

159. Ibid.

160. A common complaint. See, e.g., Bernstein, *Ethical Life*.

161. Rose, "Parts and Wholes," 99–100.

162. For a detailed argument to this effect, see Bernstein, *Ethical Life*.

Rose, however, ethics must be handled speculatively because it is always suspended, "neither surrendered on the one hand, nor posited on the other."[163] Rose's ethics is therefore both "universal and aporetic," hence its reliance on "some dynamic and corrigible metaphysics of universal and singular."[164] Despite the obvious power of Habermas's work, at the very last moment it capitulates to the reigning diremptions within reason.[165] It does not fully address its own contribution to the rationalization it otherwise criticizes,[166] nor sufficiently appreciate its own position within society, the internality of thought to being, of social theory to society.[167]

3 Politics between Moralism and Realism

In addition to the equivocation and suspension of the ethical, the broken middle as an idea and analysis also develops Rose's substantive, immanent normative ideal of mutual recognition (§3.1), her idea of modern *phronesis*, and her intellectual mood striking the right balance between utopianism and despair. Again, subtle differences in metaphilosophical expectations (of which intellectual mood is a part) can have substantive theoretical effects. Rose's political orientation avoids messianism and *Realpolitik*,[168] moralism[169] and brute power. Its balance of ethics and realism resembles Weber's ethics of responsibility, though without his ultimate skepticism about value choices.[170] This means accepting our participation in violence and resultant lack of moral innocence.[171] Rose compares Weber's *Economy and Society* to Machiavelli's *Prince* by way of their discussions on the realities of power and values in their own time. Yet the *Prince* is normally viewed as "a canny, unethical set of instruc-

163. *BM*, 154.

164. *MBL*, 10; cf. *JAM*, 59–62.

165. Cf. *BM*, 258.

166. She believes Weber, Hegel, Kierkegaard, Nietzsche, etc., did see this, hence their "facetious form." See Rose, "Dispute over Marx and Weber."

167. *BM*, 245–46. Rose's style in *BM* was an attempt to avoid this problem.

168. Cf. Schick, *Rose.*

169. For moralism, see Coady, *Messy Morality*.

170. Weber, "Politics as a Vocation."

171. This puts her in line with those who accept the existence of "dirty hands," i.e., the possibility of doing wrong in order to do right. See, classically, Walzer, "Political Action." Cf. Gorman "Nihilism," 26; Freyenhagen, *Adorno's Practical Philosophy*, 140; O'Connor, *Adorno*, 143–44.

tions for the exercise of power" and Weber's work as "value-free social science."[172] Neither is true. The fact-value distinction is not a fact but a puzzle with which to work.

> What we have come to accept as a *categorical methodological precept* or rule—with its justification in the distinction of fact from value and of social analysis from political commendation—*viz.*, the separation of types of legitimate authority from judgements concerning the goals or values of the exercise of power, knowledge of coercion from practical interest in the good, has itself a history. This history comprises the difficulty, intrinsic to the political tradition from the ancient polis to the modern republican state, of relating political goals to means, the idea of the good to the reality of the monopoly of the means of legitimate violence.[173]

From this perspective, both Machiavelli and Weber have a commitment to values (republicanism, reversing the decay of substantive politics) and research the realities of power in the light of those values. Both of them understand politics as the need to impose form (to have institutions and respond ethically to circumstances) *and* to promote "the participation of virtuous citizens in the good."[174] Thus "Weber is the Machiavelli of the early twentieth century: an ultimate concern with the political good—with goal or value rationality—is overshadowed by the analysis of the realities of formal or instrumental rationality, the legal-rational type of authority and its legitimate employment of the means of violence."[175] And his "distinction between formal and substantive rationality may then be seen as a methodological transliteration of the historical difficulty of aspiring to and representing the good between citizens" in a pluralist situation.[176] Rose implies that, in our situation, governance by formal rationality is necessary at the political level, even though it furthers nihilism and so is morally deforming.[177] Our political best is not

172. *MBL*, 87.

173. Ibid., 86–87.

174. Ibid., 87.

175. Ibid., 88.

176. Ibid., 87.

177. Bernstein, *Ethical Life*, 227–28, concedes that Habermas's moral/ethical distinction fits the world of law and policy (where norms are separately produced and *then* applied) much better than it does ethical life of individuals or civil society. Like Rose he refuses the ultimate separation of right and good or its importation into

good enough, but rather than give up on such governance, we should take what reparative measures we can, such as strengthening middle institutions or encouraging virtue where possible without tipping into the imposed *Sollen*. The refusal to separate ethics from politics in order to generate an abstract individual ethics therefore has its political corollary. "Ethics and domination, the good and violence, the community and the law, do not belong to two worlds, to two cities, to two different methodologies. The counter-distinction of ethics from politics is itself the effect, the result, the outcome, the mediation, of the relation between the negotiated meaning of the Good, whether ancient virtue or modern freedom, and the historical actualities of institutional configurations."[178] Rose added Nietzsche to Machiavelli and Weber as her exemplars of this stance because they "renew the classical tradition in ethics for the modern world."[179] They are "the three great thinkers of *power before ethics*. . . . In opposition to Christian eschatology, negotiating the dilemma of power and violence becomes the precondition for configuring virtue for the modern polity. The virtuous life involves some *impure* relation between power in the human psyche and in human association."[180] All three (Rose borrows Weber's terms) "weave the ethic of salvation into the ethics of responsibility to produce . . . [a] final definition of a mature 'calling for politics.'"[181] They thus restore "spiritual meaning, virtue, to politics as the means of violence."[182]

Rose's doctrine of the broken middle reveals the tendency in thinkers to over-identify theory and praxis by "mending the middle," i.e., by moving too quickly from theory to practice, or assuming correct theory is sufficient. Such a move fails to appreciate its own involvement in deformed reason and instrumental politics, and the intervening mediations

---

ethical life, but accepts it remains "deeply plausible" for the state level.

178. *MBL*, 88.

179. Ibid., 140. *DN*, 90: Nietzsche acknowledges he is setting up new law tables so as to keep "connections between law and morality" visible. "In this style, Nietzsche avoids erecting a new metaphysics, a new *Logos*, which would replace the opposition of law and morality; or a new morality which would, once again, be exclusively concerned with one pole of the opposition. Instead a text is designed which makes explicit and visible the historical connection between law and morality for the sake of *die Gerechtigkeit* [justice]. Zarathustra's discourse is the jurisprudence of this law beyond the opposition of rational versus revealed."

180. *MBL*, 141.

181. Ibid., 143.

182. Ibid.

between theory and the actualization of theory. This reworks Adorno's strictures on theory's efficacy. Yet the broken middle also enables a different kind of failure to emerge to view: collapsing onto one side or another of a "double danger," i.e., choosing one side of an aporia in a way that is too one-sided. The lack of straightforward connection between theory and praxis undergirds Rose's picture of politics in terms of risk and mourning: action must be risked, the deleterious consequences reflected on and mourned, and action risked again.[183] As Kate Schick has argued, although the importance of the question, "what ought to be done?" cannot be denied, an impatient and narrow focus on it as a technical, problem-solving exercise can miss historical and contextual factors and result in worse outcomes.[184] Thus Rose's emphasis on ambiguity and equivocation: the need to explore the good and bad in political and philosophical accounts and responses, neither condemning all law and politics as unjust and violent, nor assuming the achievement of justice or progress, nor being complacent and self-satisfied.[185] One aspect of the concept of the broken middle is therefore that of specifying some features of the kind of ethical and political *phronesis* Rose thinks modern society requires: acknowledging the irreparability of diremptions, tarrying with aporia, navigating double dangers, historical and contextual awareness, risking action and reflecting on practice in order to learn, navigating the impurity and complicity of any virtues.

Since Rose is engaged in phenomenology of theory, Murphy's accusation that Rose "is not interested in anything empirical unless it can be used to batter someone else,"[186] somewhat misses the mark. Likewise, Gorman's and Osborne's criticisms that her work is politically impotent fails to give due emphasis to the central place of judgment and *phronesis* involved.[187] A critical theory focused on philosophical consciousness depends on the internal connection and reciprocal influence Hegel discerned between philosophical consciousness and natural consciousness.[188] To critique one is to critique the other, even if some dots have to be joined. Hence, "we do not know what the determinate negation of par-

183. *LW*.

184. Schick, *Trauma and the Ethical*.

185. *BM*, xii–xiii.

186. Murphy, "Memorising Politics," 395.

187. Gorman, "Gillian Rose's Critique of Violence."

188. Cf. Tubbs, *Contradiction of Enlightenment*.

ticular untruths would be so long as the practice and regimes (economic, political, social) of identitarian thought remain in control. The idea of *negative* dialectics is determined by this belief; its intention is to maximize critical agency while forestalling precipitous concretion."[189] This returns us to the accusation of vagueness raised in chapter 1 and provides Rose with further defense against the charge. Not only can the desire for solutions be too hasty, it can require more action guidance from theories than they are designed to give. Nor is this problem unique to Rose, it is rather "one of the recurring internal aporias of cultural criticism: quantitative or instrumental descriptions of the goals of life need to be shown up as inadequate and reductive, yet the character of the alternative ends up being merely gestured to by unsatisfactory phrases about 'life.'"[190]

3.1 Mutual recognition and Hegelian phenomenological reconstruction

Rose's political orientation stems partly from the Frankfurt School hybrid of description and normativity, a way of handling the fact-value distinction without acceding it unproblematic authority. As we have seen, Rose is alert to the constant danger that violence and the legitimization of power will slip into brute violence and/or the justification of illegitimate power, but believes thinking through the risk is the best response to it. This approach combined with the avoidance of any imposed *Sollen* led Rose to follow Hegel in phenomenologically reconstructing mutual recognition as the immanent *telos* of modern society's ethics, law and politics.[191] Mutual recognition is their actuality, their rational core and thus that at which policy- and lawmakers should aim. It is "*the Hegelian Moment*: the struggle for recognition is a drama in which the good (full mutual recognition) and the means (varieties of misrecognition) engender each other and may be negotiated but only by acknowledgement of

189. Bernstein, *Adorno*, 353.

190. Collini, "Tale of Two Critics," 16.

191. Patberg, "Supranational Constitutional Politics," 515: "A rational reconstruction is the philosophical enterprise of identifying the presuppositions that are constitutive for a given social practice in the sense that they need to be assumed, at least implicitly and possibly counterfactually, by the participants in order that their shared practice may appear to them as meaningful and thus worthy of preservation." Rose's version of rational reconstruction emphasizes the historical element of phenomenology.

mutual implication in the violence of misrecognition."[192] Mutual recognition, even though never fully achieved, is therefore the means to help navigate the risks attendant on law, politics, public-ethical action, and action that goes against *Sittlichkeit*. *Geist* in Hegel "means the attempt to reconstruct and present these inversions of subject and substance . . . hence the *Phenomenology of Spirit* is a drama of discursiveness which ironizes its passages and its *aporiae* so as to leave its reader exposed to the recognition of being already engaged in the struggle for recognition."[193]

This further answers critics of Rose who claim she retreats into existentialism and relativism; or that she offers too little by way of concrete application; or that she is unable to think of alternatives either to the present political arrangement or to the postmodern nihilist unending agon. Given Rose's acceptance of the imperfect justice of rationalized law and the need to supplement it with institutions of the middle, impure virtue, and mutual recognition, this is rather unfair. It is true, however, that references to mutual recognition in Rose's work remain largely gestural. Recently, however, Kate Schick and Liz Disley have begun to develop accounts of recognition using Rose's work.[194] Furthermore, Axel Honneth has been developing his theory of mutual recognition for over two decades from the Hegelian Frankfurt tradition in which Rose also stood. His work therefore complements Rose's in this area. Moreover, Robert Pippin argued in a recent article on *Freedom's Right*, that Honneth's work would be better grounded and more complete if it was based on Hegelian theoretical philosophy as well as the empirical psychological and sociological work Honneth chooses as his foundation.[195] Perhaps Rose's work could complement Honneth's in this regard: given the similarities between Rose and Pippin canvassed in chapter 1, Pippin's article may be read as making explicit some connections between Rose's speculative philosophy and a more developed account of mutual recognition. I briefly discuss some aspects of Honneth's theory compatible with Rose's philosophy. Then I turn to the more specifically Rosean dimensions of recognition developed by Schick and Disley. Finally, I offer my own remarks on a Rosean account of recognition based around the centrality she accorded to recognition and appropriation.

192. *MBL*, 98.

193. *JAM*, 68.

194. Schick, "Re-cognizing Recognition," 87–105; Disley, *Hegel, Love and Forgiveness*.

195. "Reconstructivism: On Honneth's Hegelianism," 725–41.

Honneth reworks Hegel's *Philosophy of Right* with its three differentiated spheres for realizing freedom. The philosophical task is thus "historical-diagnostic."[196] A theory of justice "cannot be separated from concrete social analysis."[197] It is "neither an empirical social analysis nor pure normative assessment but some hybrid of both, what Honneth calls a 'reconstruction' of the rational core in such historically specific institutions."[198] Humans are self-determining (not absolutely but even their biology underdetermines what they can be), and so self-determination is self-constitution. Hegelian phenomenology reconstructs different ways humans have constituted themselves and discerns an intelligibility, a rationality, in those attempts *and* in the shifts between them. Determinate negation makes sense, shows a development. This does not mean every step along the philosophical journey is necessary, only that an intelligible, overall narrative can be found retrospectively and this is what guides the rationality of the reconstruction. Hegel says this intelligibility is to do with freedom; he thought, in fact, the development of freedom was necessary. This is historical rationality—there is no eternal standard to access, only the reconstruction of the logic internal to practices in the past and present. The criteria for what counts as a good reason themselves change over time. Freedom in Hegel involves dependence—his paradigmatic examples are friendship and love; it is reflexive freedom not only negative freedom. That is, freedom is the ability to act in different spheres or contexts, not merely the ability to be self-causing. Freedom is more like being able to speak a language than being able to move an arm (though it includes the latter). Being free "consists in being in a certain social relation, or unified set of social relations."[199]

I noted above the permanent tension inscribed at the heart of the broken middle because it holds together three levels of society, each with its own form of respect/recognition. It thereby differentiates itself from traditional moral philosophy, from the unity of the virtues in Greek and Christian thought, and from modern ethics' tendency to define a single principle to generate an ethical system. Thus although mutual recognition is the actuality of both ethics and law, ethics and law remain dirempted in part because mutual recognition itself is irreconcilably split

196. Ibid., 726.

197. Ibid.

198. Ibid.

199. Ibid., 727.

three ways. The three forms of respect are: love, in which a person is affirmed as unique in their needs and desires, and which exists among small groups of people; esteem or solidarity, in which a person's contributions to a shared, concrete community and/or project are valued (in the various arenas of civil society); and respect, in which individuals hold one another and themselves morally accountable and as possessing dignity, at the state level and beyond. The three levels increase in scope and comprehensiveness, but at the same time lose concreteness. The worst form of disrespect is at the level of bodily needs, desires and integrity (similar to Mill's harm doctrine). The next worst is to disregard the most comprehensive level, that of moral accountability and dignity. Finally, the least bad form of disrespect is not to recognize another's contributions to civil society and its projects. Now, "the transition from one sphere of recognition to another is always caused by a struggle to gain respect for a subject's self-comprehension as it grows in stages. The demand to be recognized in ever more dimensions of one's own person leads to a kind of intersubjective conflict whose resolution can only consist in the establishment of a further sphere of recognition."[200] Thus social conflict is not merely a struggle for brute power or self-interest but, at least sometimes, derives from "moral impulses."[201]

Honneth's theory is thus able to identify not only injustice but also social pathologies, not only harm but also disrespect. By way of phenomenological reconstruction it can be argued that recognition has emerged historically and immanently from modern European society, which explains Rose's less pessimistic stance than some forms of critical theory. In particular, Rose refuses the dilemma, often associated with Adorno, of having no norms to ground critique. Hegel's criticism of natural law was that what appeared as *a priori* values were in fact *a posteriori*. Adorno thought this left him with no immanent norms other than those of the bourgeois world, which had ended up in Auschwitz.[202] One response to this is to look for practices that can ground a different set of values and reasons—modern art for Adorno, small communities for MacIntyre, the church for Milbank, institutions of the middle for Rose. The question is always whether they are able to do the task set for them. Yet Rose blunts the force of the dilemma by refusing the initial problem as posed by

200. Honneth, *Disrespect*, 132–33.

201. Honneth, *Struggle for Recognition*, 5.

202. Finlayson, "Morality and Critical Theory," 7–41.

Adorno. The bourgeois world is not completely corrupt; notwithstanding its problems some of it is just and good, it retains some legitimacy. (Here again Rose resembles Habermas and Honneth.)

Although Rose does provide a convincing account of the fundamentals of socio-logic and systematically links it to a number of areas in very thought-provoking ways, much of the latter remain suggestive rather than detailed positions. This of course is at least partly because her life ended tragically early. Yet, some of Rose's work did have a more practical bent, by immanently showing the tensions of important areas of life—artistic representation of the Holocaust, architecture, an approach to life and death and medicine. And for works that do offer substantial accounts of specific phenomena, which succeed by Rose's criteria, one may look to the authors she cites, to other examples such as those throughout this thesis, or to those directly developing Rose's work.[203] Here, I briefly summarize the work of Kate Schick and Liz Disley who have intentionally developed aspects of recognition theory on the basis of Rose's work to further spell out some of the normative implications of Rose's social philosophy.

Schick argues that recognition theory has tended to take two forms: "hyperrationalist" or "primordial." Hyperrationalist recognition theory has actually regressed into individualism, losing its some of its initial stress on intersubjectivity, and taken on a positivist, problem-solving intellectual mood. The radical nature of agents' interdependence and vulnerability has been lost, as has the sense of the struggle of coming to know, the repeated re-cognition involved in recognition. Recognition has become a tool, applied outwardly to solve social problems by "adding more" recognition. The inward moment has sunk from view. By contrast, Rosean recognition urges the subject to discover the ways in which they are complicit in misrecognition and injustice, even while having good intentions. It highlights the vulnerability of the subject in the process of recognition.[204] Disley suggests Hegelian recognition involves love and forgiveness as central paradigms, and that both are best theorized using elements from the theological tradition (whence Hegel took

203. On international relations: Schick, *Rose*; on political theology and social action: Lloyd, *Problem with Grace*; on ecclesial organisation and civic participation, the work of Andrew Shanks; on social commentary: Williams, *Lost Icons* (for a Christian appropriation) and Maggie O'Neill (ed.), *Adorno, Culture and Feminism* (for a feminist appropriation); on education: the work of Nigel Tubbs.

204. Schick, "Re-cognizing Recognition."

them originally in his early work). Recognition thus involves *metanoia*, repentance, changing the self not merely one's mind. She thinks this is well captured by Rose's broken middle as a place of "constant change and anxiety," since recognition in its various forms are never finished.[205] The broken middle entails that taking a position always involves error, and so "violence," even within love.[206] "Imperfect and in some way incomplete (Rose's broken middle), the self in its relation with the Other is ever-changing and being remade (*metanoia*, Hegelian . . . *Aufhebung*) and is influenced by the Other and the wider community to such an extent that we cannot speak of full autonomy, though there is a clear space for ethical responsibility. . . . This ethical self is not ontologically pre-defined, but forms itself in the encounter or confrontation with the Other, who calls the self to ethical action."[207]

These developments of a Rosean-inflected version of recognition cohere well with my remarks in chapters 1 and 2 about the dialectic between recognition and appropriation, which Rose regarded as central to Hegel. Once something has been recognized, the recognition remains to be appropriated, and this applies as someone or something is repeatedly re-cognized. This involves several dimensions, all of which are important in Rose's work as a whole: time, working through, mediation, subjectivity and history. The recognition-appropriation dialectic requires time because recognition is not simply registering a fact but involves a change in the individual, "a new concept of the self-other relation, the self-self relation, and the self-world relation."[208] It is both intellectual and existential. Many accounts of recognition focus only on the initial moment of recognition or its end result, but thereby neglect the time it takes to work through the difficulties of recognition, whereas Schick and Disley start to bring this out. The labor of appropriation can be thought in terms of "working through," an important phrase for Rose[209] and driving her aberrated/inaugurated mourning distinction. Working through is a psychoanalytic term for the process in which the individual brings to consciousness and thinks through different aspects of an idea, and thereby gradually overcomes his/her initial resistance to accepting the

205. Disley, *Hegel, Love and Forgiveness*, 16.

206. Rose's term of art "violence" is somewhat confusing. It sometimes, as here, means simply error.

207. Disley, *Hegel, Love and Forgiveness*, 70–71.

208. Ibid., 2.

209. RTÉ interview.

idea. Again, this is not a narrowly intellectual exercise but involves emotions, an aesthetic sense and may involve the body more directly too. Working through over time involves finding the recognized person (or object) in more and more of his (or its) mediations, rendering him more concrete and so relating him to some sort of totality. At the same time, one is relating oneself to the recognized other and to the totality too, and thereby discovering something about how one's self is determined, which may contribute to one's freedom from determination. Equally, appropriation involves internalizing—in a deep, significant way—what is recognized, and this involves a certain kind of self-relation. The self is transformed both by open receptivity to what is recognized and by active work on the self by the self. This is why Rose regards philosophy as existentially transformative. Finally, the mediations one discerns are historically shaped and can be related to historical struggles for recognition (Honneth) and gain their meanings from phenomenological determinate negations. Yet Rose's insistence on the centrality and fundamentality of mediation against any kind of ethical immediacy may leave her account of recognition less vulnerable than Honneth's to the charge of neglecting economic and legal deformations of consciousness.[210] These brief remarks hopefully suggest the gains to be had from Rose's restoration of appropriation alongside recognition within her speculative philosophy and her version of mutual recognition.[211]

4 Conclusion

Rose's critical theory of modern society is focused around two fundamental, interacting, modern diremptions: state-civil society and law-ethics. These two diremptions combine and alter in various forms as they are filtered through class, religion, race and gender. Attention to these diremptions provides a substantive theory of modern society, a guide for framing sociological investigations, and a mode of critique of social philosophy. This focus provides a lens through which to see society and a starting point for phenomenological examinations of modernity's political history. Through them, Rose's social philosophy consciously incorporates its own logical and material preconditions. The speculative identity

210. Thompson, "Axel Honneth and the Neo-Idealist Turn," 779–97.

211. See further Brower Latz, "Towards a Rosean Political Theology of Recognition."

between law and ethics keeps in view the question of the legitimation of authority and the just use of power, both their possibilities and risks.

The modern version of the law-ethics diremption is a function of two things: the rationalization of law and the internal fissures of ethics as mutual recognition. Even though rationalized law is imperfect and fosters nihilism, it is still a necessary condition of political legitimacy and justice in contemporary society. Impure political virtue is the modern form of *phronesis*, one that incorporates its own preconditions, including the violence of state power. The chiasmus "violence in love and love in violence" expresses the shifting mixture of good and coercion found in both ethics and law and in their relation, which modern social theory must investigate ever anew. The failure of much poststructuralist theory to do so is the "pathos of the concept"—the sad fate that has befallen its ability to know and learn.

Rose's metaphilosophy is not narrowly logical but also provides an intellectual mood. In line with this Rose steers a political middle path between ignoring ethics within politics and subordinating politics to ethics. Encouraging forms of *Sittlichkeit* groups, middle institutions and mutual recognition is one way to cope with our necessarily imperfect condition. Mutual recognition is the core of her normative stance, which she thinks can be reconstructed from the phenomenological history of European societies and is therefore not an imposed *Sollen*. This takes the form of critical reconstructions, neither foundationalist nor skeptical, assessing current ethical life and theory through repetition backwards and forwards. As the actuality of law and ethics—yet imperfectly attained and distorted in its inversions—mutual recognition must heed its social mediations and inversions in order to ameliorate them, rather than seek to escape them. The dialectic of recognition and appropriation, which Rose retrieves from Hegel, is capable of opening up different dimensions of recognition that are still not fully appreciated: time, working through, mediation, subjectivity and history. Though implicit in her version of recognition, they are pervasive themes of her thought.

The broken middle is a metatheory, both epistemologically and as an immanent critique of other theories. With regard to the latter, in contrast to jurisprudential wisdom the focus shifts away from showing the legal jurisdiction underlying social philosophies and toward the complementary task of revealing the way the nature of modern society as a broken middle is both recognized and misrecognized in various theories. It thus continues the second form of ideology critique common within the

Frankfurt tradition—of pointing out the mistaking of theory for reality. Theoretical mending of the middle cannot heal society's diremptions and by obscuring this may make them worse. With regard to the former it is a version of Hegelian phenomenology and logic, which also ground Rose's view of mutual recognition. This would be consistent with the way Rose insisted on continuous interaction between theoretical and metatheoretical levels and the internality of thought and being. The broken middle and anxiety of beginning thus name the result of consistently facing both the deficit of epistemological and moral foundations in modernity, and our ability to attain, nevertheless, a measure of good enough knowledge and justice. Their vulnerability to historical accident and their internal diremptions are the equivocations of the middle. Acknowledging them allows Rose to provide a philosophical-sociological grounding to value pluralism and dirty hands, the equivocations of ethics and its suspension in (dependence on yet tension with) ethical life, and the dialectic of reflective and determinant judgment. Action and meaning in the medium of limited and historically variable reason thus take on the character of faith. As such they inherently involve risk and error but can be educated.

Conclusion

Certainly time is the occasion for our strangely mixed nature, in every moment differently compounded, so that we often surprise ourselves, and always scarcely know ourselves, and exist in relation to experience, if we attend to it and if its plainness does not disguise it from us, as if we were visited by revelation.

—Marilynne Robinson, *The Death of Adam*

THIS BOOK HAS PROVIDED an original interpretation and reconstruction of Gillian Rose's work as a distinctive social philosophy within the Frankfurt School tradition that holds together the methodological, logical, descriptive, metaphysical and normative moments of social theory; provides a critical theory of modern society; is open to religion based on the Frankfurt doctrine of self-limiting reason; and offers distinctive versions of ideology critique based on the history of jurisprudence, and of mutual recognition as the actuality of modern society based on a Hegelian view of appropriation. Rose's philosophy integrates three key moments of the Frankfurt tradition: a view of the social totality—absolute ethical life—as both an epistemological necessity and normative ideal; a philosophy that is its own metaphilosophy because it integrates its own logical and social preconditions within itself; and a critical analysis of modern society that is simultaneously a critique of social theory. Rose's work is original in the way it organizes these three moments around absolute ethical life as the social totality, its Hegelian basis, and its focus on metaphysical entanglements of law, ethics and jurisprudence. Absolute ethical life emerges from the speculative exposition of the diremptions of the broken middle and enables a critique of social theorizing that insufficiently appreciates its social determinations and/or attempts to eliminate metaphysics. The transcendental form of social theorizing leaves theory more vulnerable to this mistake than does Hegelian speculative philosophy. Since speculative philosophy is more thoroughly its own metaphilosophy, reflexively incorporates more of its preconditions, it is better able to account for its own structure and its relation to and role in society. Absolute ethical life, as a speculative unity of diremptions, acts equally as a critique of society and sociology, including the role of bourgeois property law and social contract theories reflective of it, the hollowing out of middle institutions, and rationalized forms of law and ethics that undermine mutual recognition.

Chapter 1 showed how Rose used, somewhat eccentrically, Hegel's phenomenology, triune rationality and speculative identities, in concert with recognition and appropriation, to unite method and system and develop a social philosophy that was its own metaphilosophy. Speculative philosophy's circularity is virtuous by reference to a non-totalizing totality, whereas transcendental social theory begins from a given precondition. Rose's social philosophy thus better explains the logical basis of social theory and sociological explanation, and shows normativity is intrinsic to theorizing. Chapter 2 showed Rose's appropriation of the Frankfurt-Weber analysis of modernity and self-limiting reason in relation to an aporetic ontology, philosophical modernism and religion. I showed Rose's speculative philosophy is subtly different from Adorno's negative dialectics and the implications for theoretical responses to Auschwitz. Chapter 3 examined for the first time Rose's jurisprudential ideology critique of social philosophy, using Kant as a test case. Though her criticisms of Kant largely failed, they revealed further aspects of her social philosophy: a political philosophy inspired by Hegel's *Philosophy of Right*, the use of law to gain a view of the social totality, and a metaphysically expansive view of jurisprudence. Chapter 4 showed the enduring relevance of Rose's focus on the state-civil society and law-ethics diremptions for sociological investigations and theorizing ethics and politics, and outlined the distinctive inflection Rose gave to mutual recognition.

My interpretation has five advantages over previous work on Rose. It presents Rose's work as a social philosophy with distinct forms of ideology critique and mutual recognition, and shows how it may be used without becoming an external method. It shows *Hegel Contra Sociology*, *Dialectic of Nihilism* and *The Broken Middle* as a trilogy pursuing the critique-of-society-and-sociology in relation to absolute ethical life on the basis of a Hegelian philosophy and metaphilosophy. It reveals her work as an original synthesis of all her main sources—Hegel, Adorno and the Frankfurt School, the jurisprudential tradition, Marx and Weber. It is the most comprehensive interpretation to date and only on the basis of such comprehensiveness can the full power of Rose's social philosophy be grasped. I am thus able most fully to contextualize her work's relation to religion.

Rose had a Hegelian view of reason: reason itself has changed over time because reason is involved in practices, and the only way to tell whether something is more or less rational is to reconstruct the history of its emergence. Rose emphasizes the inversions of meaning, the contradictions of reason's forms in society, as ways of understanding both the universals at which philosophy rightly aims and the aporia preventing it ever completely attaining them. Reason's self-critique is circular since the tool and object of analysis are the same. Hegel criticized Kant's critical philosophy not for its circularity, which is unavoidable, but for its way of handling this circularity, because it tried to ensure the proper use of reason as a canon before fully exploring the use of reason as an organon. The fear of error was the error itself; Kant's critical enterprise was like the attempt to learn to swim before getting in the water. Our knowing and reasoning are always already begun and must therefore improve themselves from this initiated situation. We begin in the middle. Hegel's phenomenology keeps to the immanent criteria of a form of reason (including, at the later stages, the social manifestations of that form, since the two are in fact inseparable) and negates it determinately to the next form. After some progress certain fundamental features of knowing and reasoning, on which we cannot go back, became clear. Knowing and reasoning are indeed circular, but may be more or less vicious or virtuous in this regard. The problem with transcendentally structured theories is not their circularity but their tendency to lose sight of their circularity by ossifying a precondition into too fixed a position. Transcendental social theory is thus less able to account for its social determinations than speculative social theory. In Rose's hands, Hegel's doctrine of the concept shows both that any satisfactory explanation, as a matter of logic, must refer to a totality, and shows how social wholes are more than the sum of their parts (have emergent properties).

Rose thus makes explicit the importance of Hegelian epistemology and critique of neo-Kantian transcendentalism for social philosophy. Insofar as Hegel already explicated reason as an intersubjective, cultural phenomenon rather than an operation internal to individual minds, and insofar as his epistemology is general and fundamental (not restricted to a specific object domain or discipline), Rose is simply drawing out what is already there. Nevertheless, it is particularly well suited to sociology and social philosophy, for sociology's modes, tools and concepts for its investigation will fundamentally shape the object in question. The circularity is unavoidable and is both a strength and a weakness. It is a strength insofar as it explains and provides understanding; it is a weakness insofar as sociology has shown the tendency to forget its circularity in ways that materially affect the content of study. Social philosophy must always be simultaneously theoretical and meta-theoretical; must attend to both form and content. Rose's speculative Hegelian epistemology—which emphasizes negation, experience, surprise, aporias and provisionality—is therefore the most appropriate logical basis for social theory, and in fact the basis on which it already (though usually unknowingly) operates at its best. Speculative thinking always bears in mind the difference or non-identity between object and concept, the failure of the *explicans* ever fully to account for the *explicandum*; it knows, further, that an *explicans* itself requires an explanation. Such explanations will be historical, not only structural (structures themselves have a history), and circular insofar as a good explanation of one part of society will be explained in terms of others such that the whole makes sense. The whole, the totality, remains an essential concept but it becomes an unreachable ideal, because society is too complex and too large an object to be fully known. Yet the very unattainability of the totality, which alone would give full context and so full meaning to any individual object within it and explanations thereof, is accounted for by the speculative logic of simultaneous identity and non-identity, and helps avoid the neo-Kantian forgetting of the status of sociological explanations.

In Rose's theory Hegelian phenomenology replaces Kantian transcendental deductions. Rose's phenomenology is intrinsically historical. A common postmodern mistake is to deny the historical progress possible in knowing, reasoning and morality. If sociology tends to forget its circularity, poststructuralist social philosophy tends to overdo its circularity to the extreme degree of condemning the whole Western tradition of philosophy and seeking a way out of its juridical thinking. Whereas the Frankfurt School accepted the necessity of juridical thinking and wished to sublate it within a wider and more textured form of reason, poststructuralism wished to escape juridical thinking altogether. This led to problems with ethics and politics, which Rose discussed as nihilism, "new ethics," and the longing for the singular and unknowable Event. It is now a truism to insist that universal definitions of essences are necessarily masks for power plays, but this is an overstatement, and anyway one cannot avoid definitions. Social theory must always be theoretical and meta-theoretical. Part of this dual-focus is the need to be reflexive, to know whence a definition or conceptual demarcation arises, at what it aims and what purposes it serves. A stipulative definition may clarify an aspect of an issue but it will scarcely if ever be universal. Within discourses—competing academic discourses for instance—one can keep provisionality, ambiguity and agnosticism in play; but when it comes to law or policy, definitions are enacted and imposed. This is again ineluctable. The substitution of the free-floating nature of academic disputes, in which definitions can remain in dispute, for the definitions necessary for power to operate—and to judge the legitimacy of authority—was a major failure of poststructuralism in Rose's view. It was an attempt to avoid power rather than contribute to the legitimate exercise of power. Whether or not Rose was fair to Derrida, Foucault and Levinas, some of their followers seem vulnerable to Rose's critique.

In Rose's thought Hegelian ethical life replaces Kantian morality. Social philosophy faces two dangers: imposing an abstract morality on society or too much normative reticence. The latter predominates within much sociology since normative debates can distract from sociological description. Yet such attempts at neutrality can only be provisional. The fact/value distinction is not absolute but a perennial tension to think with and through. Theoretical and practical reason are not hermetically separable. Sociological work that is relatively neutral therefore must be taken up into some wider consideration if it is to become fully meaningful. (One can always ask, "so what?" and, "what is to be done?" in response to any sociological trend or pattern.) Poststructuralism's attempts at ethics tend to fall back on Levinasian immediacy, since they hollow out rational adjudication to such an extreme degree. Postmodern political theology expects too much from small communities. Both are two sides of the same coin: fleeing from rationalization and underplaying the legitimacy of national political cultures and nation-states. Yet the middle—the complex modern relation of state and society, law and ethics—is broken in the sense that it is permanently and fundamentally dirempted and imperfect. To that extent, Rose agrees with these critics of modernity. But the brokenness of the middle does not justify flight from state, society and law, nor obviate the need to take a view of the whole. A good enough justice is sometimes possible, of which mutual recognition will be a central component. Rose sought to sublate the criticisms of law, the legal person and juridical thinking, preserving all of them as essential categories for thinking and living in modern society. Rose thereby heads off a common objection that her work lacked normative resources, without idealizing or romanticizing some kind of community innocent of the abuse of power—whether that be Judaism as the sublime other of modernity or Christian groups as immune to rationalization. She expects neither too much nor too little from ethical life and its main carriers in society. Rose may be compared to Habermas and Honneth who have been sufficiently sociological and philosophical to offer an adequate view of the whole with normative weight.

The broken middle, Rose's mature position, has five main components:

(a) A sociological thesis about modern society as fundamentally dirempted between state and civil society, and between law and ethics; between discourses of rights and actual practices of state power, between formal legal equality and inequalities of class and gender. This includes the constant tensions between individuals, civil society, and the state, and their corresponding forms of recognition. Rose's view of diremptions and mutual recognition emerged from a phenomenological history of modern society.

(b) A philosophical thesis about the nature of thinking that serves as its own meta-theory. Speculative philosophy reconstructs a view of different social wholes through phenomenological history. Such wholes are necessary for explanation but never entirely available. A fully coherent and seamlessly systematic philosophical system does not exist; philosophy, reasoning and knowing are not self-grounding but rely on social practices and institutions. Speculative philosophy is a hybrid of normative and descriptive moments able to account for the contradictions and antinomies sociology repeatedly discovers, without reducing philosophy to sociology of knowledge. Reason is also existential: it changes the subject as well as the object. The dialectic of recognition and appropriation is important to both the logical and existential aspects of reason.

(c) A framework for social philosophy based on the above philosophical and sociological elements. Rose's speculative philosophy led her to a vision of philosophy as a modernist cultural practice opening the way to modern forms of *phronesis* and *praxis*, which involves: a combination of sociology and philosophy; a self-limiting rationality; an aporetic ontology; a realist-idealist epistemology rather than positivism or relativism; a Weberian analysis of rationalized modernity; immanent critique aiming at emancipation and reflexive self-knowledge; support for a social and political philosophy inspired by Hegel's *Philosophy of Right*; the use of law to gain a view of the social totality; and an expansive view of jurisprudence as examining the links between the metaphysical, ethical and legal, oriented toward absolute ethical life and enabling ideology critique. Rose opposes the imposition of a moralistic *Sollen* on society, the assumption that theory can mend sociopolitically sourced diremptions, and warns that attempts to do so may make diremptions worse due to the complexity of society as an emergent whole or organism. The effects of such metaphilosophical assumptions and intellectual moods on social theorizing are an important part of Rose's theory.

(d) A critical phenomenology of modern theory revealing where it recognizes and misrecognizes components of the broken middle; and a critique of modern society based on where it does and does not embody expansive reason and mutual recognition. Rose criticized the inflated role of property in society, the rationalization of law and ethics (while accepting their current importance), and the diminution of institutions of the middle. The modern version of the law-ethics diremption stems from the rationalization of law and the internal fissures of ethics as mutual recognition. Even though rationalized law is imperfect and fosters nihilism, it is still a necessary condition of political legitimacy and justice in contemporary society.

(e) A thesis about some of the features of practical wisdom in ethics and politics (and thus of the kind of subjectivity appropriate to modern citizens): acknowledging the irreparability of society's diremptions; tarrying with the contradictions of ethical and political life; historical and contextual awareness; risking action and reflecting on practice in order to learn; a modern form of *phronesis* aware of its own preconditions and mediations, including violence and coercion; an intellectual mood between triumphalism and despair, a counsel of imperfection but not melancholy. There is thus no immediate ethics in abstraction from its social mediations. In foregrounding the provisionality and preconditions of both the meaning and morality of action, Rose draws out the parallels between them and religious faith; hence her use of Kierkegaard. Any intentional action undertaken by an individual is predicated on some view of the meaning of their intention and action, which rests on (is intelligible within) a view of the totality; and this view of the totality is (or should be) a mixture of sociological, normative and metaphysical elements;

and it includes, even with the most comprehensive view possible, large measures of ignorance and some confusion and error. In this sense at least, secular action and meaning are not different in kind from religious faith. The notion of self-limiting reason is the basis of Rose's comments on Hegel, Nietzsche and Kierkegaard bringing revelation into reason.

The relation between Rose's work, religion and political theology may be assessed in the light of my reconstruction of her social theory. Her social philosophy was substantially developed before her interest in religion arose. Her early treatment of religion in *Hegel Contra Sociology* is crudely reductive and religion is absent from *Dialectic of Nihilism*. In the late works it occupies much more attention: a chapter on political theology in *The Broken Middle*, a collection of essays on Judaism, discussions of political theology in *Mourning Becomes the Law*. In these instances Rose applied her developed social theory to religion and theology without being reductive or simplistic. A different tack appears in *Love's Work*, the final two essays of *Mourning Becomes the Law* and *Paradiso* (the latter two both posthumous publications). In a letter, she stated that the last section of *Love's Work* relates to John 15:13 and Romans 8:3–4: "You see I wanted to write in a way that would capture those who imagine themselves closed to Christ and to conventional religion: that is why I talk of comedy as an analogy of faith and only mention God in French. This method of 'indirect communication' I have learnt from Kierkegaard."[212] She described the final two essays in *Mourning Becomes the Law* as developing "an approach to eternity, to divine transcendence . . . contra Heideggerian finitude."[213] *Paradiso* recounts Rose's explicitly religious experiences. She was planning a book called *Poem and Prayer* when she died.[214] In a late letter, Rose described herself as a "theologian in disguise."[215] Perhaps she saw her later work as a repetition of Kierkegaard's attempt to make things more difficult for others; aimed not, however, at a religious sub-group in society, but at society as a whole. If so, the aim was clearly not to convert people to a specific doctrine—Rose retained an agnostic stance toward such questions[216]—but to raise the consciousness of her readership (or

212. Letter to Tom and Barbara, 10 February 1995, box 14.

213. Proposal for *MBL*, box 31.

214. Letter to Sir Brian Follett, 9 May 1995, box 31; "Keep Your Mind in Hell," interview with Elaine Williams.

215. Cited in Rowlands, *Theology in "The Third City,"* 11.

216. Asked during the RTÉ interview, "So you believe in something outside of the spatio-temporal continuum?," Rose replied, "Certainly, yes. But I think one has to preserve an agnosticism about it. I love what Simone Weil said, that agnosticism is the

sensitize it) to the limits of reason, especially rationalized reason; not to proselytize but to "keep culture moving and open in dark times."[217]

The last point is speculative (in a nontechnical sense), though it could help explain her work's structural openness to religion. Rose's social philosophy stands independently of these later religious concerns however. The creative uses to which political and practical theologians—Lloyd, Milbank, Raskhover, Rowlands, Shanks, Williams—have put Rose's work are interesting and valuable, and more or less in line with her own thinking, though none takes full account of her social philosophy as I have reconstructed it here. Her engagement with theology, as well as her friendships with two of the most important Christian theologians working in the English language (Milbank and Williams), no doubt fostered this trajectory of her work's reception. Nevertheless, Rose's work shows that a Frankfurt-Hegelian view of self-limiting reason may coherently lead to an openness to theological views.

Rose's social philosophy is a comprehensive structure for the logic of social theory and provides a useful heuristic lenses on the social totality for empirical research. It offers gains for both more empirically and more philosophically focused social theory. In relation to the former, as I showed with Catto and Woodhead's volume, Rose's social philosophy sets out not only important elements of good practice but grounds them in logic and their relation to one another. This provides not only confidence and clarity about methods and findings making use of contradiction and paradox, diremptions, determinate negation, speculative identity, totality, multiple methods and perspectives, and history, but also pushes at the metaphysical, ethical and political implications of such work. In relation to more philosophically slanted social theory, Rose shows how neglect of history, the philosophical tradition, jurisprudence, and empirical and classical sociology results in poorer social philosophy, unaware of its own determinations and unrealistic in its response to power, politics and ethics. Her objection to the separation of philosophy and sociology is thus justified by the consequences of their combination, as well as the fruitfulness of her own Hegelian-Frankfurt integration of them both. Rose's work thus remains a potentially rich and powerful framework for social theorizing.

most truly religious position. You must be able to say you don't know. Agnosticism is the only true religion because to have faith is not to give up knowledge, but to know where the limit of knowledge is." Lloyd, interview with Gillian Rose, 217.

217. Bernstein, "Philosophy among the Ruins," 30.

Works Cited

Works by Gillian Rose (listed in chronological order)

"Reification as a Sociological Category: Theodor W. Adorno's Concept of Reification and the Possibility of a Critical Theory of Society." PhD diss., University of Oxford, 1976.

"How Is Critical Theory Possible? Theodor Adorno and Concept Formation in Sociology." *Political Studies* 24.1 (1976) 69–85.

Review of *Negative Dialectics*, by Theodor W. Adorno. *American Political Science Review* 7.2 (1976) 598–99.

The Melancholy Science: An Introduction to the Thought of Theodor W. Adorno. New York: Columbia University Press, 1978.

Hegel Contra Sociology. London: Athlone, 1981. 2nd ed., with new preface, London: Verso, 1995.

Letter to *London Review of Books*, December 17, 1981.

"Parts and Wholes." *Proceedings of the International Conference on Parts and Wholes* (June 1983) 95–100. Copy held at University of Lund, Sweden.

Dialectic of Nihilism: Post-Structuralism and Law. Oxford: Blackwell, 1984.

"The Dispute over Marx and Weber." Lecture, University of Sussex, 1987. Gillian Rose Archives, University of Warwick Library, Modern Records Centre, MSS.377. Cassette 7702.

"Does Marx Have a Method?" Lecture, University of Sussex, 1987. Gillian Rose Archives, University of Warwick Library, Modern Records Centre, MSS.377. Cassette 7703.

The Broken Middle: Out of Our Ancient Society. Oxford: Blackwell, 1992.

Judaism and Modernity: Philosophical Essays. Oxford: Blackwell, 1993.

Love's Work: A Reckoning with Life. London: Chatto & Windus, 1995.

"A Ghost in His Own Machine." Review of *Points* and *Spectres of Marx*, by Jacques Derrida. *Times* (London), July 27, 1995.

Mourning Becomes the Law: Philosophy and Representation. Cambridge: Cambridge University Press, 1996.

"The Final Notebooks of Gillian Rose." Edited by Howard Caygill. *Women: A Cultural Review* 9.1 (1998) 6–18.

Paradiso. London: Menard, 1999.

Interview with Rose

Lloyd, Vincent, ed. Interview with Gillian Rose. *Theory, Culture and Society* 25.7–8 (2008) 203–20. First interviewed by Andy O'Mahony, on *Dialogue*, RTÉ Radio 1, 28 October and 4 November 1995. Full audio version available at www.rte.ie/radio1/podcast/podcast_dialogue.xml.

Williams, Elaine. "Keep Your Mind in Hell and Despair Not." *Times Higher Education Supplement*, April 14, 1995.

Obituaries of Rose

Bernstein, J. M. "A Work of Hard Love." *Guardian*, December 11, 1995.

Caygill, Howard. *Radical Philosophy* 77 (1996) 56.

Martins, Hermínio. *St. Antony's College Record* (1996) 112–14.

Milbank, John. *Independent*, December 13, 1995. http://www.independent.co.uk/news/people/obituaries-professor-gillian-rose-1525497.html.

Times (London), December 14, 1995.

Reviews of *Hegel Contra Sociology*

Bernasconi, Robert. Review of *Hegel Contra Sociology*. *Bulletin of the Hegel Society of Great Britain* 5 (1981) 41–44.

Crane, Jeffrey Lloyd. "Habermas and Hegel: Possible Contributions to a Unified Social Theory." *Contemporary Sociology* 11.6 (1982) 636–39.

Hawthorn, Geoffrey. "Ideal Speech." *London Review of Books*, November 19, 1981.

Knapp, Peter. Review of *Hegel Contra Sociology*. *Owl of Minerva* 15.2 (1984) 199–203.

Minogue, Kenneth. Review of *Hegel Contra Sociology*. *British Journal of Sociology* 36.3 (1985) 477–78.

Osborne, Peter. "Hegelian Phenomenology and the Critique of Reason and Society." *Radical Philosophy* 32 (1982) 8–15.

Reviews of *Dialectic of Nihilism*

Beck, Anthony. Review of *Dialectic of Nihilism*. *British Journal of Sociology* 37.4 (1986) 597–98.

Bennington, Geoffrey. "L'Arroseur Arrose(e)." *New Formations* 7 (1989) 35–49.

Grier, Philip. Review of *Dialectic of Nihilism*. *Canadian Philosophical Review* 6.4 (1986) 175–77.

Lash, Scott. Review of *Dialectic of Nihilism*. *Theory & Society* 16.2 (1987) 305–9.

Murphy, W. T. "Memorising Politics of Ancient History." *Modern Law Review* 50 (1987) 384–405.

Norris, Christopher. "Textual Theory at the Bar of Reason." *London Review of Books*, July 18, 1985.

Raffel, Stanley. Review of *Dialectic of Nihilism*. *Sociology* 19.4 (1985) 648–50.

Reviews of *The Broken Middle*

Jarvis, Simon. Review of *The Broken Middle*. *Bulletin of the Hegel Society of Great Britain* 27/28 (1993) 88–92.

Kerr, Fergus. Review of *The Broken Middle*. *Sociology* 27.2 (1993) 365–67.

Milbank, John. "Living in Anxiety." *Times Higher Education Supplement*, June 26, 1992.

Reviews of *Judaism and Modernity*

Bauman, Zygmunt. Review of *Judaism and Modernity*. *Sociological Review* 42.3 (1994) 572–76.

Wyschogrod, Edith. Review of *Judaism and Modernity*. *Modern Theology* 11.2 (1995) 268–70.

Other Works Cited

Adorno, Theodor W. "The Actuality of Philosophy." *Telos* 31 (1977) 120–33.

———. *The Adorno Reader*. Edited by Brian O'Connor. Oxford: Blackwell, 2000.

———. *The Culture Industry*. Edited by J. M. Bernstein. London: Routledge, 1991.

———. *Hegel: Three Studies*. Translated by Shierry Weber Nicholson. London: MIT Press, 1993 [1963].

———. *Kant's* Critique of Pure Reason. Translated by Rodney Livingstone. Edited by Rolf Tiedemann. Stanford: Stanford University Press, 2001 [1995].

———. *Metaphysics: Concepts and Problems*. Translated by Edmund Jephcott. Edited by Rolf Tiedemann. Stanford: Stanford University Press, 2001 [1965].

———. *Negative Dialectics*. Translated by E. B. Ashton. London: Continuum, 1983.

Adorno, Theodor W., and Hellmut Becker. "Education or Maturity and Responsibility." Translated by Robert French et al. *History of the Human Sciences* 12.3 (1999) 21–34.

Adorno, Theodor W., and Max Horkheimer. *Dialectic of Enlightenment*. Translated by John Cumming. London: Verso, 1997 [1944 and 1969].

Adorno, Theodor W., et al. *The Positivist Dispute in German Sociology*. Translated by Glyn Adey and David Frisby. London: Heinemann, 1976 [1969].

Allison, Henry E. "Justification and Freedom in the *Critique of Practical Reason*." In *Kant's Transcendental Deductions: The Three "Critiques" and the "Opus Postumum."* edited by Eckart Förster, 114–30. Stanford: Stanford University Press, 1989.

Ameriks, Karl. *Kant and the Historical Turn: Philosophy as Critical Interpretation*. Oxford: Oxford University Press, 2006.

———. "Vindicating Autonomy." In *Kant on Moral Autonomy*, edited by Oliver Sensen, 53–70. Cambridge: Cambridge University Press, 2012.

Arato, Andrew, and Jean Cohen. *Civil Society and Political Theory*. London: MIT Press, 1994.

Avineri, Shlomo. *Hegel's Theory of the Modern State*. Cambridge: Cambridge University Press, 1972.

Bauman, Zygmunt. *Modernity and Ambivalence*. Cambridge: Polity, 1991.

———. *Modernity and the Holocaust*. Oxford: Polity, 1989.

Beckford, James. *Social Theory and Religion*. Cambridge: Cambridge University Press, 2003.

Beiser, Frederick C. "Normativity in Neo-Kantianism: Its Rise and Fall." *International Journal of Philosophical Studies* 17.1 (2009) 9–27.

Benhabib, Seyla. Review of *Violence: Thinking Without Banisters*, by Richard J. Bernstein. *Notre Dame Philosophical Reviews*, July 27, 2014. https://ndpr.nd.edu/news/49514-violence-thinking-without-banisters/.

Bergo, Bettina. *Levinas Between Ethics and Politics: For the Beauty That Adorns the Earth*. Boston: Kluwer, 1999.

Bernstein, J. M. *Adorno: Disenchantment and Ethics*. Modern European Philosophy. Cambridge: Cambridge University Press, 2001.

———. "Autonomy and Solitude." In *Nietzsche and Modern German Thought*, edited by Keith Ansell-Pearson, 192–215. London: Routledge, 1991.

———. *The Fate of Art: Aesthetic Alienation from Kant to Derrida and Adorno*. University Park: Pennsylvania State University Press, 1992.

———. "Philosophy among the Ruins." *Prospect* 6 (1996) 27–30.

———. *Recovering Ethical Life: Jürgen Habermas and the Future of Critical Theory*. London: Routledge, 1995.

———. "Right, Revolution and Community: Marx's 'On the Jewish Question.'" In *Socialism and the Limits of Liberalism*, edited by Peter Osborne, 91–119. London: Verso, 1991.

———. "Speculation and Aporia." April 2, 1987. University of Warwick Library, Modern Records Centre, MSS.377, box 36, 1–7.

Bhaskar, Roy. *Dialectic: The Pulse of Freedom*. London: Routledge, 2008.

Bierbricher, Thomas. "Critical Theories of the State: Governmentality and the Strategic-Relational Approach." *Constellations* 20.3 (2013) 388–405.

Biernacki, Richard. *Reinventing Evidence in Social Inquiry: Decoding Facts and Variables*. New York: Palgrave Macmillan, 2012.

Bloor, David. "Anti-Latour." *Studies in History and Philosophy of Science* 30.1 (1999) 81–112.

Booth, Edward. *Aristotelian Aporetic Ontology in Islamic and Christian Thinkers*. Cambridge: Cambridge University Press, 1983.

Bourdieu, Pierre. *Distinction: A Social Critique of the Judgement of Taste*. Translated by Richard Nice. London: Routledge, 2010 [ET: 1984; 1979].

———. *The Logic of Practice*. Translated by Richard Nice. Cambridge: Polity, 1990 [1980].

Brooks, Thom. "Between Natural Law and Legal Positivism: Dworkin and Hegel on Legal Theory." *Georgia State University Law Review* 25 (2006–7) 513–60.

———. *Hegel's Political Philosophy: A Systematic Reading of the* Philosophy of Right. 2nd ed. Edinburgh: Edinburgh University Press, 2012 [2007].

Brower Latz, Andrew. "Gillian Rose." In *The Sage Handbook to Frankfurt School Critical Theory*, edited by Werner Bonefeld et al. London: Sage, in press.

———. "Gillian Rose and Social Theory." *Telos* 173 (2015) 37–54.

———. "Ideology Critique via Jurisprudence: Against Rose's Critique of Roman Law in Kant." *Thesis Eleven* 133.1 (2016) 80–95.

———. "More Sayable than You Think." *Open Letters Monthly*, September 1, 2016. http://www.openlettersmonthly.com/more-sayable-than-you-think/.

———. "Purity in Future Theology." In *Purity: Essays in Bible and Theology*, edited by Andrew Brower Latz and Arseny Ermakov, 252–73. Eugene, OR: Wipf and Stock, 2014.

———. "Towards a Rosean Political Theology of Recognition." In *Misrecognitions: Gillian Rose and the Task of Political Theology*, edited by Joshua Davis. Eugene, OR: Wipf and Stock, in press.

Brown, Callum. *The Death of Christian Britain: Understanding Secularisation 1800–2000*. 2nd ed. London: Routledge, 2009.

Bucklan, W. W. *A Manual of Roman Private Law*. Cambridge: Cambridge University Press, 1928.

Burbidge, John. *The Logic of Hegel's Logic*. Peterborough, ON: Broadview, 2006.

Carlson, David Gray. *A Commentary to Hegel's* Science of Logic. Basingstoke, UK: Palgrave Macmillan, 2007.

Coady, C. A. J. *Messy Morality: The Challenge of Politics*. Oxford: Clarendon, 2008.

Cohen, Ira J. General editor's foreword to *Max Weber: Readings and Commentary on Modernity*, edited by Stephen Kalberg, xi–xiv. Oxford: Blackwell, 2005.

Collini, Stefan. "A Tale of Two Critics." *Saturday Guardian*, August 17, 2013.

Collins, Randall. *The Sociology of Philosophies: A Global Theory of Intellectual Change*. Cambridge, MA: Belknap, 1998.

Conklin, William E. *Hegel's Laws: The Legitimacy of a Modern Legal Order*. Stanford: Stanford University Press, 2008.

Coskun, Deniz. *Law as Symbolic Form: Ernst Cassirer and the Anthropocentric View of Law*. Dordrecht: Springer, 2007.

Coyle, Sean. *From Positivism to Idealism: A Study of the Moral Dimensions of Legality*. Aldershot, UK: Ashgate, 2007.

———. "Legality and the Liberal Order." *Modern Law Review* 76.2 (2013) 401–18.

Cutrofello, Andrew. *Discipline and Critique: Kant, Poststructuralism, and the Problem of Resistance*. New York: State University of New York Press, 1994.

Disley, Liz. *Hegel, Love and Forgiveness: Positive Recognition in German Idealism*. London: Pickering & Chatto, 2015.

Duquette, David A. "Kant, Hegel and the Possibility of a Speculative Logic." In *Essays on Hegel's Logic*, edited by George di Giovanni, 1–16. Albany: State University of New York Press, 1990.

Elder-Vass, David. *The Causal Power of Social Structures: Emergence, Structure and Agency*. Cambridge: Cambridge University Press, 2010.

Farris, Sara R. "From the Jewish Question to the Muslim Question: Republican Rigorism, Culturalist Differentialism and Antinomies of Enforced Emancipation." *Constellations* 21.2 (2014) 296–307.

Fine, Robert. "Civil Society Theory, Enlightenment and Critique." *Democratization* 4:1 (1997) 7–28.

Finlayson, James Gordon. "Morality and Critical Theory: On the Normative Problem of Frankfurt School Social Criticism." *Telos* 146 (2009) 7–41.

Flessas, Tatiana. "Sacrificial Stone." *Law and Literature* 14.1 (2002) 49–84.

Foley, Michael W., and Bob Edwards. "The Paradox of Civil Society." *Journal of Democracy* 7.3 (1996) 38–52.

Forst, Rainer. "Civil Society." In *A Companion to Contemporary Political Philosophy*, edited by Robert E. Goodin et al., 2:451–62. 2nd ed. 2 vols. Oxford: Blackwell, 2007.

Frankfurt Institute for Social Research. *Aspects of Sociology*. Translated by John Viertel Boston: Beacon, 1972 [1956].

———. *The Essential Frankfurt School Reader*. Edited by Andrew Arato and Eike Gebhardt. New York: Urizen, 1978.

Freundlich, Dieter. *Dieter Henrich and Contemporary Philosophy: The Return to Subjectivity*. Aldershot, UK: Ashgate, 2003.

Freyenhagen, Fabian. *Adorno's Practical Philosophy: Living Less Wrongly*. Cambridge: Cambridge University Press, 2013.

Galston, William. *The Implications of Value Pluralism for Political Theory and Practice*. Cambridge: Cambridge University Press, 2004.

Gardner, John. *Law as a Leap of Faith: Essays on Law in General*. Oxford: Oxford University Press, 2012.

Gellner, Ernest. *Conditions of Liberty: Civil Society and its Rivals*. London: Penguin, 1994.

Giddens, Anthony. *The Constitution of Society: An Outline of the Theory of Structuration*. Cambridge: Polity, 1984.

———. *New Rules of Sociological Method: A Positive Critique of Interpretive Sociologies*. 2nd ed. Stanford: Stanford University, 1993 [1976].

Gorman, Anthony. "Gillian Rose and the Project of a Critical Marxism." *Radical Philosophy* 105 (2001) 25–36.

———. "Gillian Rose's Critique of Violence." *Radical Philosophy* 197 (2016) 25–35.

———. "Nihilism and Faith: Rose, Bernstein, and the Future of Critical Theory." *Radical Philosophy* 134 (2005) 18–30.

———. "Whither the Broken Middle? Rose and Fackenheim on Mourning, Modernity, and the Holocaust." In *Social Theory After the Holocaust*, edited by Robert Fine and Charles Turner, 47–70. Liverpool: Liverpool University Press, 2000.

Greiffenhagen, Christian, and Wes Sharrock. "Where Do the Limits of Experience Lie? Abandoning the Dualism of Objectivity and Subjectivity." *History of the Human Sciences* 21.3 (2008) 70–93.

Guyer, Paul. *Kant on Freedom, Law and Happiness*. Cambridge: Cambridge University Press, 2000.

Habermas, Jürgen. *Between Facts and Norms: Contributions to a Discourse Theory of Law and Democracy*. Translated by William Rehg. Cambridge: Polity, 1996 [1992].

———. *On the Logic of the Social Sciences*. Translated by Shierry Weber Nicholson and Jerry A. Stark. Cambridge: MIT, 1988 [1967].

———. *The Philosophical Discourse of Modernity: Twelve Lectures*. Translated by Frederick Lawrence. Cambridge: Polity, 1987 [1985].

———. *Theory of Communicative Action: Reason and the Rationalisation of Society*. Vol. 1. Translated by Thomas McCarthy. Cambridge: Polity, 1986 [1981].

Han, Byung-Chul. *Psychopolitik: Neoliberalismus und die neuen Machttechniken*. Frankfurt am Main: Fischer, 2014.

Hardimon, Michael O. *Hegel's Social Philosophy*. Cambridge: Cambridge University Press, 1994.

Harrington, Austin. "From Hegel to the Sociology of Knowledge: Contested Narratives." *Theory, Culture & Society* 18.6 (2001) 125–33.

Harris, Errol E. *Formal, Transcendental, and Dialectical Thinking: Logic and Reality*. New York: State University of New York Press, 1987.

Harris, H. S. "The Hegel Renaissance in the Anglo-Saxon World since 1945." *Owl of Minerva* 15.1 (1983) 77–105.

Hart, H. L. A. *The Concept of Law*. 2nd ed. Oxford: Clarendon, 1994 [1961].

Hartmann, Klaus. "Hegel: A Non-Metaphysical View." In *Hegel: A Collection of Critical Essays*, edited by Alasdair MacIntyre, 101–24. London: University of Notre Dame, 1977.

———. "On Taking the Transcendental Turn." *Review of Metaphysics* 20.2 (1966) 223–49.

Harvey, David. *A Companion to Marx's* Capital. London: Verso, 2010.

Hastie, W. Translator's preface to *The Philosophy of Law*, by Immanuel Kant, v–xxix. Edinburgh: T. & T. Clark, 1887.

Hegel, G. W. F. *Encyclopedia of the Philosophical Sciences in Basic Outline*. Part 1, *Science of Logic*. Translated and edited by Klaus Brinkmann and Daniel O. Dahlstrom. Cambridge: Cambridge University Press, 2010.

———. *Faith and Knowledge or the Reflective Philosophy of Subjectivity in the Complete Range of Its Forms as Kantian, Jacobian, and Fichtean Philosophy*. Translated by Walter Cerf and H. S. Harris. Albany: State University of New York Press, 1977.

———. *Outlines of the Philosophy of Right*. Translated by T. M. Knox. Revised and edited by Stephen Houlgate. Oxford: Oxford University Press, 2008 [1952].

———. *Phenomenology of Spirit*. Translated by A. V. Miller. Oxford: Oxford University Press Press, 1977.

———. *Phenomenology of Spirit*. Translated by Terry Pinkard. Available at http://terrypinkard.weebly.com/phenomenology-of-spirit-page.html.

———. *The Science of Logic*. Translated and edited by George di Giovanni. Cambridge: Cambridge University Press, 2010.

———. *The Scientific Ways of Treating Natural Law, Its Place in Moral Philosophy, and Its Relation to the Positive Science of Law*. Translated by T. M. Knox. Philadelphia: University of Pennsylvania Press, 1975.

———. *The Spirit of Christianity and Its Fate*. In *On Christianity: Early Theological Writings*, translated by T. M. Knox and R. Kroner. Chicago: University of Chicago, 1948.

———. *The Hegel Reader*. Edited by Stephen Houlgate. Oxford: Blackwell, 1998.

Henrich, Dieter. "Kant's Notion of a Deduction and the Methodological Background of the First *Critique*." In *Kant's Transcendental Deductions: The Three "Critiques" and the "Opus Postumum,"* edited by Eckart Förster, 29–46. Stanford: Stanford University Press, 1989.

———. "Logical Form and Real Totality: The Authentic Conceptual Form of Hegel's Concept of the State." In *Hegel on Ethics and Politics*, edited by Robert B. Pippin and Otfried Höffe, 241–67. Translated by Nicholas Walker. Cambridge: Cambridge University Press, 2004.

Honneth, Axel. *Disrespect: The Normative Foundations of Critical Theory*. Translated by Joseph Ganahl. Cambridge: Polity, 2007 [2000].

———. *Freedom's Right: The Social Foundations of Democratic Life*. Translated by Joseph Ganahl. Cambridge: Polity, 2014 [2011].

———. *The Struggle for Recognition: The Moral Grammar of Social Conflicts*. Translated by Joel Anderson. Cambridge: MIT Press, 1995.

Horkheimer, Max. "Traditional and Critical Theory." In *Critical Theory: Selected Essays*, 188–243. Translated by Matthew J. O'Conell et al. New York: Continuum, 2002.

Houlgate, Stephen. *Hegel, Nietzsche and the Criticism of Metaphysics*. Cambridge: Cambridge University Press, 1986.

———. *An Introduction to Hegel: Freedom, Truth and History*. 2nd ed. Oxford: Blackwell, 2005 [1991].

———. *The Opening of Hegel's* Logic: *From Being to Infinity*. West Lafayette, IN: Purdue University Press, 2006.

Howe, Richard Herbert. "Max Weber's Elective Affinities: Sociology within the Bounds of Pure Reason." *American Journal of Sociology* 84.2 (1978) 366–85.

Hunt, Alan. "Marxism, Law, Legal Theory and Jurisprudence." In *Dangerous Supplements: Resistance and Renewal in Jurisprudence*, edited by Peter Fitzpatrick, 101–32. Durham, NC: Duke University Press, 1991.

Hunter, W. A. *A Systematic and Historical Exposition of Roman Law in the Order of a Code*. London: Maxwell, 1885.

Independent. "Far-Right and Wrong." Editorial. *Independent*, September 19, 2014.

Ingram, David. *Habermas and the Dialectic of Reason*. London: Yale University Press, 1987.

Insole, Christopher J. *Kant and the Creation of Freedom: A Theological Problem*. Oxford: Oxford University Press, 2013.

Israel, Joachim. "Epistemology and Sociology of Knowledge: An Hegelian Undertaking." *Sociological Perspectives* 33.1 (1990) 111–28.

Jaeggi, Rahel. *Alienation*. Translated by Frederick Neuhouser and Alan E. Smith. Edited by Frederick Neuhouser. New York: Columbia University Press, 2014 [2005].

———. "'No Individual Can Resist': *Minima Moralia* as Critique of Forms of Life." *Constellations* 12.1 (2005) 65–82.

Jay, Martin. *Marxism and Totality: The Adventures of a Concept from Lukács to Habermas*. Berkeley: University of California Press, 1984.

Jones, Owen. *The Establishment: And How They Get Away With It*. London: Lane, 2014.

Kalberg, Stephen. "Marx Weber: The Confrontation with Modernity." Introduction to *Max Weber: Readings and Commentary on Modernity*, edited by Stephen Kalberg, 2–29. Oxford: Blackwell, 2005.

Kamenka, Eugene, and Alice Erh-Soon Tay. "Beyond Bourgeois Individualism: The Contemporary Crisis in Law and Legal Ideology." In *Feudalism, Capitalism and Beyond*, edited by Eugene Kamenka and R. S. Neale, 127–41. Kent: Whitstable Litho, 1975.

Kant, Immanuel. *Critique of Practical Reason*. In *Practical Philosophy*, translated and edited by Mary McGregor, 133–271. Cambridge: Cambridge University Press, 1999.

———. *Critique of Pure Reason*. Translated and edited Paul Guyer and Allen W. Wood. Cambridge: Cambridge University Press, 1998.

———. *The Metaphysical Elements of Justice*. Translated by John Ladd. Indianapolis: Bobbs-Merrill, 1965.

———. "What Is Orientation in Thinking?" In *Political Writings*, edited by Hans Reiss, 237–49. Translated by H. B. Nisbet. 2nd ed. Cambridge: Cambridge University Press, 1991 [1970].

Keane, John. Introduction to *Civil Society and the State: New European Perspectives*, edited by John Keane, 1–28. London: Verso, 1988.

Keane, Webb. "Estrangement, Intimacy, and the Objects of Anthropology." In *The Politics of Method in the Human Sciences: Positivism and its Epistemological Others*, edited by George Steinmetz, 59–88. London: Duke University Press, 2005.

Kelley, Donald R. "*Gaius Noster*: Substructures of Western Social Thought." *American Historical Review* 84.3 (1979) 619–48.

———. "The Metaphysics of Law: An Essay on the Very Young Marx." *American Historical Review* 83.2 (1978) 350–67.

Kelly, J. M. *A Short History of Western Legal Theory*. Oxford: Clarendon, 1992.

King, Anthony. *The Structure of Social Theory*. London: Routledge, 2004.

Kołakowski, Leszek. "In Praise of Inconsistency." *Dissent* 11.2 (1964) 201–9.

———. *Is God Happy?* London: Penguin, 2012.

———. *Metaphysical Horror*. Oxford: Blackwell, 1988.

———. *Modernity on Endless Trial*. London: University of Chicago, 1990.

Kolb, David. *The Critique of Pure Modernity: Hegel, Heidegger, and After*. Chicago: University of Chicago Press, 1986.

———. "What Is Open and What Is Closed in the Philosophy of Hegel." *Philosophical Topics* 19.2 (1991) 29–50.

Kortian, Garbis. *Metacritique: The Philosophical Arguments of Jürgen Habermas*. Translated by John Raffan. Cambridge: Cambridge University Press, 1980.

Kuehn, Manfred. *Kant: A Biography*. Cambridge: Cambridge University Press, 2001.

Latour, Bruno. "For David Bloor . . . and Beyond: A Reply to David Bloor's 'Anti-Latour.'" *Studies in History and Philosophy of Science* 30.1 (1999) 113–29.

Lloyd, Vincent. *Law and Transcendence: On the Unfinished Project of Gillian Rose*. Renewing Philosophy. Basingstoke, UK: Palgrave Macmillan, 2009.

———. *The Problem with Grace: Reconfiguring Political Theology*. Stanford: Stanford University Press, 2011.

Loick, Daniel. "Juridification and Politics: From the Dilemma of Juridification to the Paradoxes of Rights." *Philosophy and Social Criticism* 40.8 (2014) 757–78.

Lukács, Georg. "Reification and the Consciousness of the Proletariat." In *History and Class Consciousness: Studies in Marxist Dialectics*, 83–222. Translated by Rodney Livingstone. London: Merlin, 1971 [1968].

Lumsden, Simon. "The Rise of the Non-Metaphysical Hegel." *Philosophy Compass* 3.1 (2008) 51–65.

Macdonald, Iain. "What Is Conceptual History?" In *Hegel: New Directions*, edited by Katerina Deligiorgi, 207–26. Chesham: Acumen, 2006.

MacGregor, David. *Hegel, Marx, and the English State*. Toronto: University of Toronto Press, 1992.

Martin, David. *The Future of Christianity: Reflections on Violence and Democracy, Religion and Secularization*. Aldershot, UK: Ashgate, 2011.

Martin, Stewart. "Adorno and the Problem of Philosophy." PhD diss., Middlesex University, 2002.

———. "Adorno's Conception of the Form of Philosophy." *Diacritics* 36.1 (2006) 48–63.

Martin, Wayne. "Antinomies of Autonomy: German Idealism and English Mental Health Law." In *Internationales Jahrbuch des Deutschen Idealismus*, vol. 9, *Freiheit/Freedom*, edited by Jürgen Stolzenberg and Fred Rush, 191–214. Berlin: de Gruyter, 2013.

Marx, Karl. *Capital*. Vol. 1. Translated from the 4th German ed. by Eden and Cedar Paul. London: Dent, 1930.

———. "On the Jewish Question." In *The Marx-Engels Reader*, edited by Robert C. Tucker, 26–52. 2nd ed. London: Norton, 1978 [1972].

Meiksins Wood, Ellen. *The Ellen Meiksins Wood Reader*, edited by Larry Patriquin. Boston: Brill, 2012.

Milbank, John. "An Essay Against Secular Order." *Journal of Religious Ethics* 15.2 (1987) 199–224.

———. *Theology and Social Theory*. 2nd ed. Oxford: Blackwell, 2006 [1990].

Milne, Drew. "The Beautiful Soul: From Hegel to Beckett." *Diacritics* 32.1 (2002) 63–82.

Murphy, Tim. *The Oldest Social Science? Configurations of Law and Modernity*. Oxford: Clarendon, 1997.

Nagel, Thomas. "The Fragmentation of Value." In *Mortal Questions*, 128–41. Cambridge: Cambridge University Press, 1979.

Nietzsche, Friedrich. "Toward a Genealogy of Morals." In *The Portable Nietzsche*, translated by Walter Kaufman, 450–53. London: Penguin, 1976.

Neuhouser, Frederick. *Foundations of Hegel's Social Theory*. Cambridge: Harvard University Press, 2000.

Nuzzo, Angelica. "The Truth of *Absolutes Wissen* in Hegel's Phenomenology of Spirit." In *Hegel's Phenomenology of Spirit: New Critical Essays*, edited by Alfred Denker and Michael G Vater, 265–93. Amherst, NY: Humanity, 2003.

O'Connor, Brian. *Adorno*. London: Routledge 2013.

———. "Adorno and the Problem of Givenness." *Revue Internationale de Philosophie* 58.1 (2004) 85–99.

———. *Adorno's Negative Dialectic: Philosophy and the Possibility of Critical Rationality*. London: MIT Press, 2004.

———. "Concrete Freedom and Other Problems: Robert Pippin's Hegelian Conception of Practical Reason." *International Journal of Philosophical Studies* 19.5 (2011) 753–60.

———. "The Neo-Hegelian Theory of Freedom and the Limits of Emancipation." *European Journal of Philosophy* 21.2 (2012) 1–24.

Osborne, Peter. "Gillian Rose and Marxism." *Telos* 173 (2015) 55–67.

Ozment, Steven. *A Mighty Fortress: A New History of the German People*. New York: HarperCollins, 2005.

Pally, Marcia. *Commonwealth and Covenant: Economics, Politics, and Theologies of Relationality*. Cambridge: Eerdmans, 2016.

Parinetti, Dario. "History, Concepts and Normativity in Hegel." In *Hegel's Theory of the Subject*, edited by David Gray Carlson, 60–72. Basingstoke, UK: Palgrave Macmillan, 2005.

Patberg, Markus. "Supranational Constitutional Politics and the Method of Rational Reconstruction." *Philosophy and Social Criticism* 40.6 (2014) 501–21.

Pinkard, Terry. *Hegel: A Biography*. Cambridge: Cambridge University Press, 2001.

———. *Hegel's Dialectic: The Explanation of Possibility*. Philadelphia: Temple University Press, 1988.

———. *Hegel's* Phenomenology: *The Sociality of Reason*. Cambridge: Cambridge University Press, 1994.

Pippin, Robert B. "Hegel and Category Theory." *Review of Metaphysics* 43 (1990) 839–48.

———. *Hegel's Idealism: The Satisfactions of Self-Consciousness*. Cambridge: Cambridge University Press, 1989.

———. *Idealism as Modernism: Hegelian Variations*. Cambridge: Cambridge University Press, 1997.

———. "The 'Logic of Experience' as 'Absolute Knowledge' in Hegel's *Phenomenology of Spirit*." In *Hegel's* Phenomenology of Spirit*: A Critical Guide*, edited by Dean Moyar and Michael Quante, 210–26. Cambridge: Cambridge University Press, 2008.

———. *Modernism as a Philosophical Problem*. 2nd ed. Oxford: Blackwell, 1999 [1991].

———. "Reconstructivism: On Honneth's Hegelianism." *Philosophy and Social Criticism* 40.8 (2014) 725–41.

Pleasants, Nigel. *Wittgenstein and the Idea of a Critical Social Theory: A Critique of Giddens, Habermas and Bhaskar*. London: Routledge, 1999.

Proops, Ian. "Kant's Legal Metaphor and the Nature of a Deduction." *Journal of the History of Philosophy* 41.2 (2003) 209–29.

Rasch, William. *Niklas Luhmann's Modernity: the Paradoxes of Differentiation*. Stanford: Stanford University Press, 2000.

Raz, Joseph. *The Practice of Value*. Edited by R. Jay Wallace. Oxford: Clarendon, 2003.

Ripstein, Arthur. *Force and Freedom: Kant's Legal and Political Philosophy*. London: Harvard University Press, 2009.

Ritzer, George. *Explorations in Social Theory: From Metatheorizing to Rationalization*. London: Sage, 2001.

Rowlands, Anna. "Practical Theology in 'The Third City.'" PhD diss., Manchester University, 2007.

Sachs, Carl B. "The Acknowledgement of Transcendence: Anti-Theodicy in Adorno and Levinas." *Philosophy and Social Criticism* 37.3 (2011) 273–94.

Schick, Friedrike. "Freedom and Necessity: The Transition to the Logic of the Concept in Hegel's *Science of Logic*." *Hegel Bulletin* 35.1 (2014) 84–99.

Schick, Kate. *Gillian Rose: A Good Enough Justice*. Edinburgh: Edinburgh University Press, 2012.

———. "Gillian Rose and Vulnerable Judgement." In *The Vulnerable Subject: Beyond Rationalism in International Relations*, edited by Amanda Russell Beattie and Kate Schick, 43–61. Basingstoke, UK: Palgrave Macmillan, 2013.

———. "Re-cognizing Recognition: Gillian Rose's 'Radical Hegel' and Vulnerable Recognition." *Telos* 173 (2015) 87–105.

Schechter, Darrow. *The Critique of Instrumental Reason from Weber to Habermas*. London: Continuum, 2010.

Schopenhauer, Arthur. *The Two Fundamental Problems of Ethics*. Translated and edited by Christopher Janaway. Cambridge: Cambridge University Press, 2009.

Sen, Amartya. *The Idea of Justice*. London: Penguin, 2010 [2009].

Shanks, Andrew. *Against Innocence: Gillian Rose's Reception and Gift of Faith*. London: SCM, 2008.

Speight, C. Allen. "The 'Metaphysics' of Morals and Hegel's Critique of Kantian Ethics." *History of Philosophy Quarterly* 14.4 (1997) 379–402.

Steinmetz, George. *The Politics of Method in the Human Sciences: Positivism and Its Epistemological Others*. Durham, NC: Duke University Press, 2005.

Surber, Jere Paul. "Hegel's Speculative Sentence." *Hegel-Studien* 10 (1975) 212–30.

Thompson, Michael J. "Axel Honneth and the Neo-Idealist Turn in Critical Theory." *Philosophy and Social Criticism* 40.8 (2014) 779–97.

Thornhill, Chris. "Adorno Reading Kant." *Studies in Social and Political Thought* 12 (2006) 98–110.

———. *German Political Philosophy: The Metaphysics of Law*. London: Routledge, 2007.

———. "Law and Religion in Early Critical Theory." In *The Early Frankfurt School and Religion*, edited by Margarete Kohlenbach and Raymond Geuss, 103–27. Basingstoke, UK: Palgrave Macmillan, 2005.

———. "Political Legitimacy: A Theoretical Approach between Facts and Norms." *Constellations* 18.2 (2011) 135–69.

Tubbs, Nigel. *Contradiction of Enlightenment: Hegel and the Broken Middle*. Aldershot, UK: Ashgate, 1997.

———. "Rose and Education." *Telos* 173 (2015) 123–43.

Walsh, Philip. *Skepticism, Modernity and Critical Theory*. Basingstoke, UK: Palgrave Macmillan, 2005.

Walzer, Michael. "Political Action: The Problem of Dirty Hands." *Philosophy and Public Affairs* 2.2 (1973) 160–80.

Ward, Andrew. *Kant: The Three Critiques*. Cambridge: Polity, 2006.

Weber, Max. *Economy and Society: An Outline of Interpretive Sociology*. Translated and edited by Gunther Roth and Claus Wittich. Berkeley: University of California, 1968.

———. "Politics as a Vocation." In *Max Weber's Complete Writings on Academic and Political Vocations*, edited by John Dreijmanis, translated by Gordon C. Wells, 155–207. New York: Algora, 2008.

Wheatland, Thomas. "Debate about Methods in the Social Sciences, Especially the Conception of Social Science Method for Which the Institute Stands." *Thesis Eleven* 11.1 (2012) 123–29.

Williams, Robert R. *Hegel's Ethics of Recognition*. London: University of California Press, 1997.

Williams, Rowan. "Between Politics and Metaphysics: Reflections in the Wake of Gillian Rose." *Modern Theology* 11.1 (1995) 3–22.

———. *The Edge of Words: God and the Habits of Language*. London: Bloomsbury, 2014.

———. *Lost Icons: Reflections on Cultural Bereavement*. London: T. & T. Clark, 2002.

———. "'The Sadness of the King': Gillian Rose, Hegel, and the Pathos of Reason." *Telos* 173 (2015) 21–36.

Winfield, Richard Dien. *Hegel's* Science of Logic: *A Critical Rethinking in Thirty Lectures*. New York: Rowman & Littlefield; 2012.

———. *Reason and Justice*. New York: State University of New York Press, 1988.

Wolf, Arnold Jacob. "The Tragedy of Gillian Rose." *Judaism* 46.4 (1997) 481–88.

Wolff, Michael. "Hegel's Organicist Theory of the State: On the Concept and Method of Hegel's 'Science of the State.'" In *Hegel on Ethics and Politics*, edited by Robert B. Pippin and Otfried Höffe, 291–322. Translated by Nicholas Walker. Cambridge: Cambridge University Press, 2004.

Wood, Allen W. *Kant's Ethical Thought*. Cambridge: Cambridge University Press, 1999.

———. *Kantian Ethics*. Cambridge: Cambridge University Press, 2007.

Woodhead, Linda, and Rebecca Catto, eds. *Religion and Change in Modern Britain*. London: Routledge, 2012.

Zuidervaart, Lambert. *Social Philosophy After Adorno*. Cambridge: Cambridge University Press, 2007.